# RAMBLING MAN

By

David Place

About the author:

David Place lives and walks in the north of England.

Published by Pen2print, Ferrybridge WF11 8PL
Tel: 01977 678371 www.pen2print.co.uk

David Place

# RAMBLING MAN

For Joe and Sally

# Contents

# Part One

## 2003: Going back
### 1985, 1960, 1953

# 1

## Choices

On his way to the station he stops at Khan's to buy a newspaper. Mrs Khan sits on her high stool behind the counter, fat and benign, an eastern goddess on her plinth. She knows the purchasing habits of this tall, athletic-looking man with the rucksack whom she judges to be in his mid-fifties, and she would like to know more, for Mrs Khan lightens her long and burdensome working-days by indulging a sympathetic interest in the doings of her customers. So far, her attempts to fish in the wider waters of his life outside her shop have yielded meagre prey: his family name, a passing allusion to his daughter Annie, and the curious fact – of little moment to Mrs Khan – that his football team of choice is Doncaster Rovers.

He lives in the valley of the river Tyne some twenty miles west of Newcastle. He chose this place for its proximity to the hills and dales of northern England (from his sitting-room window, distant fell-tops change colour with the light and the seasons) and to the railway line that carried him daily to his work in the city of Newcastle. Today his journey has a different purpose. The walk down from his hillside bungalow to the small rural town where he takes the train has been a delight. It is a bright and windless day in late August. Clear skies have caused the overnight temperature to fall and a stiletto-sharp aftertaste of frost pierces the warming air. His senses are sharp, his step springy. He feels a passing reluctance to sacrifice his exhilaration to the shrill outrages and sullen angers of the press, but he is attached to newspapers; they are the fingernails that help him scratch the sores of that tiny fragment of the body politic called Stanley Walker. He knows it's wrong to scratch, but the itch of concern of the concerned citizen is an irritant that will not be denied.

He hesitates over which newspaper to buy. He thumbs through the opening pages of the *Telegraph* and the *Guardian*, two menus with the same items but cooked for different palates. How are his taste buds feeling today? Crustily right-wing or hungry for liberal compassion? He steps back from the shelf and pauses. The questions that await him are momentous, the increasing difficulty he has in answering them a cause of some discomfort. Are the Israelis his allies in democracy and a common Judaeo-Christian heritage or the puppets of American imperialism and ruthless oppressors of the Palestinian people? Are the poor always with us or only until we get the economy right? What's his take on the royals, paedophiles, teenage yobs? And now there is Iraq, with the Americans in Baghdad and British troops in Basra. What is going on there, occupation or liberation? And should he have joined his daughter on the march?

A little Stan within - a weak, dithering Stan who has become more vociferous with the passing years - shouts: 'I don't know, I don't know. Take that light out of my eyes. You've got nothing on me.' But larger Stan, Stan the concerned citizen, will have none of it. He insists that it is one's duty to know. One must know both the facts and where one stands in relation to the facts. He has friends who know where they stand and a daughter who knows where she stands. When he was a student he read Jean-Paul Sartre. For a while he believed that existentialism was his kind of -ism and political commitment was a necessary appendage of his being.

That was some time ago, and since then Large Stan has lost ground. The ideological confusion of the age is against him. Indeed, he contributed to it the first time in the voting booth of his local primary school he placed his X in a box that was not that of the Labour Party candidate. That X was Stan's own personal sign of the times.

And now he must make another choice. He reaches into his pocket, finds a pound coin and sidles round to the back of one of the grocery shelves out of sight of Mrs Khan. Heads he takes the *Telegraph*, tails the *Guardian*. Tails wins. On impulse he takes the *Telegraph* - for the sport -, steps back round the grocery shelf and approaches Mrs Khan at her counter.

A political butterfly Annie calls him, even accusing him on one occasion of 'selling out'. He replied, dousing his irritation with facetiousness, that whoever he had sold out to had got him on the cheap: his work as a university administrator was modestly paid and he failed to attend the banquet of the Thatcher years; he owned no shares, had received no windfalls, bonuses or hand-outs. Despite this his view of the age he has lived through is dominated by a sense of his own good luck and he is ill-disposed to political rancour. He was born at the right time with the right endowments. He escaped the fate of his father, worn out by his work in the pit, and - he thinks this without complacency, in his moments of blackest despair – he will escape whatever in the way of political mayhem and environmental collapse awaits his daughter. He wonders now whether it is this that exasperates her, whether they are fighting out some deep shadowy war not simply of the generations but of the epochs. Both he and she know that Stan's half-century of peace, prosperity and the benign welfare state will never recur.

'Are you alright this morning, Mr Walker?'

He looks up. He is standing by Mrs Khan's cold-shelf of home-cooked Indian dishes, his lips moving in inner debate.

'Yes, Mrs Khan. I was wondering about a nice vindaloo for tea. But for the moment I think I'll just take the paper. Oh and good morning by the way.'

Mrs Khan smiles in acknowledgement and eases her copious folds of flesh slowly, majestically, down from her stool. He moves forward to pay.

The train is less crowded than on a working day and he finds an empty double-seat on which to stage his Saturday-morning tussle with shrink-wrapped magazines and several thicknesses of newsprint. The journey from Hexham to Newcastle Central takes over half-an-hour, more than enough time for his first selective skim through the paper, stripping whatever morsels catch his eye from the still-warm carcass of yesterday's events. He will leave the solid meat of analysis and detailed reporting for the next leg of his journey, south from Newcastle. When the newspaper is exhausted he will resort to the book that was delivered to his house that very morning as he was leaving. Although he was expecting it he felt a faint foreboding for he knew that the story it contained had the power to disturb him. For a few seconds he even thought of leaving it until his return but in the end he picked it up and slid it into the lid-pocket of his rucksack.

He does a quick check of the obits. Nobody he's heard of or finds interesting enough to acquaint himself with at this late stage. He picks out their birth-dates and calculates their average age: eighty-one, gratifyingly venerable. That would give him another twenty-one years, maybe more with his level of fitness. Of course whether it's worth living to eighty-one depends on the state you're in when you get there. Would he still be climbing hills? Probably not; toddling around on the flat might be the best he could hope for, or having picnics by babbling brooks with Annie feeding him sandwiches and raging about whatever horrors are stalking the world in 2024.

But he would have his books and music and friends. Assuming they don't all take the final trip before him. That would be the worst prospect. Best not to think of it. Best to move on to sport.

The train has stopped. He can hear shouting and laughter on the platform outside. Four boys and a girl push their way onto the train. They topple into his carriage, treading on each other's heels, and make a rush for empty seats. The train whirrs and moves off. The river Tyne comes into view, its bank lined with trees, and beyond them a road, houses, a church. The youths shout and laugh at each other across the aisle, incapable of sitting still, restless with caged animal spirits. Finally, they all spring to their feet and stream back along the aisle, pushing and prodding each other, to the end of the carriage. One of the boys is complaining about their imminent return to school after the long summer break. The girl groans histrionically but sneaks a smile at Stan as she passes.

He thinks of Annie and the anger and rebelliousness of her school years. There was nothing histrionic there, it was the real thing. Her headmaster, gracing the obvious with terminological dignity, called it school-phobia. Stan can still remember the tight commiserating smile, the weak flap of his hand as he struggled to argue the benefit to Annie of a short period of exclusion. Then came the transformation: her sixth-form years of self-discipline and hard work, entry to a decent university, and her return to school as a teacher. He and Annie call it school-philia, though he sometimes wonders whether it will last. Her first two years have been hard, in a school that harbours more than its share of the damaged, aggressive and unteachable young.

'They're like I was,' she says. 'I changed. Why shouldn't they?'

And she returns to the fray, keeping faith with her idea of herself and the world as capable of betterment. He imagines her setting off on this coming Monday, the first day of her third year in the job: Annie in a hurry with her piles of registers and books, her mini that sometimes starts and sometimes doesn't, the traffic jams on the road into Newcastle...

And what will he be doing? Taking a leisurely breakfast? Or already out on the hill on a morning such as this, breathing the sharp air? The idea of Annie at work while he celebrates his freedom from work is one to which he hasn't become accustomed. It gives to his pleasure a tinge of guilt despite the fact that it was she who brought his present venture about.

# 2
## Tender is the North

'Fun,' she said.

'Fun?' he said.

'Yes, fun,' she said. 'That's what it's about after all. Having fun.'

'That's what what's about?'

He is on the point of repeating 'after all' but stops himself, knowing with exactitude how far he can push her. Even so, she is getting impatient. 'Oh, come on, Dad. You know what I mean. We all need some fun in our lives.'

Stan pauses, then says: 'I'm sure we do but less of it than you think.'

'You're too subtle for me, Dad. I can't see what's wrong with having fun, and as much of it as possible.'

'I'm not saying there's anything wrong with it, Annie. I'm saying it's not as important as you think. It's a trivial word for a trivial thing. Now if it's pleasure you're talking about, then I'm with you. Pleasure's the word I prefer.'

She shrugs her shoulders. 'Pleasure, fun, call it what you like…'

'You see I get a lot of pleasure from my reading and listening to music but I wouldn't call these things fun.'

He knows he is being pedantic but he goes on: 'Then there's my hill-walking…'

'OK, Dad, I get it. Let's call it pleasure. I just want you to have more of it. And now's the time surely.'

She is beginning to sound tetchy. Stan decides it's time to back off. 'You may be right, Annie. No doubt you are right. But I need time to think. You forget I'm a bureaucrat and a man of caution. I like to file things away and come back to them later.'

'You'll soon be an ex-bureaucrat and that's exactly the point of this conversation.'

She grins in acknowledgement of his capitulation, nudges him in the ribs and stands up from the sofa. She is short and sturdy; standing there looking down at him with her feet apart and solidly planted, her fists on her hips, she has the air of an improbably pretty flyweight-boxer.

'Early retirement and your sixtieth birthday a few months down the line. Calls for some serious celebration if you ask me. In other words fun. It's good for the soul.'

He looks into his soul, a solid filing-cabinet of a soul containing a drawer marked Big Questions-Big Answers. He flicks through the files - Know Thyself, Live Virtuously - searching for the one labelled Have Fun though he knows it's gone missing. He says: 'Alright then. I need a few leads. What does my fun-coach suggest?'

'You could travel.'

'Ah of course. Travel, the opium of the retired classes. Why didn't I think of that?'

She is clearing the low table. She pauses, a tea-cup in each hand, torn as so often with him between amusement and exasperation. 'You boring old curmudgeon you. What's wrong with travel? You don't do enough of it Dad.'

'Nothing's wrong with travel, my dear girl, though I can't see that it makes people any less boring. When was the last time you heard anyone say anything remotely interesting about their latest jaunt to Machu Picchu or the Valley of the Kings? Travel may broaden the mind but I see no evidence that it deepens it.'

He stops in mid-rant, reminding himself that reasonableness is the policy of the moment.

'However, I suppose you're right. Indeed, I've been thinking along similar lines myself. I'm as partial to a puff of opium as the next man.'

'Sounds promising. Tell me more.'

'Oh, it's nothing definite yet. It's early days. I'm barely out of the job. I need time to think.'

'You think too much. It's time to act. Why don't you do a tour of

Europe? You could go to the opera houses. You could brush up your languages.'

'And who says I need to brush up my languages?'

' I say. You're a disgrace, Dad. A degree in languages and you haven't spoken French or Spanish for years.'

She turns round and heads for the kitchen. He shouts after her: 'No, but I read them. That's what matters: books, ideas, great literature. Not idle chit-chat on the Costa Brava.'

He can hear her laughing as she washes the cups. She returns and sits by him on the sofa.

'You know, Dad, you're a lucky man. You're not rich but you're not badly off and you've been pretty thrifty. You could go just about anywhere you want. Africa, Asia. Do you remember that programme we watched on the silk road? You could go to Samarkand...'

'Whoa, hold on there, not so fast.'

'Or what about mountains? The Rockies, the Himalayas, the Andes. You love mountains.'

'That's not quite what I had in mind. I was thinking something perhaps a little less ambitious. I'd actually thought of doing some walking.'

'You can walk in the Himalayas. You're exceptionally fit for your age. You could do it.'

'Except that what I'd had in mind was something closer to home.'

'Ah, I see. Closer to home.'

She is beginning to sense where this is heading.

'Yes, I thought... and you must understand that as yet it's only a thought, nothing's decided on... I thought I might go and walk the Pennine Way.'

She can hardly believe her ears. The Pennine Way! Her father has spent much of the last thirty years tramping the hills of the Lake District, the Yorkshire Dales and Northumberland. She sometimes thinks he has waged war on every sod of grass in the north of England.

'But Dad, you go walking every weekend. You must have walked the Pennine Way several times over. Why don't you do something different? There are cheap flights to everywhere. Why potter around your own backyard when the whole world's waiting for you? God, you're so parochial.'

The accusation is not new. He has a sudden memory of some previous occasion with Annie exasperated, calling him an old stay-at-home who never left his own patch, blurting out - then covering her mouth too late like a child shocked by her own temerity - that he'd even married his childhood sweetheart.

He says: 'Pottering around my own backyard! I'll have you know, my girl, that the Pennine Way is two hundred and seventy miles long and it crosses some of the roughest country in England. It may not be the Himalayas but it's nobody's backyard. Of course you're right to say that I've already walked most of it. But only in bits and pieces and over the years. I want to do the whole thing at one go.'

He is suddenly animated. He takes Annie's arm and pulls her close. 'It'll be a sort of summing-up of my walking career. Of my life in fact. I'll walk the length of the North of England, the place where I've lived, the place I love. I'm not parochial. I'm provincial, and that's a fine thing to be. Remember Tennyson: 'Dark and true and tender is the north'. He knew what he was talking about. I'll do the world later, I promise you. There's plenty time. I've got years ahead of me. But for the moment this is what I want to do.'

That was three months ago and he is now doing what he wants to do. On the carriage seat beside him his cherry-red rucksack has been packed with meticulous regard for economies of space and weight. The boots in the new boot-bag (a retirement present from his former colleagues) have been cleaned and waxed. He feels the lightness of being of those who carry their life's necessities with them: prehistoric hunter-gatherers, desert nomads, Mongolian herdsmen. The previous weekend he completed his training regime with a fourteen-mile hike in the Cheviot Hills, and last night Annie cut his hair just as he likes it, close to the scalp and square and clean across the neck. He feels fit, efficient, aerodynamic.

He will travel by train to the little village of Edale in the Derbyshire dales. From there, for the next three weeks, he will tramp the bleak and lumpy spine of Northern England to the Scottish border. He will endure privations, he will freeze, sweat, and ache. He will get lost and feel afraid for, despite the long years he has spent walking these hills, he is an indifferent navigator. Life will be reduced to the mundane practicalities of finding a bed for the night and provisioning his body for locomotion. But he knows that in this shrinkage and constraint he will find expansion and freedom, and that – at least for longer periods than usual - he will obtain remission from the agitations of the age and intimations of his own mortality. His walk will end at the village of Kirk Yetholm in Scotland from where he will return by bus to the place he left this morning. He will have completed the loop of his native province, the territory he calls home. He wonders whether the deep satisfaction he derives from this idea has evolutionary roots. Are there primitive tribes who circumnavigate their land for no practical purpose other than to repossess it in their own minds? He makes a mental note to add anthropology to the topics to pursue in his retirement.

# 3

## Hot tips

Leaving Newcastle Central Station on this bright, late-summer morning is like emerging in slow motion from a breaking egg. The vast, shadowed cavern of Victorian arches and pillars recedes, the horizon lifts and the ground falls away to the river Tyne below. Daylight blazes in. The train that Stan has taken creaks as it moves, as though stiff-jointed from its night in the sidings. It stops on the King Edward Bridge. It is barely a minute out of the station. The couple across the table from Stan raise their eyebrows at each other in synchronised exasperation. The man whispers something to the effect that 'they' couldn't run a whelk stall. Stan assumes that 'they' are the train company. (What's his position on privatised railways? Does safety suffer in the rush to profit or will entrepreneurial flair improve the service?). He smiles across at the couple in solidarity with a sense of victimhood he doesn't feel. A fault of his, he reflects, this tendency to concur so readily with others. In reality he finds it a pleasure to be suspended above the shimmering river, free of the packed and cluttered city and seemingly of gravity itself. He picks out the Tyne and Millenium bridges elegantly half-hooped over the river, and the new Sage music-hall that is nearing completion, a plump, segmented pupa, smooth and shiny as silk, sunning itself on the south bank of the Tyne.

He gazes inland to the west, the direction from which he has travelled this morning. Beyond the Redheugh Bridge the river curves out of sight, but he knows its course through the urban-industrial reaches of the city, past suburban townships and rural villages, narrowing and dividing beyond Hexham into its twin tributaries, the rivers North and South Tyne that flow down from the desolate hills and moors of Northumberland. He will be crossing this country in a few weeks time. He traces in his mind the line he will take, descending from the summit of Cross Fell, walking north along the

South Tyne valley to the Roman wall and through the border forests, climbing onto the long high ridge of the Cheviot Hills before descending into the valley of Kirk Yetholm.

This mind-travel through the landscapes of the North of England is a form of day-dreaming that has buoyed him through many a dreary working-day. He sometimes wonders whether it - and its realisation in the walking expeditions that take up most of his week-ends - hasn't drawn the sting of his ambition and hindered the development of his career. On many occasions, the bulging briefcase that he took home on Friday night remained untouched until the late hours of Sunday; then its contents were hastily skimmed, leaving him inadequately prepared for the working-week ahead.

A voice over the intercom apologises for the delay. At that moment the train begins to move. There is laughter in the carriage and the woman opposite smiles at Stan, sharing her relief. The man beside her rests his head back on his seat and composes his features for sleep. The decor of bridges and shining water slides away behind the containing wall of the track.

Clever but lacks ambition: that seems to have been the judgement, more or less, throughout his working life. Bill Dyer put it well at his retirement presentation. A master of the retirement encomium, Bill, but honest too, unable to resist the occasional barb lovingly encased in a velvet sheath of diplomacy and equivocal praise.

'Like the long-distance walker that he is, Stan always kept something in reserve. You felt he had a bit more to give but what he did give was so good it didn't really matter.'

There are knowing smiles all round, wine glasses are raised to lips, canapés nibbled and fiddled with. But the smiles are affectionate too for he is well liked. At the end the handshakes were probably warmer than usual, the injunctions to keep in touch more sincerely felt.

Durham: the castle and cathedral spreadeagled against the sky, a plunging glimpse of streets and clustered terraces as the train crosses the viaduct. It is gone in seconds, the soaring grandeur of medieval Europe giving way to a broken landscape of arable fields, trees and houses.

'That was Durham, wasn't it?'

It is a few seconds before he realises the woman is speaking to him. The man beside her is asleep. Stan smiles and says: 'Sorry, I'm dreaming. Yes it was.'

'Lovely, isn't it? I'd no idea it was so grand.'

She has a strong Scottish accent that gives a confirming vigour to her words. He is pleased with her reaction, for his attachment to Durham goes far back and he takes a proprietorial pride in its beauty. His maternal grandmother was born on the rural outskirts of the city and it must have been from her that he gained his first image of the castle and cathedral on a hill in an arm of the river Wear. He remembers crayoning it into his drawing-book, the hill bright green, the river blue, and the castle an orangey-brown mess of ill-proportioned battlements and crooked towers. He didn't know what a cathedral was and when his mother told him it was a sort of church he squeezed a lop-sided version of the local Wesleyan chapel onto the side of the hill.

The woman continues, as though anxious to explain her ignorance: 'We usually fly abroad for our holidays. I don't really know the north of England.'

She gives a little laugh. She looks about Stan's age and is carefully dressed in a smart print-blouse and matching ear-rings. Her fine features and slender body have sharpened into a look of gaunt fragility but her laugh is clear and fresh, as though her voice has escaped the decay of her youth. She tells Stan that she and her husband are travelling to York for a family wedding; the bride comes from York; they themselves have never been there; there will be relatives they haven't seen for years. Stan nods and smiles and makes interested noises. The conversation falters. She begins to smooth the cover of the magazine that lies on the table in front of her, finally picking it up and flicking through the pages.

On the front cover of the magazine, emblazoned in white letters, are the words Ten Tips for Married Bliss. The claim is endorsed by a picture of a supernaturally beautiful couple who look very married (she is wearing an elaborate bridal gown and he a top-hat and tail-coat) and very blissful. They recur in an inset photograph in which they are stripped down to pants and bra of the most exquisitely tight and lustrous kind. The woman's breasts are touching the man's chest while his hands rest nonchalantly on her hips. From his confident smile and the bulge in his pants whose tasteful delineation – no more than the subtlest of hints – is the result of a cunningly chosen camera angle, it is clear that he is ready to demonstrate the efficacy of a crucial one of the ten tips.

The woman folds back the cover of the magazine, exposing the inside pages to Stan's view. He sees that tip number-four urges spouses to be tolerant of each other's opinions. He laughs quietly to himself. At least he got that right! And on the best authority! A good listener his wife called him - understanding, open-minded. That was in the early days. Later on, as things cooled, she began to confuse listening with agreeing.

'You don't listen, Stan. That's the trouble. You just don't listen.'

But he did. He listened, he understood, he disagreed. Though no more than most husbands, he believes. It was a marriage like many others, far from a mismatch but not quite a match, a good deal of common ground harbouring some fundamental difference of temperament that was the grit in the shoe. They lived with it, accommodating their differences and bound together by their shared pastimes and their love of their daughter. He believes they would have continued to live with it had it not been for the take-off of her career as a writer. That and Pip Slaley, who was a part of the take-off.

He takes up his newspaper but feels too distracted to read. He gazes out of the window. A motorway rushes to meet the railway track; speeding cars and lorries home in on the side of the train before slipping overhead and out of sight. Fields with grazing cows slide past. He is trying to remember where they are now, Cathy and Pip. He should know, for she told him that they were going off somewhere at the end of August. He's becoming forgetful. Was it France? Italy? The Greek Islands? He continues east, performing a rapid tour of the globe until he arrives at Florida. He remembers now; she made a joke about it in her phone-call: 'Palm Beach and Disneyland. And we can't even pretend it's for the sake of the kids!'

In recent times they have recovered something of their old friendliness and confidentiality. Stan even wonders whether her frequent complaints about life in London and her nostalgia for the North aren't a covert admission that all is not well in her present marriage. It is a thought that arouses in him confused feelings that include an insistent, demeaning wish that it might be true.

She had phoned him to tell him that her latest book was out and that she had sent him a copy through the post. It had arrived as he was leaving home that morning. A memoir she called it, then laughed at what she felt to be the pretentiousness of the term. Memoirs were for elder statesmen and the distinguished generally, not for writers of modest repute with a handful of novels for children to their name. When he asked her why, after all this time, she felt the need to go back to the events of their childhood, she said: 'Therapy. The exorcising of ghosts.'

'But it was so long ago,' he said.

'They never lie down, Stan. At least they haven't for me.'

He too knows that they never lie down. That is one reason for the sour ripple of apprehension he felt as they spoke. The other reason was some faint, irrational fear of being exposed to the public gaze, for he knew that he himself figured largely in the book. How many people would read it? How many thousands of eyes would scrutinise whatever version of his childhood self emerges from its pages?

When he made this point to her she laughed and expressed astonishment that he should worry about his image of fifty years ago. In any case, she assured him, he comes out of it all pretty well.

He believed her. There was no reason he shouldn't come out of it well for Cathy never knew the whole story.

'If the book has a hero, you're it, Stan.'

He didn't tell her that this was precisely what he feared.

'I think we must be arriving somewhere. Will it be Darlington?'

Stan wakes from his reverie. He nods and looks out at the slowing buildings beside the track. The woman tells him again that she and her husband are leaving the train at York. She glances sideways at the man still sleeping beside her, smiles and shakes her head.

'He can sleep anywhere.'

Stan says: 'It's a useful thing to be able to do.'

The conversation fails to spark and the woman returns to her magazine. Stan notes that tip seven urges the desirability of shared interests. Another box ticked! Walking, reading, theatre, music: they shared the lot. Interests were not the problem. Even her writing, an all-absorbing passion that might have come between them, at first brought them together. He was her first reader, offering views that were sufficiently tentative to appease her touchy pride and sufficiently insightful to be of use. A good reader, she continued to acknowledge, even after his stock as a good listener had begun to fall.

Yet he still finds it odd to think of her as a writer, this woman he first knew as a ten-year-old child in his native village of Calcroft. When they met again in later life, having lost touch for over twenty years, she was working as a full-time secretary. It was perhaps this that obscured for him the seriousness of her vocation. When in an unguarded moment he referred to her writing as her 'hobby', he was astonished by the fierceness of her correction. 'Work' she insisted on calling it, real work, the only work she ever wanted to do. He remembers the day – it must have been sometime in the mid-eighties - that she first mentioned an idea she had had for a novel, the novel that was to become her first published work. What remains most vividly in his mind is not the excitement and eagerness with which she embarked on her new plan; it is the exasperation she felt towards him. She could not understand his less than whole-hearted attitude towards his own work, his readiness to subordinate his career to other things. It was the exasperation of a woman who knew that it was she, locked in her mediocre round of part-time work and domesticity, who was the one with a sense of vocation.

# 4

## Work and play

'You don't listen, Stan. That's the trouble. You just don't listen.'

As she speaks, she changes gear in order to ease the car up the steepening slope. In her irritation she snatches at the gear-stick too early and he has to raise his voice over the revving of the engine.

'I do listen and I know exactly what you're saying. You think I should go for the London job because it's better paid and you think it offers better prospects. The trouble is I don't want to live in London. It's too big, too crowded, and there are no hills.'

From the back seat of the car Annie shouts: 'Shut up you two. You're always quarrelling.'

Cathy says: 'We're not quarrelling, darling. We're having a discussion about where Dad should get a new job.' She continues, her voice taking on a tone of strained reasonableness for the sake of Annie: 'But what's the alternative Stan? You can't spend your life working in obscure provincial colleges. You're better than that. You've gone as far as you can go in the sector.'

'And that's precisely why I'm applying for jobs in universities.'

'In *one* university, Stan. One *provincial* university. I can't see why you have to place all your hopes in the Newcastle job. What's so special about Newcastle? You could at least apply for the London one. I know it's not ideal but it is London after all. There may be no hills but there are lots of other things we like - music, theatre, museums. We'd just live a different life.'

At that moment the car emerges from the narrow defile of Holden Clough. The enclosing hillsides fold back like the pages of an opening book and they are running along the level top of the Snake Pass with open moorland on either side. Pale shadows cast by the broken cloud drift stealthily over moors and hills. They are barely fifteen minutes from their home on the outskirts of Manchester.

Cathy, perhaps realising she has chosen the wrong moment to promote the virtues of the metropolis, gives a little sigh of pleasure. Stan keeps quiet, letting the landscape do his arguing.

At breakfast that Saturday morning she had suggested that Stan and Annie accompany her on what she called 'a research trip'. They could combine it with a walk and a picnic. Her imagination had been caught by a newspaper article about an aircraft that had crashed on a hillside not far from their home during the Second World War. The daughter of one of the airmen killed in the crash, a woman now in her late sixties, had visited the site and recounted to a local reporter the story of her childhood bereavement. For Cathy the story struck some deep chord in which the bleak Pennine landscape on their doorstep became entwined with the tragedies of wartime and her own childhood. Within days she was sketching out key scenes for a work of fiction based on the incident. Her provisional title was *Missing Dad*.

The ground is still stiff with cold as they set off on their walk. The last of the winter snow dimples the heather. Annie runs ahead, gathering it up in handfuls and throwing it back at Cathy and Stan. Stan chases after her and sweeps her, screaming and wriggling, into the air. When he puts her down she says: 'Dad, turn round and look away. I'm going to hide. Count to twenty and then you can come and look for me.'

She goes off into the broken ground of peat channels and banks of heather that lie on either side of the path. Her red woollen hat with its blue pompom remains intermittently visible, bobbing along between the clumps of heather. Finally it stops, Stan shouts: 'We can still see you. Your pompom's showing.' The hat and pompom immediately disappear. Cathy laughs, tilting her head slightly back. With her short, light-brown hair, full mouth and smooth, unblemished skin, she appears younger than she is, still attractive despite her constant worries over her thickening body. She sets off along the path, eager to be on the move, while Stan cuts across the heather to find Annie. When he and Annie rejoin the path, she is well ahead. Annie chases after her but Stan hangs back.

He is reluctant to engage in further conversation about his job prospects. He feels Cathy's impatience and restlessness is a judgement on the modesty of his ambitions. He likes his present life. His family's situation, living just beyond the edge of the city with the hills and moors of Derbyshire within easy reach, seems to satisfy some part of himself where need and imagination meet. Whatever the frustrations of his working day, the hillside that swings into view at a particular point of his journey home has the power to lift his spirits. On returning at night from some concert or opera in the centre of Manchester, he will often walk out beyond the last street-lights of his small suburban town and, with melodies still swirling in his head, stand there inhaling the wind that blows off Kinder and Bleaklow. Where else would he feel so fulfilled in his love of cinema, concerts, and barren heaths? He has refined his work as senior administrator in a technical college to a level of competence and efficiency that leaves him with time to indulge his love of reading. Works of literature, history and politics feed his curiosity about the world and the human condition. Their truths burn as brightly in Glossop as in London, Paris or New York. His weekend rambles with friends and colleagues are an itinerant debating-society in which ideas and positions are fiercely disputed amidst landscapes of wild and rugged beauty.

The northern conurbations of Manchester, Leeds, Sheffield and Newcastle would all offer such a life, and these are the places on which he has concentrated his hopes of finding a new job, a job that is better paid and, in Cathy's words, 'more challenging'. Of the applications he has sent off, all have failed except the Newcastle one.

The path slants across a heather-covered slope down to a stream. The slope is south-facing and completely free of snow. In the varying light caused by the shifting clouds the heather changes colour from rust to copper to a deep chocolate-brown. It is here that they come across the crash site. Fragments of metal sheeting, one of them bearing the faded roundels of the RAF, litter the sloping side of a deep and wide channel of peat. In the bottom of the channel a skeleton of rods and pipes lies half submerged. Annie's foot kicks against a tube tangled in with the heather like some mutant root. Cathy takes out an old school exercise-book and begins to make notes and drawings. Annie comes towards them carrying a metal disc the size of a dinner plate that is pierced by a circle of holes.

'What's this, Dad?'

'I'm afraid I can't tell you, Annie. I don't know much about aeroplanes. But it looks as though it might have been a bit of the propeller.'

'Can we take it home? I want to put it in the garden.'

Stan says: 'Why do you want to put it in the garden?'

'Because I want to. It's nice.'

Cathy says: 'I think it would be wrong to take it, Annie. We should leave it here.'

'Why?'

'Because it's a part of the aeroplane that crashed. The poor men in the aeroplane died, so this place is a sort of grave. We shouldn't take things away from it.'

'Are the men buried here then?'

'No. They were taken away and buried in a churchyard but I think we should still leave these things here.'

Annie grimaces but half-heartedly, as though not wholly convinced that she wants this unidentifiable piece of aeroplane in her garden. She turns round and, walking with an exaggerated stagger as though carrying a heavy weight, returns it to the place she found it. She then carefully re-arranges the heather over it.

'There now, bit of propeller. You stay there and don't let anyone take you away. Mummy and Daddy think you shouldn't be moved.'

Stan and Cathy burst out laughing. Annie looks at them, trying to disguise her pleasure at their reaction behind a show of solemn disapproval. Stan finds her ability to mock them a delight. In a sudden rush of affection he strides towards her and lifts her into the air. She shouts at him to put her down and one of her flailing arms catches him under the chin, causing him to bite his lip. He sets her back on her feet, trying to control his irritation, and watches her run off, kicking at the clumps of heather that line the peat. As he raises his handkerchief to his lip, Cathy asks if he is alright.

'She packs quite a punch for an eight-year old,' he says.

'It was an accident.'

'Sure.'

But he isn't. This isn't the first time Annie's playfulness has flipped over into bad temper and aggression. At school her behaviour has become wayward and recently she has begun to resist going to school at all. Cathy thinks it is anxiety. She has a theory that Annie is afraid that while she is at school one of her parents will leave home and disappear. She thinks it is a result of their squabbling.

For they squabble often. The apportionment of domestic tasks is a spark that can ignite conflagrations. In order to create time for her writing Cathy has reduced her part-time employment while Stan has taken on an increased share of the household duties. They are like opposing commanders, manoeuvring for space and time, trailing their armies across difficult terrain, sniping and skirmishing but always avoiding the final confrontation.

She has completed two novels for children, both as yet unpublished. The stream of publishers' rejections has sapped her confidence but not her will. Stan is astonished at the single-mindedness with which she organises her life, determined that no single hour free of the demands of motherhood, housework and paid employment will be wasted. She can work as readily at the cleared kitchen-table as at the desk that stands in the bedroom they have converted into a shared study. In the evening, the busy rattle of her typewriter competes with the strains of Stan's music collection and the sounds of the television set.

She finishes her note-taking and they continue their walk. Ahead of them they can see the feature they have identified on their map as the place for a picnic, a small waterfall like a white sheet hung out above the stream to dry. When they reach it they find that it falls into a deep pool formed out of a basin of rock. From the pool the water slides swiftly over the lip of the rock into the stream where little fish dart like slivers of shadow across the gravel bottom. Down here they are out of the breeze and can feel the first warmth of spring when the sun breaks through the clouds. They spread their waterproofs on the grassy bank and sit down to eat, munching and chewing and drinking in a daze of contentment, feeling the sun surprisingly warm on their faces as they gaze into the flashing depths of the pool.

He was surprised when he was offered the Newcastle job. He felt that he had interviewed well but not well enough, having failed to strike the authentic note of thrusting enthusiasm that the interviewing panel seemed to expect. There were also aspects of his CV - his brief and abortive attempt at postgraduate research, some years spent teaching English in France and Spain – that he feared would be less than enticing to a panel of career administrators.

He was wrong. The chairman of the panel told him later that they had been impressed by the boldness with which he had shifted his career-path into administration and by the range of skills he had picked up along the way. He found this gratifying; it was a view of him that clashed with his habitual self-deprecation. It would also please Cathy by justifying her estimate of him as being superior to his estimate of himself.

After the interview he stayed overnight in Newcastle and spent the evening with Pip Slaley. Although they had kept intermittently in touch since their Grammar School days, it was the first time they had met in over ten years. The figure he saw approaching across the restaurant floor seemed identical to the Pip of their last encounter; he had the same slight frame, the same fine blond hair and elegant, almost dandyish dress, the general air of some rarefied English heart-throb of the nineteen-forties.

'Stanley Walker! How good to see you.'

His voice is surprisingly deep and strong, confidently heedless of the customers gathered at the bar. While they wait for their drinks he apologises for being late and enquires after Stan's wife and daughter, expressing the hope that he might meet them now that Stan is coming to work in Newcastle. Once at their table they talk easily, taking up their lives at the point at which they had left them years ago when Pip was struggling to establish himself in the world of journalism. He is now the features editor of a regional newspaper based in Newcastle but is desperate to move on, his ambition being fixed on working for one of the national dailies in London. He has just emerged from his second divorce.

'I think a new start is called for, Stan. Maritally, professionally, and geographically. Much as I love it up here, I feel I need to be closer to the heart of things.'

'What do you mean by the heart of things?'

'The shows, the exhibitions, the seething life of the metropolis.' He pronounces this last phrase with a self-conscious pomposity that distances him from his own cliché.

'There is no 'heart of things'. There's just the seething life of the metropolis and the less seething life of the provinces. Personally, I prefer the latter. It's more relaxed.'

'It's not for me, Stan. I crave excitement. I was made for higher things than reporting on flower-shows and pop-concerts in provincial cities. A man's reach should exceed his grasp and all that.'

His conversation is facetious and self-mocking, echoing with allusions, ironies and bad jokes. 'I had a dream.' His voice wavers briefly in imitation of Martin Luther King. 'I wanted to review books for the Guardian and plays for the Observer. I might yet realise the dream. I have contacts, strings I can pull, not to mention my astonishing, multifarious talents.'

33

He continues talking as they order their food. The waitress, an embarrassed intruder, smiles and shuffles her feet. He is still the precocious schoolboy in love with words and his own performance. But he is frustrated too. 'I'm over forty, Stan. I'm beginning to feel *un peu long dans le dent* as our friends across the channel might say.'

'They don't. And it's *la dent*,' Stan corrects him.

'Bloody pedant! You were always better than me at French.' He laughs out loud. Diners at the next table stare across. 'And at French women if I remember correctly. What was her name?'

'Marie Salasca.' Stan speaks quietly, trying to rein in the noise of their conversation.

'Ah yes, the delectable Marie. But in the end, you returned to your roots and the girl next door.'

'Not quite next door. Cathy lived half-a-mile away on the other side of a railway bridge. That was foreign territory by the standards of Calcroft.'

'You know, Stan, you intrigue me. When we were at the Grammar School we all had you marked down as the one who would go far. It costs me to say this, for as you know Pip Slaley and self-effacing modesty are not natural bedfellows, but you were the sharpest of us all by a clear head. I would have expected…how can I put this without being hurtful…?' He screws up his features in a parody of pained sensitivity. Stan laughs, he is beginning to enjoy himself. He says: 'You're wondering how I ended up as a paper-pushing bureaucrat in an obscure provincial college.'

'Well, Stan, I was about to put it more delicately than that, but yes. Why?'

'Well you see Pip…' Stan leans across the table and lowers his voice to a confessional murmur. 'It's a spiritual thing.'

Pip guffaws. Heads turn. Stan continues: 'You see, my principal aim in life is to achieve inner peace. Now, while work is an economic necessity and a source of activity and interest, it is also a threat to aforementioned inner peace. It is an imperial power, occupying places in the mind where it is not wanted, bringing oppression and stress in its wake. So… after one or two false starts I find a type of work at which I seem particularly adept. I'm quick at it, I get things done. I rarely take its problems home with me. I hold its imperialist incursions at bay…'

'You mean you work short hours?'

'…The space that is thus protected I fill with music, reading and rambling in the hills of the North. The result? Inner peace. Or at least as near as I can get to it given the pesky obligations of work and home.'

'Mm… interesting. But not the way I see things.'

'I think we're different, Pip. Different in our attitudes to work and maybe in other things too. I've never known what I wanted to do as a profession. I sometimes think I just lack strong desires. Whereas I remember that you were set on being a journalist from the moment I first met you. You knew what you wanted, you had great ambitions. And you were determined to get off the patch and travel the world.'

'But you too, surely. You went away. You had those years abroad.'

'But I've come back. I like the North of England. It's home.'

'It's not for me Stan. I'm too restless.'

He adopts a tone of mock portentousness: ' 'For always roaming with a hungry heart, Much have I seen and known'. You remember?' Then, in response to Stan's blank stare, he says: 'It's Tennyson, Stan, *Ulysses*. 'And drunk delight of battle with my peers, Far on the ringing plains of windy Troy'. You must remember that, 'the ringing plains of windy Troy'. We loved it.'

Stan feels a twinge of annoyance at his slip of memory. He thinks back to their old friendship at school, a conspiracy of two in a world indifferent to poetry, swapping quotations, adopting poses. He laughs but fails to summon up an appropriate rejoinder. He says lamely: 'Even Ulysses returned home.'

'Yes Stan. He returned home to his Penelope, as you have returned to your Cathy. But alas, my Penelope has fled so I must continue to wander. 'I cannot rest from travel: I will drink Life to the lees'. Remember?'

'It's coming back.'

'I fear you're forgetting your poetry, Stanley Walker.' Pip pokes at his pile of spaghetti and begins to twist his fork. 'Nothing good can come of it. Nothing good at all.'

# 5

## Home and Abroad

The mouth of the man opposite twitches. His eyes open and for a few seconds he stares unseeing at Stan, then straightens up and looks out of the window.

'Where are we?'

The woman tells him they have just left Darlington station and asks if he is feeling better for his nap. He nods and yawns. Although he appears barely taller than her, he is almost twice her size across. Below the short sleeves of his shirt, his arms are thick and well muscled. He probably works out of doors - a farmer or builder Stan guesses. One of his hands reaches beneath the table and Stan senses that he's taking hold of the woman's hand. She turns to look out of the window, her lips half-open in a faint, reflective smile.

The train slows to a creep, then stops. Five minutes, ten minutes pass. The man begins to fret, making irritated tutting noises and twisting his head to look back down the aisle of the train in ostentatious pursuit of non-existent officials. The woman sighs and says to Stan: 'We are being picked up by our relatives at York. I'm afraid they'll have a bit of a wait. We've had a lot of trouble with the trains on this trip, haven't we Bob.'

Bob takes this as a signal to vent his frustration with the vagaries of public transport in modern Britain. Stan sees a hobby-horse approaching and swerves to avoid being trampled underfoot. He says: 'I'm very fond of York. I used to go there as a child.' The woman nods and smiles but Bob ignores his remark and charges on: 'I don't know why we can't run decent railways. We invented them after all. It wouldn't happen in France. They know how to run a railway system there. Have you travelled on French trains?'

Stan says: 'I have and they're very impressive. They're highly subsidised, mind you. I don't know whether the tax-payers over here would tolerate the cost.'

'The private companies here are subsidised too. They get more in subsidies than the old British Rail.'

Stan goes quiet, unsure of his ground. This is not what he wanted. His diversionary tactic has failed and the sound of galloping hooves is becoming deafening.

The train begins to move. Bob's tone lightens and he says: 'Still. I mustn't get onto politics or I'll never stop.' He turns to his wife and says: 'Will I?' She smiles at him and picks a few specks of invisible dirt off his shirt. Stan recognises these calming rituals and decides to make his own contribution. He says placatingly: 'You're right about France of course. They do these things very well.'

The woman says: 'We like France a lot. Do you know it?'

'I studied French at university. I used to go there frequently but not in recent years.'

This is an act of notable risk-taking for he has suffered grievously at the hands of garrulous francophiles convinced that his degree in French guarantees his fascination with their tales of holidays abroad. He braces himself for more provençal lifestyle-talk: the refurbished old farmhouse, pastis on the terrace at sunset, wily but characterful peasants possessed of the secret of the good life.

The woman beams with pleasure. 'So you speak French? I do wish I could speak foreign languages. Bob and I have tried hard over the years…'

'Well, you have,' Bob chips in.

'…but we don't seem to get very far. We had our honeymoon in Paris, didn't we Bob? We still go back sometimes to the little hotel where we stayed. It's kept going all these years. We had a lovely time on our honeymoon.'

Outside he can see the faint outlines of the Yorkshire Dales in the distance. The upturned hull of Penhill floats on the haze of morning heat. Beyond it lies Wensleydale and, beyond that, Great Shunner Fell; he will soon - on a morning such as this he hopes - be climbing its long southern flank on his journey back north.

'Do you know Paris at all?'

She is smiling. One of her ear-rings glints in the sun that slants in through the carriage window.

'Quite well. When I was a student I lived in the area of Les Halles.'

She looks blank. He adds: 'Les Halles was the old central market. They knocked it down to build a big new shopping complex and the Pompidou centre.'

She says she knows the Pompidou Centre but cannot remember what was there before it. She thinks it a pity when things like old markets disappear, and she wonders whether Paris isn't losing some of its character. She tells him of a picturesque square that she and Bob once came across while walking through Paris. She cannot now remember its name but it was very pretty, very quaint, a bit like one of those impressionist paintings.

Place de la Contrescarpe, Marie Salasca across the table from him, her smile grave and affectionate, the promise of a renewal of their passion warm in his veins...

Bob seems to be getting restless. He stretches and yawns and makes little grunting noises in his throat. He murmurs something about needing to stretch his legs. The woman ignores him and turns the conversation back to France, asking Stan how he came to study French and what other languages he speaks. He is embarrassed by her question. His spoken languages are in poor repair; he neglects his French, his Spanish is a rusting hulk, his German a sunken wreck. He reaches for the quickest reply and says he enjoyed French lessons at school. The woman says she hated French lessons but now regrets that she didn't take them more seriously. Bob says he could murder a cup of coffee and begins to get to his feet. The woman says: 'Would you mind keeping an eye on our things while we go for a coffee?'

'Of course.'

'I do envy people who can speak foreign languages,' she says. 'I wish I'd taken those lessons more seriously.'

She places her hands on the table and pushes herself up. Bob is already in the aisle; he takes her arm and helps her out from the table. Stan watches them move off, the man resting his large hand protectively on the woman's shoulder. He feels a stab of nostalgia for the lost companionability of marriage. At sixty years of age, he tells himself, it is unlikely he will embark on another affair and almost inconceivable that he will marry again. But such is the power of the romantic dream, such the prompting of his fading but still insistent lust that even as he thinks this he knows he does not accept it. His mind strays again to Marie Salasca. He tries to imagine her in her sixties but cannot get past the memories he carries of her from his youth. He is surprised now that he failed to keep in touch, given the impact she had on his life. 'I wish I'd taken those lessons more seriously,' the woman said. How seriously did he take them before Marie Salasca? Not very. Afterwards of course it was a different story.

# 6

## French Lessons

The air in the classroom is congealing with heat and boredom. Stan looks at his watch under the desk; it is stuck on half-past three. The next half-hour stretches into eternity. He risks a sideways glance through the window beside him. Some fourth-year girls are on the tennis courts, their legs golden-brown against their short white skirts. He feels the familiar warmth in his abdomen and crotch spreading like a slow explosion.

'Walker! Concentrate on the matter in hand, please. How would you translate the next sentence?'

Mr Derry is staring straight at him - wearily, without animosity, almost sympathetically, for he too is bored, worn down by the heat and his day-long struggle with forgetful, frivolous and obtuse minds. This should be one of the high points of his day: prose composition with the lower sixth, the ones who have *chosen* to study French, the ones who are 'university material', the future linguists of the nation. But the day has been long and hot. Stan feels that only professional decorum stands between Mr Derry and a frank admission of his solidarity in tedium with Stan and the lower-sixth French group. They are fellow victims of the weather and the state's absurd insistence on chaining its youth to the wheel of scholarship and learning.

'Well, Walker?'

Stan is looking down at the page before him, searching feverishly for the point in the text that Mr Derry is referring to. He finds it; the next sentence is easy: 'Guy shook his head and left the room.' He looks up and recites the sentence that has already arranged itself in his head: 'Guy secoua la tête et quitta la pièce.' Mr Derry nods, repeats the phrase and asks for other possible translations. The class remains silent. Mr Derry remains silent. Only the muted thwack of racket on ball and the distant shouts of the fourth-year girls is a reminder that sound is still possible. The silence lengthens, is absorbed into the atmosphere and returned to the class as heat and embarrassment. Mr Derry knows this and exploits it. Silence is one of his favourite pedagogical tools, silence prolonged to the point at which skins prickle, brains churn, minds turn inwards to contemplate, aghast, their utter emptiness. Beneath the desk Stan sees that the world has moved forward by three minutes.

'Any idea, Walker?'

This is a common pattern: question, silence, appeal to Walker. Stan is Mr Derry's star pupil and he wishes he weren't. Mr Derry has ambitions for him, hoping that he will go on to study French at Oxford or Cambridge, but Stan has other ideas, preferring history and English literature. Of course he hasn't told Mr Derry this. He sometimes thinks things would have been easier – easier for him, easier for Mr Derry - if he had been less adept at French, if he didn't have a brain that soaked up words, phrases and grammatical constructions like a sponge. But he knows at bottom that he wouldn't want that for he would then miss out on those little pleasures of vanity and mock modesty that accompany what he now finds himself saying: 'I think you can say *hocher la tête*. Unless that means to *nod* your head. I'm not sure.' Behind him he can hear Pip Slaley muttering under his breath: 'You bloody creep, Walker.'

'It can mean both,' says Mr Derry (Stan knew it could), 'depending on the context.' He turns to the board and starts to write out the phrases while pronouncing them over his shoulder.

'And a third way of saying 'shake one's head' is *branler la tête*.'

He adds the phrase to the list. Some of the class open their vocabulary books and copy the phrases down. Others take the opportunity, while Mr Derry's back is turned, to look around and stretch their arms to the ceiling, or simply to stare at it, stunned by the pointlessness of knowing multiple ways of saying 'shake your head'. Stan absorbs *branler la tête* into his sponge and looks out at the girls on the tennis court, seeking out the shapely ones with their tight little breasts and brown legs, feeling the warmth rise into his penis.

As Mr Derry turns round to face the class again he is muttering something about the 'vulgar meaning it has in the reflexive form.' Stan's mind has wandered and he is not sure what 'it' refers to but he thinks it must be the verb *branler*. There is a subtle change in the atmosphere of the classroom, a faint tremor on the air, as of an awakening. Vulgar meanings have that effect on the lower sixth. The serpent Prurience stirs in the dank pit of their boredom. There occurs a lifting of weary heads, a flicker of attentiveness across dull features. Mr Derry hesitates, appears to be on the point of satisfying this transient thirst for knowledge, then moves on.

'O.K. Let's have a look at the next sentence.'

Heads droop. Features re-compose themselves stoically for silent suffering. Stan looks at his watch. It is twenty to four.

After the class he went with Pip Slaley to the library to consult the dictionary. They tried the large Harrap, the most likely source of enlightenment, but could find nothing in its renderings of *branler* – 'to swing, shake (one's legs etc.); to wag (one's head)' - to satisfy their curiosity. Pip snaps the dictionary shut, takes out his comb and re-arranges his quiff in the reflection of a glass book-case.

'Who writes these bloody dictionaries? Don't they want us to know any French?'

Stan shrugs his shoulders and says: 'We could ask Marie. We can just catch her before she leaves the staffroom.' He says this without conviction, having already lost interest in the matter. In any case, he doesn't really think they can ask Marie for he can imagine their embarrassment if the answer to their question turns out to be what he suspects.

But Pip likes the idea; any pretext for approaching Marie is welcome to him and the question of embarrassment is irrelevant. Pip isn't easily embarrassed.

Marie Salasca is the school's French *assistante* and for the whole of this school year she has held the boys of the lower sixth in a spell of awe-struck admiration and hopeless lust. She is twenty-one years

43

of age, older than the boys but not so much older as to render their dreams of more intimate relations with her totally unrealistic. Her jet-black hair and complexion the colour of milky coffee speak to their wintry northern souls of the warmth and sensuality of her native Provence. The rumour that her place of birth was in fact Algeria simply adds further lustre to her exotic aura. She is tall and slim, with breasts whose fullness is accentuated by her flat stomach and narrow waist. According to Pip who affects an intellectual preoccupation with what he calls 'the science of sex-appeal', it is this slight disproportion between the slenderness of her body and the fullness of her breasts that is the source of her erotic power.

Alas, Marie is also aloof. She has met with a cool disdain all efforts to tempt her out of her shell of professional rectitude onto more intimate ground, though as the year has progressed and winter has given way to spring and spring to summer, it has been noted that she has become more open and friendly. Pip, who takes pride in his ability to turn a sharp phrase, says that she has 'warmed with the weather'. It is also known that Marie's engagement to a young man in France has failed to withstand the rigours of separation. According to Pip, she is now 'a free agent in the market-place of sexual exchange' and he has announced his intention of 'putting in a bid'.

It is difficult to know how seriously Pip takes his own pronouncements on relations between the sexes, though it is accepted that his knowledge is beyond the ordinary. The sexual experiences of the lower-sixth boys are sizeable in number but limited in scope. They have kissed, stroked and groped their way through countless encounters in the local cinemas, back-alleys, woods and lanes; they have glimpsed their final destination and the means of arriving there but for reasons they only half understand few of them have completed the journey. It is 1960. They are the products of a demure decade. The nineteen-fifties have now shuffled off into historical obscurity but the age of sexual liberation has yet to dawn and the majority of them still bear their virginity like an unwanted disease.

Pip is one of the exceptions to the general rule. His completed journeys are a regular feature of the lunch-break gatherings in which Stan, Pip and others take off to a far corner of the school playing-field so that the smokers among them can indulge their vice as far from the windows of the school staff-room as it is possible to get. They sit and lie on the grass, the smokers with their backs to the school building, pulling on their cigarettes and flapping their hands to disperse the evidence of their criminality. Pip squats among them with his legs crossed, holding court. He is slight in build with blue-grey eyes and fine blond hair that he combs into a wave above his forehead. He is the only one among them on whom the black school blazer and grey trousers appear a triumph of sartorial elegance. He has the habit, as he speaks, of raising his finger to emphasise particular points of his stories which are recounted in a language of self-conscious preciousness that he has quarried from a surprising breadth of literary knowledge.

'I have a tale to tell that may be of some interest to you worshippers at the shrine of Venus,' he announces, his finger in the air demanding attention. He then embarks on an account of his latest 'amorous assignment' with some 'Emma Bovary of the coalfield' who has been captivated by his air of aristocratic grace and elegance. Amid the groans and shouts of 'bullshit, Slaley', there is some amused laughter. Pip proceeds regardless. His self-confidence is absolute, his subject-matter and the manner of its telling stir some deep, turbid well of emotions in his audience – envy, prurience, sexual contempt - that compels their attention.

In Stan, Pip arouses amusement and irritation in equal measure. It is irritation he feels now as they stand in the school library, with Pip giving his quiff a final flick and straightening the sleeves of his jacket. Stan is feeling priggish. He dislikes the casual opportunism with which Pip has turned a search for the meaning of a French word into a way of pursuing his designs on Marie Salasca. Why then does he, Stan, intend to accompany him? He has to admit that his irritation has another cause; he feels that he has been subjected to an unwelcome challenge. For the fact is that he too has designs on Marie, though 'designs' is perhaps too strong a word for the mixture of hopeful fantasising and weak resolutions to approach her – no sooner taken than abandoned – that has been a feature of his mental life for much of this school year. In Marie's classes of French conversation Stan is the most competent speaker. Her relief and pleasure at having a pupil who can sustain a conversation, however mundane, in accurate French has created a bond of friendly respect between them that Stan would like to transform into something closer and more personal.

It is thus in a spirit of unwilling rivalry that he joins Pip on his short journey along the corridor from the school library. He half hopes that Marie will already have left the building for he fears that what is about to happen may set back rather than advance his own cause.

As luck would have it they meet her as she emerges from the staffroom. Pip quickens his stride to get ahead of Stan, and says: 'Marie, I wonder if we could have a few minutes of your precious time.'

'Of course. I have plenty time.'

'Nevertheless, we mustn't detain you too long. You will want to get home.'

Stan finds Pip's attempts at graciousness rather wheedling and feels that he has struck the wrong note. Marie is looking at him in the same cool, appraising manner she has in class when listening to his faltering attempts to speak French (for, much to his regret and frustration, Pip's verbal facility is limited to his native tongue). She carries a set of books across her chest and Stan notices again the little physical imperfections – the rough and bitten fingernails, the slightly pitted skin around her cheekbones - that clash with the image of her that he routinely carries in his head. These things make her seem less remote yet more alluring, as though the cold beauty of some immaculate sex-goddess has been transformed into warm and vulnerable flesh. He feels suddenly ashamed of his complicity in Pip's plan.

Pip has immediately asked her for the meaning of the term 'se branler'. He puts the question in a tone of frank innocence accompanied by his most winning smile. Marie flushes slightly round the neck but answers without hesitation: "Se branler'? Let me see. It means the same as 'masturber'. How do you say in English 'masturber'?' Stan goes hot with embarrassment, though this is exactly what he has been expecting. Pip remains unmoved, staring her straight in the eye and continuing to smile as he says: 'It's the same word – masturbate.'

'Ah oui.'

Whatever brief discomfort she may have felt has passed. She holds Pip's look and nods. Her face is expressionless.

'But in French 'se branler' is slang when it means the same as 'masturber',' she says. 'You have a slang word in English for 'masturbate'?'

She is taller than Pip and only slightly less tall than Stan. She has been resting her shoulders against the wall beside the staffroom door but now, as she speaks, she stands upright and tilts her head back as though she wishes to observe Pip from a greater distance and height. For the first time Pip hesitates. 'Er, yes of course... there are various possibilities. Now what would be the most common?' He turns to Stan, whom he has so far shut out of the conversation, but Marie continues to stare straight at Pip, forcing his attention back to her.

She says: 'Surely you have not forgotten.' Her eyes narrow and her voice hardens. 'It must be such a common habit among schoolboys.'

Two little stains of pink appear at Pip's temples, a slight discoloration of his smooth, pale skin that Stan has noticed is the closest he ever comes to a physical display of tension or embarrassment. He is silent for a moment and then, forcing his features into a smile, he says: 'Among *some* schoolboys perhaps. Those who can't do any better.'

'Ah yes, perhaps,' she says. She then turns to Stan, making it clear that she has no interest in the direction that Pip's remarks have taken.

'And you Stanley Walker, it surprises me that you do not know the meaning of this word. You are so strong in French.'

Stan feels as though he is suddenly transparent, his seedy imaginings exposed to that calm, frank gaze that rests on him like a mocking caress. He mumbles: 'It wasn't in the dictionary. At least that particular meaning wasn't in the dictionary.'

'I see. So your English…how do you call it? …prudishness... it affects even your makers of dictionaries.'

Stan's mind is racing. He says without thinking: 'Oh, you know what these dictionary-makers are like. Perhaps they were never schoolboys.'

Her eyes flash with amusement and she smiles for the first time since they accosted her.

'Ah yes, very good. That must be it. They were never schoolboys.'

Suddenly she laughs, emitting a trill of gaiety that contrasts with her usually earnest demeanour. Stan, who does not find his remark very witty, is surprised and gratified. Marie grips her books tighter to her chest and prepares to leave. As she turns to walk along the corridor to the school's main door, she says: 'That reminds me. I have something for you, Stanley Walker. It was a suggestion by Mr Derry. It is a book. I shall give it to you tomorrow after your conversation class.'

Stan was dumfounded. Marie Salasca had graced him, Stanley Walker, with her favour! She had smiled at him and laughed at his weak joke! She had clearly preferred him to Pip Slaley! And now she had a book for him. What could it be? And, equally important, what might it lead to? These were the two questions that held him for the rest of the day, and much of the night, in a fever of puzzlement and excited fantasising.

The book that she gave him was entitled *L'Etranger* by Albert Camus.

As she hands it to him - standing by her desk at the front of the classroom, the rest of the pupils having left the room - she says that Mr Derry has told her about Stan's reading programme and she thought that the book might interest him. Stan finds this implausible. It is true that Mr Derry, having decided that Stan is the only one of this year's lower-sixth French group who has a chance of entry to Oxford or Cambridge, has made special efforts to encourage him to widen his reading. But as yet Stan has failed to be encouraged; there is no reading programme; there are two novels by Pierre Loti and Henri Troyat, borrowed by Stan from the school library at the instigation of Mr Derry, that have rested unread at Stan's bedside for almost a month. Mr Derry has made no further enquiry about them. It simply isn't credible that he has told Marie that Stan has a reading programme. She is playing a game.

But what game? Stan looks into her dark eyes, searching for clues. She places her hand on the desk and rests her weight on it, bending her upper body from the hip. His desire to touch her, to rest his hand on the curve of her body and slide it up to the breasts that press against her white blouse, is almost irresistible. He feels something like panic at the madness of the idea and checks himself. What should he do? He mustn't act stupidly and ruin everything but he must do something to advance his cause and bring the situation to some sort of resolution. At the very least he must ask her to go out with him.

But at the last moment his courage fails him. He mumbles his thanks to her and walks off. He is instantly angry with himself for having missed his opportunity. He has condemned himself to more days and nights of fruitless longing and to the agonising uncertainty of not knowing what, if anything, she wants of him.

Albert Camus was spared the fate of Loti and Troyat; Stan set about reading the book that very evening, intending to finish it as soon as possible so that he could return it to her. He still felt that he needed a pretext for approaching her; then, having approached her, he would work the conversation round to the point at which he could ask her to go to the cinema with him.

His love of English literature has not extended to French. The need to consult a dictionary every few sentences makes the process of reading laborious and unrewarding. But this time he makes quick progress. The language of the book is surprisingly simple and he needs less help from his dictionary. When, at the beginning of the second chapter, he comes to the episode in which Meursault, the hero of the novel, makes love to Marie Cardona after a visit to the cinema, he feels sure he has seen the point of Marie's gift, the hidden message that she wants to convey. He instantly realises that the idea is crazy, unbelievable, a result of the concurrence of the fictional episode with a fantasy that has played out in his mind many times. But the idea will not leave him alone. It accompanies him to bed, where it wraps him in its hot and sticky embrace throughout a night of fitful sleep. It comes down to breakfast with him, urging him on to action, yearning to be made real, like some restless, wandering spirit seeking bodily incarnation.

It is his need to shake off this continuing torment that overcomes his fear of rebuff and drives him to act. He pursues her later that day as they all come out of the dinner-hall onto the school playing-field. He is aware of Pip and the smokers watching from their corner of the field as he catches her up.

'Marie.'

She turns to face him. Although there is no-one close by, he speaks quietly, as though afraid that Pip and the smokers will overhear.

'I thought…I wondered if you would like to come to the cinema with me.'

She looks at him in her imperturbable way, the slightest of smiles playing round the corners of her mouth. Her self-possession is terrifying! She says: 'No. I think not. But thank you for asking.'

The disappointment he feels is lightened by something else that he realises is relief. At least he has asked her and he now knows the answer to the question that has been torturing him. He can turn round and go and join his friends, crack jokes, talk nonsense, have fun. Life can return to normal.

But she continues: 'Do you have a bicycle?' He nods, uncomprehendingly. She says: 'I have a bicycle. I bicycle almost every evening when the weather is good. It isn't often good in this terrible climate of yours. It seems such a pity to sit in the cinema. We shall go for a ride on our bicycles.'

Thus it is that he finds himself cycling along a deserted country-road on the outskirts of Calcroft (the winding-gear of the pit is visible above distant trees) with the beautiful Marie Salasca from Provence who, according to rumour, was born in North Africa. For a while he has a curious sense of dissociation, as though he is standing outside his own body watching some other Stanley Walker talking and turning the pedals, with beside him this bird of paradise who has inexplicably alighted among the pit-heaps of South Yorkshire. He has prepared phrases in English and French - opening gambits, statements about life that he imagines to be smart or profound - for he is afraid that conversation might fail to take hold. But he is delighted to realise that his fears were groundless. She speaks easily, mainly in English with occasional forays into French when the words fail to come, and he speaks easily in return, exclusively in English. As they stop and sit on a stream bank at the edge of fields and woods, his cup of delight runs over, for she confesses to him that she likes Englishmen; she likes their reserve and (compared with Frenchmen for, as she sagaciously points out, all things are relative) their lack of vanity.

'Your friend Philip Slaley, he is too much like a Frenchman — beau parleur, pas sincère. How do you say 'beau parleur' in English?'

It is the first time Stan has heard the phrase but he senses what it means. 'A smooth talker,' he says.

'Ah yes, a smooth talker. Just like a Frenchman.'

Stan remembers her recently failed love-affair and wonders whether it explains the note of bitterness. But when she eventually mentions a man by name, it is her father.

'My father, he was a smooth talker too. He had many women. He broke my mother's heart. We lived in Algeria at the time. They divorced and my mother and I went back to live in France where my mother was born, the Lubéron in Provence. Do you know it?' Stan shakes his head. He has only been to France once, on a school trip to Britanny when he was in the fourth year. She says: 'I was six years old.'

She goes quiet. In order to break the silence Stan says: 'What did your father do?'

'Do? He stayed in Algeria where he had his own business. He was born there, like me. He was a true *pied noir*. He stayed and continued to chase the women.'

Stan feels uneasy. The self-satisfaction of a minute ago is draining away. One moment he and Marie Salasca are sitting on a grassy bank in the country on a sweet-smelling, balmy evening in June, he transfixed by her beauty, she speaking flattering words about his countrymen; the next, she is telling him she does not like men who chase women! Is it a warning to him? He must be smart and subtle, pretend indifference to those eyes like dark jewels, those lips that are so full and soft that he can imagine their touch on his. Above all he must say nothing that might reveal his secret intent.

But then how will his secret intent become known and achieve realisation?

He says: 'What is a *pied noir*?'

She explains, looking at him in her earnest, teacherly way that has the curious effect of making her appear more desirable than ever. She describes for him the French colonisation of Algeria. His heart sinks. A lesson in history! He is being given a lesson in history by Marie Salasca, when all he wants to do is take her in his arms and press her back into the deep, yielding grass and kiss those sumptuous lips. His mind is churning frantically in an attempt to think of some way to bring the conversation back to more congenial matters, such as admirably reserved Englishmen who are lacking in vanity. But then she says something that shakes him out of his self-absorption.

'And now they are killing people. And being killed.'

She notices his look of surprise and says: 'The war! You must know that there is a war in Algeria. The French army and the *colons* - my father and his people - against the Muslims. My father has seen people killed. His neighbour's son was kidnapped. He was twenty years old. They found him on their doorstep, tied in a sack. His throat was cut.'

He knows there is a war in Algeria. He has seen news items on television and headlines in newspapers. But he has never read the stories beneath the headlines. Politics doesn't interest him, and French-Algerian politics is an echo from another, too distant world. Yet for Marie Salasca it is close and real. It is the slaughter of her father's neighbour's son. Tied in a sack! They cut his throat and tied him in a sack!

She surprises him further by telling him she sympathises with the liberation movement, the FLN, despite their methods. She supposes it all goes back to her attitude to her father who is a domineering and sometimes violent man. When she was a child she saw him beat a family servant whom she loved. The memory of Ali, and the helpless pity and fear she felt at his pain and humiliation - an ageing man on his knees with his arm protecting his head - have remained with her. From that moment on, her love for her father was poisoned by fear and the beginnings of hate. Later, when she was older and living in France, her mother told her of her father's infidelities that had ruined their marriage. That was some years ago now and she hasn't been back to Algeria since. She has cut all ties with her father.

'You know that Albert Camus was born in Algeria? He was a *pied noir* too. In 1957 they gave him the Nobel prize and afterwards he made a speech. He said that he couldn't support the FLN because their terrorist acts might result in the death of his mother. His mother still lived in Algeria, you see. For Camus, Algeria and its *pied noir* community was his mother whom he loved. For me it is my father, and my attitude to Algeria is different. It is more a mixture of love and hate. The trouble is Algeria will not leave me alone. It is a beautiful country and I still regret it. Remind me, how do you say 'regretter' in English?'

'We say 'miss'. You mean you miss it.'

'Yes, I still miss it. When we went to live in France, my mother and I, the children in my French school mocked me for being a *pied noir*. They asked me to show them my black feet. 'T'as les pieds noirs? Montre-nous'. They laughed at me. I hated them. That is all in the past now but I still do not feel truly at home in France. I do not feel truly at home anywhere. Before my mother told me the truth about my father I used to visit Algeria every year. It was necessary for me, necessary for my *bien-être*, my well-being. That is why I love the writing of Albert Camus. He understood the power and the beauty of Algeria.'

He has never heard a girl talk like this. His thwarted desire and his frustration at the turn the conversation has taken are infiltrated by another feeling that is new to him: a sense of his own frivolity in the face of her intellectual earnestness and experience of life.

She pauses and then says: 'What do you think of the book I gave you?'

He feels caught out. He is on the point of saying that he liked it because the French was easy and he didn't have to read with an open dictionary beside him, but he stops himself for he realises that the book has meant more to him than that. It has left a residue of thought and feeling that lies, unexamined, in some silted depth of his mind. Under the pressure of her question, he forces it to the surface and, falteringly, into words.

'I think I understand Meursault. I recognise something in him. Perhaps it's just his laziness... No, laziness isn't right. It's more like apathy or indifference. I think it's something we all feel sometimes. Or maybe it's just me…' He pauses, watching her reaction, still the pupil awaiting encouragement. She nods slowly, as though assuring him that it is not just him.

He goes on: 'There is an episode in the book where Meursault's boss offers him promotion, a new job in Paris. Meursault turns it down because he can't see the point of it. I understand that. It's like when Mr Derry keeps pushing me to apply to go to Oxford University. I know it's important to think of such things but I have to force myself to take them seriously. Much of the time they don't seem to matter.'

This seems to interest her; her eyes focus more intently on his face. He says: 'And sometimes nothing seems to matter. It's not because I'm unhappy or anything like that. It's just the way things are. Nothing seems to matter because of the way things are. That's the only way I can put it. And I think Meursault feels like that.'

For a moment she gazes down at the grass on which they are sitting, then around them at the trees and, beyond the trees, at the electricity pylons and the winding-gear of the pit. When she looks at him again, she is smiling. Her smile is warm and sympathetic. She says: 'Ah oui, mon ami, I think you have seen the truth of the book.'

When, in September, he announced to his parents that he was going to apply to university to study French, they were both pleased and baffled by his scholarly progress. To go to university was certainly a fine thing but to choose to study French there was not what had been foreseen. His mother suspected the influence of the French girl he had spent time with earlier in the summer and whose return home to France had left him so unhappy. For his father it simply confirmed Stan's earlier disappointing decision to study arts subjects at A-level. Dad was good at arithmetic and had a book called *The Marvels and Mysteries of Science* which Stan devoured as a child. For Dad science made sense; it was true knowledge with practical uses. But he couldn't see the point of French, particularly the works of literature that were beginning to absorb much of Stan's attention. According to Stan's cousin Frank, who had worked at the pit-top since the age of fifteen and was studying at night-class to be an electrician, French was 'neither use nor ornament'. Stan's parents were less blunt, and contented themselves with wondering aloud where it would get him and whether he would end up 'frenchified' like Melvin Nesbitt, the newsagent's son. Melvin had spent time abroad and returned smoking cigarettes that gave off strange odours and wearing clothes which, together with his rather bulging eyes – the consequence of a thyroid condition – gave him a bizarre resemblance to Peter Lorre in *Casablanca*. He was unable to adapt to life in Calcroft and, in his mid-twenties, he developed mental problems and spent much of his remaining years in the psychiatric ward of Doncaster Infirmary.

Perhaps Stan's parents felt that Melvin was a poor recommendation for the cosmopolitan life.

## 7

## Home territory

The train is approaching York. Stan can see the grey triple towers of the minster in the distance. The old names of the city – Eboracum, Yorvik - run through his mind together with confused memories of the day-trips of his childhood and youth. Beside the track the low brick buildings and water tanks of a sewage works give way to rows of houses, then a glimpse of the river Ouse. A rowing eight are sliding back and forth on their seats, forcing their boat forward in little spurts that instantly slow down, so that for a split second they appear to be stationary before the next forward thrust. As the train overtakes them their boat seems to stop and slide backwards before slipping away behind his shoulder.

The woman and her husband are gathering their things from the table and the luggage-rack. She says: 'Well, it's been very nice meeting you. I hope you enjoy the rest of your trip.' The man lowers a travelling-bag to the table. He nods at Stan and says: 'All the best.'

Stan wishes them well and hopes they enjoy their stay in York. They turn to join the slowly shuffling crush of people leaving the train. He glimpses them again on the platform, Bob trailing a large suitcase on wheels, the woman carrying the travelling-bag and looking back towards the train. A moment later they vanish into the crowd.

Their seats are taken by a boy in a red tee-shirt and jeans, and a young woman whom Stan takes to be his mother. She places a pile of belongings – a magazine, a mobile phone and a carrier bag full of packets of food – onto the table and sits down with a loud puff of relief. As the train pulls out of the station, the boy waves wildly to someone on the platform while the woman leans across him, waving and mouthing silent goodbyes. Then she sits back in her seat and wafts her hand in front of her reddened features.

South of York he is on home territory. To the east, flat plain stretches to Hull and the Humber estuary, to the west are Leeds and Bradford, conjoined by their relentless Victorian expansion. Almost a century ago his father was born on the outskirts of Leeds, where the city puts out long fingers of terraced cottages, mills, churches and chapels into the first shallow valleys of the Yorkshire Dales; and it was at Leeds that Stan chose to spend his years as a university student. The headmaster of the grammar school, Mr Boothroyd, had given the sixth form a talk, telling them what a fortunate generation they were and how they had opportunities that had not been open to the majority of their parents. The state would support them financially to study the subjects of their choice at the finest universities in the land. All they had to do was to convince those universities that they were worthy of being given the chance. Furthermore, they would find there was more to university life than studying books. They would make new friends, join societies, play sports; they would enter into a new world in which their intellectual, social, and physical capacities would blend together in that ideal end-product of human evolution, 'the rounded person'.

Stan didn't much like Mr Boothroyd. He felt uncomfortable with his smart suits and ties, the whiskers that looped down over his cheeks, his drawling accent, his frequent references to the Oxford college at which he had studied 'Greats'. During Stan's first year at the grammar school, when he had rebelled against the school's attempts to make him abandon his beloved game of football in favour of rugby, Mr Boothroyd had been nasty and snobbish, suggesting, in subtly veiled but unmistakable terms, that rugby was the game played by a superior class of people, a class of people that Stan should aspire to join. If Mr Boothroyd was a rounded person and if Oxford was the place at which the rounding had occurred Stan knew that Oxford wasn't for him. He knew there were other universities of less ethereal hue and that were closer to home in more senses than the merely geographical - universities like Leeds.

The boy opposite him has unrolled a pair of earphones and now sits listening while chewing gum. Wires trail from his ears. Stan can hear the rhythmic buzz of the music. The boy begins to tap lightly on the table top with the fingers of one hand. He gazes out of the window, wearing a dreamy half-smile, as though hypnotised by his own satisfied senses. Chewing, tapping, listening, watching the world go by. Stan suddenly feels happy. Life is simple. Outside, the summer is mellowing into a golden autumn, ahead of him lie the hills.

The only shadow in his path is the book. He decides he must read it before starting his walk. With the remainder of his train journey to Edale ahead of him, followed by a night in a guest house there, he should have time. He gets up to retrieve it from his rucksack.

Back in his seat he stares down at the cover. The title, *Publicans and Sinners*, is displayed in stark red lettering against a black-and-white image of a child standing before a building that bears the name 'Railway Hotel'. At the bottom of the cover is a quotation from one of the reviews: 'A moving account of the *annus horribilis* of one woman's childhood'. He looks out of the window, disconcerted by the quotation, taken again by a reluctance to start reading.

The cooling-towers of power-stations stand in steaming huddles on either side of the railway track. He knows their names: Ferrybridge, Eggborough, Drax, the ganglia of the national grid, radiating power-lines like stretched nerves. As the train glides forward the two to the right change positions like groups of stately dancers on a rotating ballroom floor, sidling together, then apart again, before wheeling slowly out of sight. Most of the pits that supplied them have closed since the great strike; grassed-over spoil-heaps stand like the burial mounds of the once powerful King Coal.

In a short time the train will pass through his native village of Calcroft. He looks out for the approaching signs: a farmer's barn by a row of cottages and, just beyond it, a stand of trees where he played as a boy and where, years later, Marie Salasca deftly relieved him of his virginity to the thunderous roar of a passing express. But what he is really searching for - pressing his head sideways against the carriage window and staring hard ahead - is the building that is represented on the cover of the book. Beside the building there is a bridge under which the train will pass, and it was on that bridge, fifty years ago to this very month, that he stood gazing intently towards the Railway Hotel, hoping for a glimpse of the girl who was later to become his wife.

The village is upon him and gone in seconds, the bridge a mere flash of brickwork, the Railway Hotel glimpsed in the click of a shutter, with its windows boarded up and its roof holed where tiles have slipped. He relaxes back into his seat.

Fifty years! And he can still remember the moment he first heard her name, still remember the three of them sitting at the table having their tea, with the leaden sky of that damp summer day outside and his father about to say something. You always knew the signs when he was about to say something: a puckering of the lips, a tightening of the muscle in his jaw, warming up for the act of speech. It was a necessary ritual perhaps because Dad's talking parts didn't get much exercise. The table at which they ate their meals was an altar to silence broken by the tinkling of spoons and knives on mugs and plates and by muffled exchanges between Stan and his mother. Partly it was Dad's work that made him silent, the exhaustion of the pit and his part-time job at the Railway Hotel. But it was more than this. Stan thinks now that he suffered from depression though it was a word they didn't use. People like them didn't get illnesses like that. For them Dad was just quiet, didn't waste words, kept himself to himself. Or he was a miserable old devil who needed to pull himself together. It depended on how indulgent you felt. Mostly you just accepted it as a part of life. It was one of the fixed points of Stan's childhood world: schooldays and weekends, football in winter, cricket in summer, the streets and ginnels of Calcroft, auntie Brenda's back ache, auntie Peggy's Geordie accent, his mother's kindness, his father's silence.

He knows the exact date on which it happened: the second of June, 1953, the day of the coronation of Queen Elizabeth II. The coincidence seems to invite a prophetic reading for, to the ten-year-old Stan, the girl whose name he was about to hear was queenly; her behaviour was often capricious, her motives inscrutable. But she was vulnerable and anxious too. Stan's mother said she was 'needy', and for a while Stan liked to think that it was he whom she needed.

So Dad is about to say something. The silence deepens as Stan and his mother pick up the signs of his imminent foray into speech.

'There's a new manager arrived at the Railway.'

Mam looks up with a wary expression on her face. She doesn't like Dad doing another job in addition to the pit. She says they can manage, they don't need the extra money. But Dad is stubborn, driven by fear of the poverty that ravaged his childhood. Stan knows she will be torn, half wanting the new manager to tell Dad he doesn't need him and half fearing Dad's reaction – the slump into bitter silence - if he does.

Finally she speaks: 'Oh. What's he called?'

'Stapleton. There are three of them. Him, his missus and their little lass.'

'What's the lass called?'

'Stapleton. Like her dad. The wife's a Stapleton too.'

Dad grins. Mam laughs, partly with amusement, partly with relief. The atmosphere lightens, as though some pressure in the air has been relieved. Dad has that effect; he controls the weather of the house.

'I know that, you daft article. What's her first name?'

'Catherine.'

'Catherine. That's a nice name. What are her parents called?'

'He's Robert. She's Helen. He wears a dicky bow.'

He looks at Stan and winks as though dicky bows are the key to some private joke between them. Stan grins back. He feels happy. Dad's having a good day.

'Ooh lord, a dicky bow,' says Mam. 'You don't see many of them in Calcroft. I'll bet they don't come from round here.'

'No. They're from down south. Mr Stapleton said he used to manage a hotel in Suffolk.'

'Suffolk! That's a long way. What's made them come all the way up here?'

Dad shakes his head. 'Can't say. I only popped in for a couple of minutes. To see how things stand with me.'

Mam hesitates a few seconds, then asks: 'And what did he say?' Though she already knows the answer from Dad's cheery mood.

'He says he'll be needing some help. At least to begin with though he can't promise anything in the long term. It depends how the business goes.'

He raises his mug of tea to his lips. Mam nods but keeps quiet. She starts to brush the crumbs into a little pile on the table-cloth. Then she smiles her what's-done's-done smile and says: 'And what's their daughter like? Did you see her?'

'No, she's still down south finishing off her schooling. But I saw a photo. She's a pretty lass. She's ten. Like our Stan.'

Mam laughs and looks at Stan. 'Do you hear that, son. You'll soon have a new class-mate.'

Stan is curious about this girl from the south who has a nice name and whose dad wears a dicky bow, but he's not going to admit it. He reaches out to the biscuit plate, pondering his reply, playing it cool. Then he says: 'Aye but she's only a lass.'

And there it stands, a memory diamond-sharp, deposited by that crumbling, slithering landslip of a year that swept him on into new and frightening territory. As yet, however, as Dad spoke and Stan and his mother listened, grateful for his cheerfulness and volubility, Stan's world was still in place; the ground was firm, the first tremor barely perceptible, a mere flicker of interest in a girl's name in that summer of nineteen-fifty-three.

# 8

## What's in a Name?

Earlier that day he had watched the coronation at his uncle Harold's since at the time his parents did not have a television. Harold had closed his shop and invited them to join him and auntie Rachel. While they were watching - Stan, his mother, uncle Harold and auntie Rachel (for Dad, contemptuous of royalty, had preferred to work on his garden) - an incident occurred that left a deep impression on Stan's mind. The camera, which was panning slowly down the aisle of Westminster Abbey, came to rest on Winston Churchill.

'Ah but he's a great man, isn't he?'

The speaker was auntie Rachel. Stan looked at her, trying to gain further guidance from her expression. She was a good-looking woman with long, dark hair and lips whose fullness was accentuated by the ruby-red lipstick she always wore. It was said that strong men would agree to shop for their wives in the hope of catching a glimpse of auntie Rachel behind the counter at uncle Harold's store. She continued to stare at the screen, nodding slightly in confirmation of what she had said. Stan looked towards his mother and uncle Harold but their faces revealed nothing and neither of them spoke.

He was puzzled. Mr Churchill a great man? His family didn't like Mr Churchill. He wasn't sure how he knew this for his parents rarely talked politics. But somehow, from somewhere or somebody, perhaps from passing comments made by his father about things heard on the radio or read in the newspaper, he had absorbed this certain truth: his family did not like Mr Churchill. So why was auntie Rachel, who was also their family, saying he was a great man? Whatever it was that Mr Churchill had done to earn their dislike hadn't put auntie Rachel off.

As they walked home from uncle Harold's Stan could have asked his mother, who was his oracle, for the solution to the riddle. Perhaps he did, but if so he has forgotten her answer. All that remains with him now is the memory of his puzzlement and, later that day, of the obscure sense he had of a connection between Auntie Rachel's comment on Mr Churchill and the name of the young girl uttered by his father over the tea-table. It was as though Auntie Rachel's words had opened up a crack in his world into which his father - with his story of Catherine Stapleton, the hotel in Suffolk where she had lived and the father who wore a dicky bow - had slipped the blade of a knife, widening the crack until he could see through.

Of course he had known that there was a world outside Calcroft, a world in which people voted Conservative, wore dicky bows and preferred rugby union to football, but he suddenly felt that that world was closer at hand than he had ever realised. Furthermore, his perception of it had changed; from being a world towards which he was indifferent, even faintly hostile, it had become one that was infused with a strange allure. And that allure was embodied in one word above all others - Stapleton. He knew a Catherine – Catherine Grix, the younger sister of Billy Grix, one of his classmates. But Stapleton was new. He found the name elegant. He tried to imagine what sort of girl could have such a name and whenever he did this the same shapes and ideas rose within him. It was as though the name was a key that unlocked only the boxes labelled 'tall', 'dark-haired', 'willowy'. It seemed impossible to be short and dumpy and to be a Stapleton. Or to have freckles and frizzy hair like Maureen Burns who lived in the next street and fancied him, passing him notes in class that contained declarations of undying love and that always ended with a drawing of a heart pierced by an arrow.

During the following day he found himself wandering, as though by accident, past the Railway Hotel. It was a tall red-brick building with a long front that had stone columns on either side of the main entrance. Stan thought it was the finest building in the village. He wanted to stop and look through the windows though he knew she wasn't there for according to Dad she had stayed with her grandparents in Suffolk to complete her school year. It was only later that summer that he first saw her.

It was his cousin Keith who suggested they should go to the bridge by the Railway Hotel. Keith lived three doors away from Stan with uncle Ted and auntie Kate, and he and Stan had been born a week apart. He was short and fat with pink, podgy cheeks like a baby's. In Stan's eyes Keith was a bit of a genius. He loved drawing and drew ships, birds, castles, anything you liked, with a speed and accuracy that were astonishing. He could do voices and would pitch Stan into fits of giggles by having conversations with him in auntie Peggy's Geordie accent and calling him 'hinny' at the end of every sentence. He mimicked the opera-singers that he heard on Uncle Ted's old gramophone, singing their songs in a sort of imitation Italian that he made up as he went along. He called this his Mario Lanza act and said that if he decided against being a draughtsman (this being the career that uncle Ted had recommended to him on account of his drawing ability), singing in opera would do just as well.

But Keith's main pastime – more than a pastime, a passion – was train-spotting. On summer days he was a familiar figure on Calcroft bridge, watching and waiting, pencilling the numbers of passing engines into the notebook he kept in his pocket. At weekends Stan would sometimes accompany him on spotting expeditions to Doncaster Station and its outlying works that were known locally as the Plant. The Plant was one of their reasons for believing that Doncaster was a town that had an honourable place in the sun of national life. Great steam locomotives had been built there, including the greatest of them all, *Mallard*. Stan can still remember the astonishment and pride he felt when Keith told him that it was the fastest steam engine in the world. It had been driven at 126 miles per hour on a stretch of the London to Edinburgh track - the track that ran through Calcroft - and this was a world record.

But as he stands on Calcroft bridge on this day in late August, it is not steam engines that preoccupy him. The weather is hot. The railway lines, emerging from beneath the bridge, shimmer away into the distance like rivulets of molten silver. Keith wanders back and forth across the road, leaning his arms on the brick parapet of the bridge and staring ahead for the smudge of smoke on the horizon that is the first sign of an approaching train. Stan remains on the same side of the road as the Railway Hotel. From the top of the bridge he can see the front and one side of the building. Behind it there is an asphalt yard surrounded by a high brick wall. Only a fraction of the yard can be seen, a rough triangle of space bounded by the surrounding wall and the side of the hotel.

And it is there that he catches a glimpse of her, a figure with blond hair darting across the sunlit yard and stooping to pick something up, a white smudge against the black asphalt that must be a ball. She disappears instantly behind the bulky side of the hotel. He stands transfixed, willing her to emerge again while already adjusting in his mind his idea of Stapleton beauty. The tall, dark-haired and willowy girl of his imagination gives way to one who is slight and blond. He doesn't mind the transformation; he finds blond hair glamorous. He imagines her face, extraordinarily pretty with even white teeth and a rosebud mouth framed by the blond hair.

Keith is explaining something to do with a steam engine called *Hornet's Beauty*. It is the only one of its class that he hasn't seen and he has been told that it's in the paint-shop at the Plant; they must go and see it. Stan nods and grunts in reply while keeping his eyes fixed on the yard which is now like a lit stage abandoned by the principal actor.

He waited in vain. Trains came and went. Keith babbled happily on about the different classes of steam engine and spotting expeditions with uncle Ted to York and Newcastle. Stan continued to stare into the yard of the Railway Hotel. It remained empty, an abandoned stage. At tea-time they decided to leave. On their way back home Keith, whose technical knowledge was precise and voluminous, patiently explained the mysteries of Walschaerts gears and Kylchap blast pipes while Stan revolved in his mind stratagems for meeting Catherine Stapleton. If all else failed he knew that he simply had to wait for the first day back at school. There he would not only see her, but appear before her to his best advantage, a prize pupil (top of the class in English and Arithmetic) and a skilled sportsman and member of the school football team.

# 9

## Life Lessons

Mr Tomkiss loves the school piano. He even practises on it during the dinner-break. On warm days when the hall windows are left open, trills of notes float out and hover on the air as the pupils of Calcroft Juniors shout, run, fight, and kick footballs around the playground. Keith has told Stan that the music Mr Tomkiss plays is called 'classical' and it must be this classical stuff that he is playing now as they all file out of morning assembly and head for their classrooms. As he passes the piano, Stan sees that the piece is called *Marche militaire* and it's by somebody called Schubert. He likes it and feels a tingling sensation at the top of his spine. He puts this down, not to the music but to his excitement at the prospect of meeting Catherine Stapleton.

He hasn't yet seen anyone who could be her. It is impossible to spot a new face in the serried rows of morning assembly and in the crowded corridor afterwards. He pushes his way along to the fourth-year classroom and is one of the first in. There are five rows of double desks. He has agreed he'll grab one on the back row for Keith and him.

He is nervous with anticipation in a way he hasn't felt before. He sits down and watches the rest of the class who are now straggling into the room talking and shouting. The faces are familiar: Dicky Hardy, Maggie Worrall, John Charlton, Billy Grix. The noise rises as the room fills up. Desk lids begin to bang. They keep coming in: Smiggie Smith, Jennie Cooper, Maureen Burns. Then a stranger, a girl! Her head is turned away and she has blond hair! He feels a rush of excitement that fades instantaneously as he realises that her hair is in ringlets! The girl in the pub yard had blond hair but it wasn't in ringlets! He tries to recall her dash into the sunlight. It all happened so quickly he wonders now whether he is right about her hair. It was difficult to tell at that distance and he caught only the very briefest glimpse of her. He re-imagines the scene, trying to bring the girl's hair into focus, willing ringlets to materialise. At that moment the girl entering the classroom turns to find a desk in the row next to his. As she stops by one of the desks she gives a nervous smile and glances around as though seeking permission to sit down. She has a pretty mouth with neat even teeth. His spirits rise again. It must be her! New pupils are such a rare occurrence at Calcroft Juniors that it must be her!

Keith arrives, hot and puffing as usual. He starts talking excitedly about some film he's seen at the Regal with Spencer Tracey in it. Stan doesn't have to reply to Keith; he'll talk to himself for a few minutes. He looks around the room. Everybody's in now and there are no more new faces. It must be her!

'Good morning, children.' The new class-teacher, Mrs Archer, stands erect by her desk in a smart two-piece suit. She wears glasses and her hair is a mass of tight grey curls like twists of steel. Her words fall and die, unheeded.

'Quiet children, please.' She's almost shouting now. The noise subsides.

'I'll try that again. Good morning, children.' A wave of grudging, half-stifled 'good mornings' washes around the classroom. There is a silence while Mrs Archer decides whether she will try a third time. Instead, she introduces herself and says that she hopes they will all have a happy year together. Then she sits down and takes out the register. She explains that she would like them all to reply 'Present, Mrs Archer' to their names, and begins to read out the list in alphabetical order: David Atkinson, Shirley Bassett, Maureen Burns, John Charlton...Stan listens intently for the new girl's name, hoping that it won't come yet, willing it to the back of the alphabet. James Cooney, Jennie Cooper... the familiar names settle like homing pigeons on the seated figures around him. Billy Grix, Dicky Hardy, Helen Hudspith. As the thin, precise voice moves through the list he feels himself getting more excited. He gazes at the back of the girl in the next row waiting for the name Catherine Stapleton to descend and fuse with those golden ringlets. James Krake, Harry Langton, Keith Miller, Shirley Patten. The name approaches at gathering speed. Dorothy Reckitt, Joan Tetlow, Stanley Walker.

He feels deflated and cheated. No Catherine Stapleton! She's not there! The voice pauses, then repeats: 'Stanley Walker?' He jumps with sudden recognition. 'Yes...er...present, Mrs Archer.' Mrs Archer bends forward and looks over the top of her glasses. 'Wake up, Stanley. You're back at school you know.' Faces turn round to grin at him. Keith giggles and digs him in the ribs. Mrs Archer resumes: Gary Williams, Margaret Worrall, Margaret Young. The girl with the ringlets answers: 'Present, Mrs Archer.'

At home that evening it was the time of silence for Dad was on night shift. When he was on night shift he would get back from the pit at six in the morning, go to bed for a couple of hours, then get up and potter around. If it was one of his Railway Hotel days he would go to tap barrels in the cellar and stack the shelves in preparation for the opening time of the pub. In summer he sometimes went into the garden: after digging coal, digging earth, or squatting against the wall of the house, staring at his rhubarb and leeks. At two o'clock in the afternoon, after his dinner, he went back to bed until eight o'clock. The walls and ceilings of the pit-house were thin. Lying in bed you could hear every word and movement downstairs, a shout could wake you. Stan would come home from school to a house becalmed. 'Your dad's on nights,' Mam reminded him as soon as he was over the doorstep. They would sit at the tea-table speaking in low tones; the tinkling of crockery seemed a desecration. After tea he went out, eager for freedom and noise: football on Lovatt's field or, as the evenings drew in, games under the street lamps and expeditions with firing-cans out into the darkness beyond the end of the village. Sometimes he watched for his father leaving the house. He would push his bike along the path to the gate, swing his leg over and start the mile-long journey to the pit. Once he was out of sight Stan would go inside to clearing skies and a lightening atmosphere.

But tonight he's at home when Dad comes down, heavy with sleep and the dark mood of the pit. The air, thick with tension, seems to press on their ear-drums. Dad eats his supper quickly: gravy, potatoes and cabbage, the remains of the weekend's joint. His snap-tin and dudley containing his favourite pit-drink of cold tea are ready waiting on the edge of the table. Through the window the evening light is just beginning to fade. It floods the room with a warm golden glow. Stan feels sorry for his father who has to leave all this behind in order to go down the pit but he wants him to move so that life can begin again. He sits in the armchair, his face behind a copy of *The Rover*. He's having trouble concentrating. He looks over the top of the comic, eyeing the clock on the mantelpiece. Twenty to nine. He knows Dad will leave at a quarter-to, ten-to at the latest. Then all of a sudden he is gone, taking his leave in silence, picking up the snap-tin and dudley on his way out.

Stan relaxes and breathes more freely. It's time to find out about Catherine Stapleton if he can only find a way of getting round to it. His mother is sitting by the window knitting, catching the last of the daylight. He waits for her to speak or look up. He is embarrassed by his interest in Catherine Stapleton and wants her to mention the name first. He stares hard at her, waiting for her to ask him about his day at school. This could take time. His parents are not very curious about school. They are proud of his cleverness but school is part of a world they take for granted and rarely enter. She is now concentrating on her knitting, holding it up to the light and counting the stitches. He can hear the shouts of children playing on the street – familiar voices, familiar games. He wants to go out and join them. But he also wants to know. He must get things moving. He says: 'We've got a new class-teacher at school.'

'Oh yes. What's he called? Or is it a she?

'She's called Mrs Archer.'

The conversation flags. She hasn't even looked across at him. He continues: 'We've got a new girl in the class as well.' She'll surely take the bait now; Dad has mentioned the Stapletons several times in recent days so the name is in the air. But to his surprise, she says: 'And what's she called?'

He feels irritated and says with a touch of bitterness that makes her look up: 'Margaret Young.' There's a burst of laughter out in the street followed by shouts and the sound of wildly racing feet. He plunges on. 'That girl from the Railway. What do they call her? She wasn't there.'

Mam puts her knitting down and smiles: 'Oh yes, Mr Stapleton's girl, Catherine. Didn't your dad tell you? I thought you were there when he mentioned it. She's going to a private school in Doncaster.'

A private school! It was the first time he'd heard the phrase. He didn't know what a private school was but it obviously wasn't Calcroft Juniors. Mam had carried on talking; she was saying something about how Catherine's grandparents had put money away for her education. Mr and Mrs Stapleton had sent her to a special type of school where you pay to have your children educated, a school not for the likes of the Walkers. Mam thought it wasn't just but society was like that...

He only half-heard the rest. Society was like that! Not for the likes of the Walkers! What did she mean, not for the likes of the Walkers? She had said it with a laugh and a smile that seemed to say: 'What do we care?' But he felt baffled and hurt. It was as though the ache he felt at his separation from Catherine Stapleton had undergone some sudden transformation, been prolonged into a wider world called Society and returned to him as a judgement on him and his kind.

# 10

## The Glory that was

The train is standing in Doncaster station. The woman and the boy have left their seats. 'We have a bus to catch,' she said as she waited for him to remove his earplugs and wind up the wires with leisurely care. Stan watches them hurrying back along the platform to the station underpass. As they disappear down the steps they seem to slip into some groove in his mind, worn there by his remembering, that leads back to himself and his mother. He imagines them taking the bus and travelling through the streets of the town as he and his mother did long ago after their shopping expeditions in the centre of Doncaster. He found the familiar journey long and boring though it lasted barely twenty minutes, and he would pass the time by closing his eyes and guessing whichever local landmark the bus would be passing when he opened them. They would play one of their silly games, laying wildly escalating bets – a hundred pounds, a thousand pounds, uncle Harold's shop, the crown jewels – on the accuracy of his judgement. From the turn in the Doncaster Road that led to Calcroft High Street, he knew every building and open space from the Fox Inn that stood on the corner to uncle Harold's store where he and Mam would get off the bus and continue along the road to the short terrace of pebble-dash pit-houses where they lived.

This is how he still sees it despite the changes wrought by the decades: the businesses that have come and gone, the Railway Hotel and two of the three workingmen's clubs boarded up since the great strike, the new take-away outlets for kebabs and curries, the police station bulldozed out of sight and mind, leaving a gap in the street like a missing tooth. On his last visit two years before, uncle Harold's shop had become a carpet centre that opened at irregular hours and seemed to do little trade. On its side wall, defying the assaults of the weather and the local council's graffiti squad, one could make out in faint grey lettering the words 'Tory scum. Death to Thatcher.'

He finds it odd now that he should have been surprised and hurt by his mother's revelation of Catherine Stapleton's private education, yet reason tells him there must have been a time of innocence before he knew the way society's cards were stacked. He tries to imagine himself back into the state of social knowledge of Stanley Walker aged ten years eleven months. He had heard of Mr Atlee and Mr Churchill. He had listened in to conversations and radio programmes, and even read bits of *The Daily Herald* that dropped inside the Walkers' front-door every morning. Somewhere in his mind props were being erected for the staging of that dramatic conflict, that bitter war of the pronouns between them and us.

He could see clearly the wreckage around him: uncle Vic coughing till the veins bulged purple in his neck and spitting gobbets of blackened phlegm that boiled and hissed on the coals of the living-room fire; the Hedley children across the road with their worn and patched clothes that were always too large or too small, their father who never worked, and their house with its bare linoleum floor and its stink that seemed to bar the door whenever he called on Alfie Hedley to come out to play. It was about this time that uncle Herbert was left disabled by an accident down the pit. One of the steel doors that controlled the ventilation of the pit was lowered before the paddy-train, in which Herbert's shift was travelling to the coal-face, had got clear of it. It sliced into the seat in front of him, killing the two men sitting there and mangling Herbert's body almost beyond repair. It took what for his family was a miracle of medical science and care to return him to them nine months later, able to hobble and talk but never again to work.

Despite all this, private schools had escaped his notice. They belonged to a social hinterland that was still largely off his map. His family were not very political and he had never had reason to think that society's cards were stacked against him. Loving parents, a father who didn't shirk the pit, a warm and protective herd of aunts, uncles and cousins were sufficient insulation against the realities of poverty and sickness. A sharp brain and the 1944 Education Act did the rest. That and the NHS that cured his whooping cough and salvaged his crumbling proletarian teeth.

But there was something else, something that he realises, looking back, gave to his humble biography a touch of world-historical dignity, for it proved that Karl Marx had got it wrong. This was patriotism, the balm that soothed the wound of his and his contemporaries' class resentment. They lived in the best country in the world, they'd won the war, and a quarter of the globe was still coloured red. Everything he heard and read told him this, even *The Rover*. Whether it was Alf Tupper, the people's athlete, licking Johnny Foreigner on the track or the devil-may-care fighter-pilot Braddock giving Jerry a pasting in the air, its heroes demonstrated that British was best. The Second World War was a source of such pride and inspiration that he regretted having missed it. When, as an undergraduate, he came to read Stendhal's *Le Rouge et le Noir*, he recognised instantly Julien Sorel's nostalgia for the heroic period of the Revolution and Empire that he had been born too late to know. The dragoons of Napoleon's army that the child Julien sees passing through his native Franche-Comté en route to confront the Austrians in Italy, resplendent in their long white coats and plumed helmets, were for Stan the fighter-pilots of East-Anglian airfields zooming off daily to engage in aerial derring-do over the English Channel.

He pestered his parents with unanswerable questions about Atlantic convoys, the battle of El Alamein, and the relative merits of Messerschmidts and Spitfires. And with a question – the inevitable one – that his mother answered so well it changed his understanding of life.

'Mam?'

'Mm?'

'Was Dad in the war?'

'We were all in the war, son.'

'I mean was he in the army or the navy or anything like that? Or the air force?'

'No, he wasn't. They didn't conscript miners because their work was important for the war effort.'

'Did he just keep on being a miner then?'

'Yes. Everybody round here did. He was in the ARP mind you. So he did his bit. Though if you ask me, working down the pit was enough.'

'What's the ARP?'

'The Air Raid Police. He had to go out into the streets at night to make sure everybody had blacked their windows out.'

Stan knows about this; they've been told about it at school. She goes on: 'Not that there was much chance of them bombing Calcroft unless it was by accident.' She gives a little laugh. 'Though there was an aeroplane crashed once. A German plane it was. They reckon it went off course after bombing Hull. You could see it burning from the bedroom window.'

He feels let down. He wants Calcroft's war to be more than one crashed aeroplane and his dad wandering the streets telling people to black out their windows.

'Mam?'

'Yes, son.'

'Why was Dad's work important in the war?'

'Our Stanley! You're a devil for asking questions. Why was pit work important? Well, it stands to reason, doesn't it? You can't do anything without coal. Trains run on coal. Ships run on coal. You can't even *build* trains and ships without coal, can you? I mean all that steel from Sheffield that they use to make things with. They need coal to heat the furnaces, don't they? You can't make steel without coal. You can't do anything without coal. Getting coal is the most important job there is. And the hardest.'

He had never heard her wax so eloquent. He was impressed. This was the cherry on the cake! Not only did he live in the finest country in the world but he had a father who did the most important job! He had a lot to be grateful for.

Despite this, all was not quite for the best in Stan's heroic little world. His mother's news of Catherine Stapleton's private school was a blow to his childish complacency. It appeared that somebody out there, somebody called Society, wasn't as convinced of his family pedigree as they should be. In fact they were so unconvinced that they felt Catherine Stapleton and he should be kept apart. But the thing that was really surprising, and that he only dimly discerned at the time, was that this knowledge didn't lessen his interest in Catherine Stapleton; it made it more acute.

He was in his father's garden shed when she appeared. He must have been kneeling, mending something perhaps or screwing studs into his football boots, for he remembers looking up to find her standing there in the sunlight glare of the door, a slight figure in a blouse, skirt and tennis shoes. She looked startled to come across him and said: 'I've come to see Joe. I've got a message for him from my dad.' She doesn't say who her dad is or who she is but he knows.

He rises to his feet and says: 'I'll see if he's in.' As he brushes past her he catches a faint smell of something he can't put a name to, something fresh and flowery that seems to go with the flowery pattern on her blouse.

'Would you tell him my dad would like him to do a couple of extra hours this evening if he can manage.'

Stan goes through into the living-room. Dad is slumped in an armchair asleep. His mouth hangs open. His face seems moulded out of grey wax with a darker smear of stubble around the cheeks and chin. He is wearing an old collarless shirt that leaves his neck exposed. The stretched tendons and swollen veins have a vulnerability that Stan has never noticed before, as though they might snap or puncture. Below the rolled-up shirt sleeves the unflexed biceps hang like white pouches. Stan backs quietly out of the room and goes into the yard.

'My dad's asleep. I'll tell him when he wakes up. What time do you want him to come?'

'Six o'clock, opening-time. You will remember to tell him won't you?'

She looks worried, furrowing her brow and squinting as though dazzled by the sun though she is now standing in the shadow cast by the house. The skin of her bare arms and legs is pale gold. Her face is a deeper colour, light brown with a touch of dry, fading sunburn on her cheeks from the summer just past. Her eyes and mouth seem slightly too large and this gives to her expression a frank and direct quality that flusters him. He wants to reassure her. He wants to keep her there. He searches around in his head for something to say. She turns to leave. He says: 'Do you want him to stay until closing time?' She stops and says: 'I suppose so.' There is something in the tone of the words that hurts him, a hint of indifference or disdain. His desire to keep her there, to narrow the gap between them, is like a wound that must be closed. All he can think of to say is: 'OK then. I'll tell him.' But she is already on the path to the gate. At the gate she turns; she looks worried again. She says, as though it's something she has just remembered: 'My dad says I can invite you to play at the Railway Hotel if you like.'

For all his fascination with Catherine Stapleton he hesitated. He did not usually play with girls, and this one with her soft, glowing skin and her way of speaking like people on the BBC, was like no other he had met. She changed the rules of a game he hardly knew how to play in the first place. But he went, and he continued to go, braving the taunts of his friends and the capriciousness of Catherine Stapleton herself. It was a momentous decision. The events that followed from it shattered his childhood, and he can still feel their touch across the years.

*

In the book that lies on the table before him lie memories waiting to be re-awakened. On the whole he would rather they weren't. But he knows this is irrational and even cowardly. It happened fifty years ago after all. And fifty years is a long time.

# Part Two

# 1953-54: There are Two Sides to Every Story

# 11

## Bed-time blues

*The child lies in bed gripped by fear. She has a strange sensation, a feeling of being suspended in darkness like a solitary star. Darkness is everywhere: in the empty sitting-room beneath her, in the floors of empty rooms above, in the moonless night outside. She lies still, her body hunched up against the chill of the bed. This she knows is the crucial moment, the moment of precarious balance when she will either sink into sleep or remain anxiously awake. As her eyes become accustomed to the dark, the shapes of her bedroom furniture resume their shadowy half-life. The curtained window gives off a faint glow. She begins to feel calmer. She must now close her eyes and mind to the world around, shut out all consciousness of those upper floors where water tanks drip, doors creak, and trapped winds sigh and whistle through the autumn night.*

*She begins to count her heartbeats. Gradually they slow and fade to a gentle pulsing in her ear that she can barely feel. She continues to count, visualizing the numbers in her head, looking inwards, shutting things out. She unfolds her body, spreading its island of warmth to the chilly seas around. She continues to count. Weariness creeps through her, her mind begins to drift. The numbers dissolve into images and fragments of dream...*

*There is a sudden crash and she is instantly awake, joined by a taut wire of anxiety to the floors above. Her ears strain to catch further sounds, her mind travels the empty corridors and rooms as she tries to fit the noise that has woken her to some familiar feature of the house - the attic door that bangs open in the slightest breeze or a fall of plaster from one of the decaying ceilings.*

*The silence is no longer silent. The darkness gives out a faint murmur like waves breaking on a distant shore. She is in a long, wide corridor lined with the shadows of her bedroom furniture. She sees the glowing window far away. Dark space swirls above and below her. The long room seems to breathe and expand, the walls are receding away from her, then closing in. She is inside some vast, bloated intestine that swells and shrinks, swells and shrinks. She holds herself rigid, stifling her breathing, torn between fear of moving and the desire to turn on her bedside light. In a sudden spasm of desperate will, she reaches over and presses the switch. The room leaps back to its former shape. The chair, table, and wardrobe are in their usual positions, four-square and solid in the bright glare of the lamp. Harmless, mundane.*

*I was that child. The year was 1953, the year of the coronation of Elizabeth II. The place was called the Railway Hotel. As I've proceeded with the writing of this memoir I've begun to view the Railway Hotel as its true protagonist. Even now, after half a century, its creaking staircases and empty bedrooms, its abandoned and crumbling outhouse – especially that - recur not only in my memories but also in my dreams. I have read of valleys that have been flooded and dammed, and whose inhabitants are haunted by the remembrance of their submerged villages with their streets, churches and houses. That is the Railway Hotel for me - out of sight but never out of mind, more than a building a facet of my own being, an inner demon that will not die and that sends out its mournful whale-song from the drowned world of my past.*

From his too. Memories rush in. He tries to shut them out and concentrate on the text before him, give her story priority over his own. But his willed attention to the words on the page is a sluice-gate through which the dammed images seep. He sees the backyard where they played, a derelict bedroom in which they stood looking down on Calcroft's main street while she told him of her fear of the night. He sees the old outhouse on a dark, late-winter evening, the beam of his torch lighting their way in... Sentences slide past, their meanings unregistered by his divided mind. He reaches the bottom of a page before realising that a whole paragraph has escaped his attention. He goes back. He must concentrate, refocus.

*It was on a bright May morning in that year of 1953 that my father, Robert Stapleton, announced that we – my father, my mother and I – were moving house. I don't remember now feeling any disappointment or apprehension. I liked the house in which we were living well enough but was aware of its disadvantages. It was in fact a small hotel in rural Suffolk called Fairview Lodge that was owned by my grandparents and managed by my father, their only son. Our living quarters were a sectioned-off part of the hotel that was cramped and sometimes noisy for the hotel bar was immediately beneath us. Whenever I stepped out of the front door of the hotel and walked along the country road into the nearby village, I saw thatched cottages and houses washed in delicate shades of pink that I imagined might be more pleasant to live in. But when my father said we were moving to a new house, these were not the houses and this was not the sort of place that he had in mind.*

*Fairview Lodge had failed to thrive during the years of austerity and when my grandparents, unable to afford the renovations it required, decided to sell the hotel in order to fund their retirement, my father was left with much reduced prospects. He obtained a job as manager of the Railway Hotel, situated in the mining village of Calcroft close to the town of Doncaster. When I, beginning to sense the drawbacks of the move, asked him why he had applied for such a post in such a part of the country, he replied that beggars can't be choosers;*

he had tried to obtain similar positions closer to home but without success; the Railway Hotel would keep the wolf from the door while he managed to find something more suitable.

At the time I didn't fully understand the tale of genteel penury that brought us to Calcroft. I only knew that I hated the place on sight. After the rolling, wooded countryside of Suffolk with its pretty villages, everything about Calcroft was alien and mean: the grid-like streets of grey pebble-dash houses; the spoil heaps and winding-towers of the pit that dominated the view from the rear upstairs-windows of the hotel; the steam trains that ran fifty yards from the house, clanking, hissing, and whistling through the night and, on days when the wind was in the wrong direction, puffing plumes of black, grit-bearing smoke over the backyard of the hotel. I remember my mother, Helen, rushing me out of the house on one such occasion to help her gather the washing in.

'Just look at the state of it,' she cried, pointing to the rash of tiny black spots on the sheets. 'It makes you wonder what our lungs will be like after six months in this place.'

I imagined my lungs, all pink and healthy from the air of the East Anglia countryside, turning greasy and black. For a while, when I went out onto the street or into the backyard, I held my breath for as long as I could. When I finally had to breathe, it was as though I was submitting to some invading, noxious force.

I didn't belong here. I was out of place and lonely. I complained, I wept, I raged. As far as I was aware I was the only child in the village attending a private school and that fact quarantined me from the other children as irrevocably as the plague. The private school in question was called Nightingale House and its pupils came overwhelmingly from the most prosperous quarters of Doncaster. If they were at all inclined to take a bus journey of several miles to join their new class-mate in her odd little pit-village, they failed to reveal

*it. Nor did I wish it, for in those early weeks I have to admit I
was ashamed of my new home.*

*The Railway Hotel wasn't strictly speaking a hotel at all. It
had been one at some time in the past but somewhere along
the way it had changed into a mere public-house, parts of it
having been converted and the rest left to decay. It was a long
and complicated red-brick building with cellars, a ground floor,
and three floors of bedrooms. We didn't so much live in the
building as camp out in it. Our living quarters were a sitting-
room and back-kitchen at one end of the ground floor. They
were connected by a corridor, flanked by two disused reception
rooms, to the bar, Tap Room, Smoke Room and Concert Room
at the other end of the building. Dad, trying to make the best
of things, joked about it. He called the Railway Hotel the family
pile and likened us to impoverished aristocrats.*

'Would you like to see the family pile?'

She had that expression of earnest appeal, with the furrowed
brow and the eyes squinting slightly. He could tell she was nervous
and he wanted to reassure her. The trouble was he didn't know
what she meant. The family pile? Pile of what? He smiled and said
'Sure', as though being asked to look at family piles was one of
those things that happened to him on a fairly regular basis.

*My mother was not amused. The Railway Hotel was beyond
a joke; it was resistant to all her efforts to recreate the haven
of middle-class chic and knick-knackery that we had known
at Fairview Lodge and that was her prevailing standard of
domestic elegance. I too complained. It wasn't fair I told my
father, nobody had told us about the Railway Hotel. At least
they hadn't told me and I was the one who was suffering from
its inadequacies. At night-time the ascent to my bedroom on
the first floor was a test of nerve and courage. Dad, who took
a keen interest in the first ascent of Mount Everest during that
summer of 1953, referred to the first floor as 'base camp'. It*

*was the last outpost of civilization beyond which lay the chaos of the upper storeys - abandoned bedrooms in which no-one slept, corridors of bare, dust-encrusted boards which feet never trod, broom cupboards from which the last brooms had long since departed. As that summer came to an end and the September nights drew in, these cavernous, echoing wastes became the source of my childhood terrors* climbing the stairs – bare boards, no carpet - to the top floor. The room they enter is completely empty; the wallpaper is faded and stained; plaster has fallen from the ceiling exposing the laths. The room seems to contain its own medium of floating atoms, neither air nor dust, that scintillate in the sunlight streaming in through the window. He is surprised by the dust and dereliction concealed by a building he has known only by its palatial exterior. From the front of the Railway Hotel they look out onto Calcroft's main street and, across the street, onto Mr Lovatt's greyhound stadium with the railway line running close beside it.

It was then that she told him of her nightly ordeal, how she hated going to bed, her fear of these empty rooms and of the bare, creaking staircases. He listened, then said: 'You should come out at night and go to bed later. That way you'll be tired and you'll fall asleep. It's good fun on the streets after dark. You won't come to any harm. Not in Calcroft. It's a nice place, Calcroft.'

Back on the ground floor they met Robert Stapleton, a gangling, slightly stoop-shouldered man with sandy-coloured hair and a moustache. Stan noticed he was wearing a cravat instead of the dicky bow his father had led him to expect. He had pale-blue eyes that seemed distant and dreamy, in contrast with the briskly cheerful manner with which he greeted Stan. He shook his hand and said he was 'delighted' to meet him; he had heard great things about him from his father Joe. Stan felt embarrassed and did not know what to say. The handshake had surprised him and the elaborate courtesy of Mr Stapleton's manner seemed to demand a response he did not know how to give.

He returned often that autumn to the back yard of the Railway Hotel. Cathy insisted on instructing him in the arts of tennis, a game she played with a fierceness and joy in victory that made no concession to his beginner's fumblings. He was fascinated by this sylph-like creature who was yet boisterous and athletic. When he jokingly suggested that they play *his* game, football, she responded at first with wild enthusiasm. Her enthusiasm quickly turned to frustration at her inability to win the ball from him. She danced around him, pushing and elbowing, her right leg flailing out at the ball that he cleverly managed to keep out of her reach. Finally she knocked him off-balance with an elbow in his ribs and charged away, the ball at her feet, cackling with triumphant glee. Stan looked up on impulse and saw Robert Stapleton standing at an upstairs window gazing down at them. On catching Stan's eye he smiled and waved, then turned away. Stan was surprised and gratified by this attentiveness from a man who was old enough to be his father and who came from another social world.

# 12

## Night-life in Calcroft

*My father was a man in whom great hopes had been invested by his parents. They had struggled to send him to private school and had expected the appropriate reward of a son established in one of the more lucrative professions. His failure to distinguish himself academically had placed this prospect out of reach and he always felt keenly his lack of success in their eyes. During the war he had been unfit for active service due to a chronic problem of the lower back and had worked in the catering corps. Although this fitted him to take over the running of Fairview Lodge after his father developed a heart condition, Grandad's gratitude for this turn of events was tempered by disappointment at the thwarting of his own paternal vanity.*

*Dad was a modest and philosophical man who did not allow knowledge of his failures to sour his character. On our arrival in Calcroft he bore what was, in all observable respects, a much reduced situation with calm and good humour. He saw the Railway Hotel as a temporary measure, a holding operation forced on him by the suddenness of his parents' decision to sell the hotel in Suffolk. For all his lack of pretension, he knew that he had the experience and ability to move on to better things, and that this would occur sooner rather than later.*

*My mother saw things differently. Though herself originally from the north of England and with a sister still living on the outskirts of Manchester, she bore the move to Calcroft with none of Dad's stoic good grace. She thought of her time in Suffolk as the best period of her life. Her meeting with the handsome young Robert Stapleton and their years sharing the rural-bourgeois idyll of his parents had given her a fulfilment and a status from which the Railway Hotel was a sad falling-off. The wood-panelled bar and lounge of Fairview Lodge, where she had spent three evenings a week overseeing the bar staff and conversing with the better-off inhabitants of the surrounding villages, had given way to the Tap Room of the Railway Hotel and a clientele who were hewn out of different and, in her eyes, altogether inferior material. Her galleon of social aspiration, with its pennants all–flutter, had run aground on this barren shore, and my mother was bereft.*

*The highlight of her social week, indeed the only light, was Tuesday evening when she and Dad took time off from the pub. They usually went dancing to the Co-op ballroom in Doncaster with other members of our local aristocracy: Harold and Rachel Davidson, who owned a general store in Calcroft, and Alec Bowen, the manager of the village branch of the Yorkshire Penny Bank, and his wife Miriam. Once they had all arrived there was a final swirl of activity as Mum sent my father scurrying round the sitting-room and bedrooms searching for lost purses and dropped ear-rings. At these moments I saw the elegance of my mother in her dancing dress and sensed in my father something of the pleasure and admiration he must have felt when they were young but which had wilted before her acerbity and self-pity. He called her his 'svelte beauty' and would pick loose hairs off her dress, bending back from the hips to appraise the finished picture, then helping her on with her coat with the exaggerated ceremoniousness the men adopted as the appropriate style for the occasion.*

*Rachel and Harold Davidson invariably arrived before Alec and Miriam, and would sit chatting with my mother and father while they waited. I found them an odd but interesting couple, he voluble, cheerful and opinionated, she quiet and self-contained. She was strikingly attractive with a wide, full mouth and tumbling dark hair that reminded me of Jane Russell who I'd seen several times in films. As Harold held forth to my father and mother on matters of business and local gossip, she would watch him impassively through her lazy, half-hooded eyes, occasionally checking his indiscretions with a 'Now Harold, Robert and Helen don't want to know about that.' Harold would immediately stop or change tack. He seemed almost in awe of her as though he couldn't quite believe that he was married to this beautiful woman, for he himself was unremarkable to look at. My father was at his most tactful in such situations, managing somehow to reassure Harold that his conversation was interesting to the company while seeming, with a smile and slight nod of the head towards Rachel, to express his appreciation of her intervention.*

*Harold had benefited in life from a great stroke of luck, having been left his store by its previous owner Alfred Morton, a childless bachelor for whom he had worked. He had retained the name Morton's on the front of his store in grateful tribute to his benefactor. His favourite saying was that he had swapped a coal-mine for a gold-mine, for he had initially taken the job of Mr Morton's delivery boy in order to avoid working down the pit. 'Lucky's my middle name,' he would say, beaming with a pleasure in life that was saved from complacency by a sort of naïve delight tinged with incredulity at the blessings that fate had bestowed on him. I liked Harold. He was kind and good-natured, and his optimism contrasted with the bitterness of my mother and the worry and tension of life at home. I believe that this contrast was one of the sources of my own later desire to succeed. I wished that we too could be lucky and if not lucky, then successful by some other means. The important thing was to be successful because success brought happiness, the happiness of Harold.*

The happiness of Harold! The luck of Harold! They were part of the family folklore.

'If you ask me, Harold has made his own luck,' his mother would say. Dad always agreed: 'Aye, you're right there.'

'When Harold took over the running of the shop, Morton's was on its last legs.'

'Aye, he turned out to have a good head for business.'

And he would return to his newspaper or whatever task he was engaged in, happy to confirm Sally's pride in her brother but quickly running out of words.

Not all the family saw things this way. Uncle Vic, embittered by the lung disease that had ended his working life, was said to harbour resentment of Harold's good fortune while Stan once overheard auntie Aggie express the view to his mother that Harold would have come to nothing without the help of Mr Morton. At the time these little eddies of envy and malice barely disturbed the calm surface of family life, for on the whole Harold's warmth and geniality forestalled ill will.

In any case, it didn't last. The luck, that is.

*Within the dreary tale of those early months in Calcroft the ritual of my parents' Tuesday-night outing to the Co-op ballroom was the crucial event, the twist of plot that injected unexpected excitement into my life. One of the part-time staff employed by my father was a miner called Joe Walker. My father depended on Joe for most of the heavy labour involved in managing the pub's cellar, particularly the handling of the massive wooden barrels called hogsheads that each contained fifty-four gallons of beer. Dad's lower-back problem, which I suspect that at the time of his appointment he concealed from the brewery, prevented him carrying out such tasks and he was in a state of constant apprehension that Joe's main employment at Calcroft Main pit would prevent him from being available for work at the Railway Hotel.*

*Joe had a son, Stan, of whom he was immensely proud. Although taciturn to a fault, Joe had been known to wax, if not lyrical, at least moderately effusive about Stan's talents as a scholar, footballer and all-round 'good lad'. It must have been this that led my father, worried by my isolation and* unhappiness in Calcroft, to suggest that I invite Stan Walker to play with me at the Railway Hotel.

Stan's first visit was a curious affair. I was on my home ground but nervous. I no doubt reacted by appearing offhand and a bit snobby as was my way. It was only gradually that I began to relax. He had about him a mild and unthreatening amiability that made my defensiveness unnecessary. A meeting that started off as a guided tour presided over by the mistress of the house ended with a heart-to-heart conversation during which I confessed my nightly struggle with the terrors of the Railway Hotel. He listened in the curious way he had, with his head cocked slightly to one side and his eyes intently focussed on my face as though they too were listening. Then he said: 'You should come out to play at night. It'll make you tired and help you to sleep.' His tone was matter-of-fact and sympathetic. When I objected that my mother would never allow it, he said: 'Don't tell her. Come out on Tuesday when your mam and dad go dancing.'

'How do you know they go dancing?'

'My dad told me. He's sometimes on the bar Tuesday nights. They go with my uncle Harold and auntie Rachel, don't they?'

And this was how, on a mild and damp autumnal night, I come to be slipping out of the back-door of the Railway Hotel and hurrying across the yard to join Stan Walker at the gate. I am almost breathless with excitement and nervous tension. But curiosity, the need for adventure, and relief at putting off the ascent to my bedroom drive me on.

We cross the street to Lovatt's Greyhound Stadium. This was a ramshackle affair consisting of a racing track and wooden stand that housed a thousand or so spectators, the whole thing being surrounded by a circular fence of ten-foot-high wooden boards following the cinder path that curves round the back of the stadium, walking into the dark, away from the street lights and entry turnstiles. He feels anxious. She seemed excited at first but now she's gone quiet. What will she think? Will she get a kick out of it like he does? Or will she just think it's boring and silly? He begins to wish he hadn't asked her to come out. *My tension dissolves and slips away, to be replaced by a growing elation in my new-found freedom. Stan keeps stopping to look through cracks and holes in the fence. We have arrived during a period between races and the crowd of spectators gives off a low murmur of conversation punctuated by laughter and the shouts of the bookies. Finally he gives a grunt of satisfaction.*

'*This'll do. Just the job.*'

*A cylindrical metal container resembling an oil-drum stands upright at the foot of a board that has been broken off at a height of six or seven feet. Stan says: 'Somebody's been here before us. Done a nice job too.*'

*He climbs onto the drum and peers over the top of the broken board.*

'*We're in luck. They're just putting them in the traps.*'

*He remains watching for a few moments more then steps down. He takes my arm and pushes me towards the drum* hesitating to touch her, still feeling the distance between them. Then taking her arm. The first time he's held her like this. *It is one of my most vivid memories of that year: the green oasis of the dog-track bathed in its pool of dazzling light; the strength and beauty of the greyhounds that, even as I raised my head above the broken board, were leaping from their traps; the sudden roar of the crowd which seemed like a disembodied power thundering out of the dark sky. I joined in the cry, shouting encouragement to the speeding dogs while gripping the fence and jumping up and down on top of the oil-drum. I felt exultant and free. For the first time since my arrival in Calcroft I was happy!* Her shouts, his relief. He starts shouting with her though he can't see the dogs through the fence. She gives a last wild cheer and jumps down. 'That's amazing! They're so fast!'

Pride in his local knowledge and the gift he has given her. Sudden elation!

*It was the start of my secret night-life with Stan Walker. As I look back on it now I can barely believe the contrast between the modest little adventures we had and the joy they gave me. Was my life really so constricted and dull that it could be transformed by peering over Lovatt's fence at skittering greyhounds! Or sitting by the railway line that passed close by the dog-track, watching passing trains! For this is what we did next. According to Stan we just had time to see the ten-to-nine express before returning to our oil drum for the last race of the evening. Then we had better go home.*

*We continued along the cinder path and sat on a low wall that ran alongside the railway line. To our left was Calcroft bridge and, beyond it, the line that ran away to York, Newcastle and Edinburgh. It was from this direction that the train would come. We could hear it miles down the track, a faint pulsing that faded away then returned, louder and closer, its rhythmic beat pummelling the night air, thumpety-thump, thumpety-thump. There was a lamp-post beside the track and during the split second that the engine would take to pass through the fan of light cast by the lamp we must catch its number and name. We can hear it getting closer and closer, we can feel its power in the tremors beneath our feet. I am staring hard at the dark mouth of the bridge. Stan shouts: 'It's here' and it is upon us, bursting out from under the bridge trailing a ragged mane of smoke and steam. Its streamlined casing gleams briefly in the light; we glimpse the name, Kingfisher, and the red glare of an open firebox with the fireman bent over his shovel. The lit carriage windows stream swiftly by. It is gone.*

*The dogs and the ten-to-nine express became one of our regular outings. We were sometimes accompanied by Stan's cousin Keith whose boundless passion for steam engines at first dismayed me. Gradually I began to understand it and even joined him on his*

*train-spotting trips to Doncaster. The great Pacific engines that
surged back and forth along the line that ran through Calcroft, or
that stood steaming at their rest in Doncaster station, or that
emerged sleek and shining from the paint-shop of the Plant in
their green livery, edged with black and orange lines, began to
exert a spell that in later life I realised was one of my first
experiences of aesthetic pleasure. With their beautiful and
mysterious names that set my imagination alight – Hyperion,
Chamossaire, Sun Chariot, Isinglass – they gave to the
sprawling, workaday assemblage of soot-blackened brick and
stone that was Doncaster station and its outlying works an
attraction that repeatedly drew me back.*

*I began to abscond from the Railway Hotel on nights other
than Tuesday. As long as my mother and father were in the
bar I would risk it. Stan and I would sit by the railway track in
the enfolding darkness, hugging each other to keep warm and
listening for the approaching thunder of the train. We began
to exchange kisses that became less clumsy with practice.*
Should he? Dare he? He can feel her shivering slightly beneath his
arm. Then suddenly she says: 'You can kiss me if you like.' But at
the last moment she turns her lips away and he kisses her ear. *In
very cold weather we retreated to the outhouse of the Railway
Hotel that we called our den. The ground floor of this building
was divided into two rooms, one of which, according to my
father, had been used for laundry work during the Railway
Hotel's glory days as a functioning hotel. It contained a square,
brick-built structure into which was set a large metal bowl
above a fireplace. Here we lit a fire and, with the aid of Stan's
torch and candles filched by me from a store-room of the pub,
we arranged various pieces of usable furniture before it. There
was a rickety table on which we placed our candles and an old
horsehair sofa on which we sat and cuddled.*

*Fire fascinated us. We lit fires on the patch of spare land
behind the dog-track that we called Lovatt's field. We lit fires*

*in Ostler Milk tins pierced with air-holes that we swung round on wire handles to make the coals glow brightly. We recaptured what must have been the deep joy of primitive man in this his greatest discovery - the magic, dancing sprite that filled his dark winter nights with light and warmth.*

# 13

## Secret Lives

*I am with my father and Stan Walker in the sitting-room of the Railway Hotel watching television. The three of us are bound together by a mood that is at once subdued and fascinated, transfixed by the events unfolding on the glowing screen before us. It is the memory that best captures the emotional atmosphere of those late-November days during which my friendship with Stan Walker was beginning to flourish under the benign influence of my father. Dad had invited Stan to join us, having learnt that the Walkers did not yet have a television set. And now we sit - Stan and me on the sofa, Dad in his armchair - watching the running, leaping and diving figures of twenty-two men battling for possession of a football. Suddenly there occurs on the screen one of those brief, flashing moments, over before it has begun, which lodge themselves in the consciousness of a nation. Ferenc Puskás, a Hungarian footballer hitherto unknown to us, scores the goal that punctures the imperial hubris of English football, a goal of such simple and efficient beauty that we all shout out in wonder* rolling the ball back under his foot, neatly and quickly, out of the reach of Billy Wright who goes charging past like a bus that's missed its stop, then driving it into the top of the net. *My father, whose natural urbanity gives way to a tense excitability when the nation's sporting honour is at stake, leaps up from his chair and turns to me and Stan.*

*'Did you see that! Did you see that goal!'*

*His tone is a mixture of disbelief and something akin to indignation that such a thing should be possible. He paces the carpet between the television set and his chair, lamenting the England performance, drooping his shoulders in a comic caricature of his own glumness. I giggle and say: 'Sit down Dad, you're blocking the screen.' He finally sits down and begins to bewail the scale of the disaster. Six-three! England have lost a football match by six goals to three on the 'hallowed turf' of Wembley Stadium where they have never before been beaten. Matthews, Mortensen, Billy Wright, the flower of English sporting manhood put to the sword. And by whom? By the Hungarians!* Robert in his chair, looking across at Stan and smiling now. 'What did they say he was called?'

Stan says: 'Push-kash.'

Until a few days before, he had never heard of the Hungarians. Even reading their names in the sporting pages of that morning's Daily Herald had failed to give them reality, the unpronounceability of the names confirming their anonymity as a nation beyond the edge of the footballing universe. The fact, also gleaned from that morning's paper, that they had won an Olympic gold medal for football did not impress him for everyone knew that Olympic football was for amateurs and the second-rate. It is only that evening, settling into the sofa with Cathy beside him and savouring the pleasure of having been invited into the Stapleton's home, that he hears those names shaped into sound, and sees the men who bear them become real. The men themselves then mutate before his very eyes into sporting prodigies whose artistry compels admiration and awe from even the most patriotic English soul.

In subsequent days he and his friends, in their improvised playground matches, competed to adopt the names of Puskás and Hidegkuti. Even his cousin Keith, whose weight and girth condemned him to a near-static defensive role, swinging his right leg at whatever passed close by – which was sometimes the ball, sometimes the boy with the ball – even Keith was inspired to assume the mantle of the great Sándor Kocsis.

*Football! My father loved it, Stan Walker loved it and I - less smitten - loved their love of it. I wanted to share in this passion that was the cement of our steadily building fellowship of three.*

During my time in Suffolk Dad had often taken me to see
Ipswich Town play at their stadium at Portman Road. On my
part it was more an act of duty than of enthusiasm. Young as I
was, I think I sensed the loneliness that lay behind this desire
to have me with him and foster in me an interest in the game
he loved. He succeeded to a degree. I could recite the names of
the Ipswich team, I knew my full-back from my centre-forward,
and I could thrill to those moments of sudden beauty such as
the goal scored by Ferenc Puskás on that fateful day for English
football, 25*th* November, 1953. But the passion for the game
that moved my father seemed to be exclusively the preserve of
men. In the long queues of male bodies that passed through
the turnstiles of Portman Road I was an anomaly both in my
sex and in my take-it-or-leave-it attitude to the game. It never
occurred to me then or since to think that Dad regretted not
having had a son though I can see now that there was more
than a hint of paternal pride and concern in his attitude to
Stan. He took a serious interest in his achievements as a
member of the football team of Calcroft Juniors and would
question him about results, form and his fellow players. He
revived our trips to football matches, this time to watch
Doncaster Rovers and with Stan accompanying us. On
Saturdays when the Rovers were playing at home, he would
get extra help in at the Railway Hotel and leave the business
in the hands of Joe Walker. He, Stan and I would then take the
bus to Doncaster and join the throng of spectators streaming
along the road that led to the Belle Vue stadium.

These are my happiest memories of my life in Calcroft: Stan
arriving at the Railway Hotel with his red-and-white striped
scarf, the three of us setting off in high spirits, the chatter, the
expectation, the thrills and spills of the match itself. My father
threw off the fretful atmosphere of the Railway Hotel and
entered with gusto into the day's adventure. He would greet
Stan with a 'What's the state of play, old boy?' an enquiry that

*covered everything from Stan's health to his latest exploits on
the football field. They would discuss the match to come, the
form of the players, the likely result. This is how I like to
remember him, boyishly enthusiastic and convivial. His
relations with Stan were full of that easy grace and friendliness
that endeared him to those who knew him well. It was a manner
bred in him by his background and education and came as
easily to him as breathing. But it also bespoke much that was
real in the man.*

Background and education. He was aware of it constantly though
he could not have formulated it in these terms at the time. It was
there in Robert's dress, in his gestures, in the turn of a phrase.

'A pretty tall order. Do you think they can do it?'

The game is over and they are strolling back from the stadium to
the place where they catch their bus back to Calcroft. The tall
order is something to do with Doncaster Rovers and their prospects
for the season. But it is the phrase itself that Stan remembers.
Although he has heard it before, in Robert's tone and accent it
suddenly seems odd, as though he's appropriated it for his type
and class.

In recent weeks Stan's education in the socially defining nuances
of English speech has made great progress. He knows from Cathy
something of her father's background, his years in a private school
that she bafflingly calls a public school and his work as manager of
his parents' hotel. He has realised that certain ways of speaking
that he had thought particular to people on the radio are in fact
characteristic of real people like Cathy and Robert Stapleton. He
is struck by Robert's manner which is courteous in a way that he
has never come across before except in characters seen at the
cinema or on television. He often addresses Stan as 'young man',
'old boy' and 'my dear boy', and has a direct and open smile, the
smile of someone who is interested in Stan and views their relations
as a friendship. Stan notices the difference from the smile of his
wife Helen which is a quick and dutiful turning up of the corners of

the lips, the routine gesture owed to the son of a valued employee. They are different in other ways too. Stan senses in Helen a disapproval of his burgeoning friendship with her daughter, a friendship that Robert tolerates and even seems to encourage. *It was a manner that also concealed much, as we were to discover, though in this my father was no different from the rest of us. We all have our secret lives, those thoughts, fantasies and passions buried deep within that never reach the daylight of everyday living. The essential difference among people is between those who can live with them and those who cannot.* Was it that same day, on that same return journey from Belle Vue stadium, that an incident occurred that revealed to him another, different Robert, someone cold and remote whom background and education had failed to reach? Memories merge; the walk to and from Belle Vue was a ritual performed so frequently, the emotions that accompanied it recurred with such predictability – excitement and anticipation on the way there and, whatever the result of the match, growing weariness on the way back – that it has become fixed in his mind as a single journey.

Perhaps on this particular day the walk had seemed unusually long and tiring for Cathy was complaining that she needed an ice-cream. She adopted a childish whinge, half in jest half in earnest, that irritated Robert and then compelled him, in a sudden volte-face, to reach into his pocket for money. Cathy took the coins and darted off into the nearest sweet shop with Stan following. When Stan re-emerged, leaving Cathy waiting for her change, Robert was standing stock-still outside the doorway of the shop gazing across the street. His mouth was open in a fixed half-smile of recognition. Stan's eyes followed his gaze. The pavement opposite was a fresco of anonymous hurrying figures, men, women and children, most of them spectators returning from the match and flowing towards the centre of the town. Passing traffic intermittently blocked the view. On realising that Stan was standing before him

Robert said: 'Oh, there you are old boy. I was lost in thought. I see you got what you wanted.'

But the smile had gone. He was now staring hard at Stan, his blue eyes as cold as ice, his features rigid with tension. Stan had the sudden conviction that something had passed between Robert and the person he had seen, some gesture or sign that Robert feared Stan had witnessed. Cathy came out of the shop. Robert turned to her and laughed. 'There. Are you satisfied now?' Cathy grinned and dipped the tip of her nose into her ice-cream. 'You can have that bit.' Robert laughed again and licked it off. Then he grabbed the pair of them by the necks of their coats and pushed them along the street. It was an action that would normally have given Stan pleasure, this way Robert had of including him in his gestures of rough, fatherly affection. But now it felt false and ingratiating. He was being urged into silence about an event he barely understood and he felt sure that the aim of that silence was to keep whatever he knew from Cathy.

And he did keep it from her. For what he knew was next to nothing. He had no inclination to tell her that on their way back from the football match - while she was in the ice-cream shop and then only for a period so brief that Stan is now beginning to think he may have imagined it - her father had given him a funny look!

The incident might have been washed away by the flow of events and Robert's unfailing goodwill if Stan had not been reminded of it a few weeks later. One day, in a bout of wild acrobatics with Cathy in the den - bouncing on the sofa and swinging from a rope they had fixed to a ceiling beam - he fell and twisted his ankle. The knife-slash of pain gave way to a deep throbbing ache that reached up to his groin. Fighting back the tears that he must not show to Cathy, he hopped and shuffled his way to the back door of the Railway Hotel. It was Robert who came through into the sitting-room in response to Cathy's search for help. He removed Stan's shoe and sock and examined the swelling foot. He told Stan he had studied first aid during his years in the army catering corps. His touch felt light and expert.

'Nothing broken. I'm pretty sure of that. But we ought to get you along to the doctor. Cathy, you'd better go and tell Stan's mum and dad what's happened.'

He helped Stan out to his car, an old Austin that the Stapletons rarely used and that they kept parked by the side of the pub. In the car neither of them spoke. The pain in Stan's leg had faded to a dull ache in his ankle. At the doctor's surgery they sat and waited, remaining silent. In order to make conversation - for he already knew the answer to his question – Robert asked Stan what exactly he had been doing to injure himself. Stan explained again. He probably sounded embarrassed for he knew that Helen disapproved of him and Cathy playing in the outhouse. Soon after the Stapletons' arrival in Calcroft Cathy had put her foot through a rotten floorboard and gashed the inside of her leg on a nail. Helen had tried to rule the outhouse out of bounds but had yielded with great reluctance before Cathy's resistance. Robert must have picked up his unease, for he tried to sound reassuring.

'Oh well, don't worry. It sounds a bit of a dangerous game you were playing but we're all tempted to play dangerous games now and again.'

He looked down at Stan. His face was expressionless. He added: 'It's only human. Don't you think?'

It was not the words that took Stan back to that moment on the street in Doncaster, nor the expression on Robert's face, which remained impassive and impossible to read. It was the puzzlement that he, Stan, felt. This was the second time he had sensed some hidden motive in Robert's behaviour without understanding what it was. He felt flustered and unable to reply. He was relieved to hear his name called by the doctor's receptionist. He stood up and hobbled across the waiting-room floor before Robert could offer to help him. A sprained ankle he could cope with!

## 14

## In the Bleak Midwinter

*Christmas was coming. At my prep school, Nightingale House, the atmosphere quickened with anticipation; a carol service was held and a tree decorated with tinsel and coloured globes appeared in the school hall for the last week of term. At the Railway Hotel a similar tree similarly decorated appeared in the Concert Room. Robert announced his intention of hiring entertainers – a singer, a comedian and perhaps a conjuror or hypnotist – for the Christmas period itself.*

*But were the geese getting fat? That was the question that hung in the dark December air, hovered over the Christmas tree in the Concert Room, and charged the atmosphere of the festive season with a febrile anxiety.*

*I had understood soon after our arrival in Calcroft that the Railway Hotel was going through lean times. The trouble was that the pub had difficulty competing with the local working-men's clubs, which offered cheap drinks and free entertainment and were the creation of the pitmen themselves. The arrival of my mother and father to manage the Railway Hotel had not helped; some of the regular customers had defected to the clubs, others to the Fox Inn which stood at the other end of the village and was managed by an ex-miner. I gathered that this loss of custom was not unusual when public houses changed their managers but I also understood that my mother and father were having difficulty reversing the process.*

*The fact is they were not popular. Looking back I can see why Mum failed the test. She found it difficult to disguise her disappointment with the situation in which she found herself. That and her sharp tongue, which she was not always able to control, could hardly have endeared her to the clientele on whom the business depended. But my father's case was more puzzling. Although well liked by some, with others he seems to have had difficulty establishing the cordial relations required of the successful pub landlord. At the time, I was not in a position to witness the ways in which this failure manifested itself, nor was I of an age to understand it. Now, fifty years older and if not wiser at least more knowing, I can only assume it was that familiar feature of our nation's social geology: the formation of mountains of class antipathy out of the molehills of accent and social manner.*

He doubts it was antipathy. More likely discomfort with a man who, though personable and willing to please, was foreign to their tribal customs. Robert's predecessor at the Railway Hotel, Fred Merriman, had had his loyalists and hangers-on, satellites on whom he exercised a planetary pull. He shared their love of betting and organised trips for them to Doncaster races, he served them beer after closing-time while dimming the pub lights to hoodwink patrolling bobbies, he lent them money to tide them over to pay-day (Stan's father had seen the little note-book in which he kept his list of 'subs'). When Fred left they left, spinning off into the outer space of the clubs, where the beer was cheaper, and the Fox Inn where the manager, a working-man like themselves, better understood their needs.

Stan's father foresaw the difficulties Robert would have.

'He's a nice enough chap but he doesn't belong at the Railway.'

Stan accepted the judgement as he did all his father's rare but trenchant statements about life. He remembered his own sense of Robert's strangeness when they first met, the feeling that Robert's manner and speech required of him a response he did not know how to give. For all that, he had come to see and appreciate his goodwill and generosity and his encouragement of his friendship with Cathy. That was until the day of their return from the football match. That one brief incident, that flash of glaring coldness slipping instantly back into the old geniality when Cathy emerged from the shop, had changed his perception of Robert. The picture had become blurred at the edges. All those features that had once been clear and sharply defined - his courtesy and kindness, the friendly interest he took in Stan's doings - were now shadowed by the possibility of a Robert who was not the unfailingly affable person he appeared to be.

*So the decline in the Railway Hotel's fortunes continued during the time of my father's stewardship. Within a few months of our arrival the drop in takings had been mentioned - delicately and in a way that reassured my parents that the situation was far from grave - by Mr Gent, the brewery's area manager who visited them once a month. His visits were awaited by Mum and Dad with an apprehension that became particularly acute as November gave way to December. I understood that the approaching Christmas period was a crucial time for my parents, during which it was hoped they would witness an explosion of festive spending by the customers that would make good to some degree the disappointing takings of their first half-year in the pub and herald more prosperous times to come. They felt that Mr Gent's December visit might include a little homily to this effect, together with some indication of their and the Railway Hotel's place in the brewery's future plans.*

*Mr Gent appeared a week before Christmas, a harmless-looking little man – at least six inches shorter than Robert – with thinning hair and a faded grey suit. He had a tentative, almost nervous smile that seemed to apologise for an appearance that failed to square with the terror he struck into the hearts of failing publicans throughout the West Riding of Yorkshire. The message he carried was hardly appropriate to the season. Indeed it was the main burden of my mother's indignation once he had departed that he hadn't even had the decency to delay the bad news until after Christmas.*

*According to Mr Gent the brewery was beginning to wonder whether the Railway Hotel was commercially viable. This was*

107

*not intended as a criticism of my parents, Mr Gent was quite emphatic on that point; he was sure they were devoting to the business their very best efforts. But trading conditions were difficult they must understand; the competition from the clubs was fierce and the miners often preferred them to the better class of establishment such as the Railway Hotel. It was not always easy for people from outside the area and of a more…how shall he put it?… a more elevated… Well, it was not easy for such people to gain the loyalty of the miners. However, there was no immediate worry, there was time to turn things around and the Christmas period was a good moment to renew their efforts. And once again he must assure them that he felt they were doing their very best; it was no straightforward task to run a successful public house. He took his leave on this sympathetic note.*

*This conversation took place in the sitting-room where I was buried in the depths of my favourite armchair pretending to be absorbed in a book. Mr Gent's toleration of my presence impressed me. I decided I quite liked him. Although he sometimes had bad news to convey he was obviously a very understanding man.*

*The anxiety left by Mr Gent's message was compounded by the strain caused by the demands of the pub during what was the busiest time of the year. The atmosphere in the home was tense and brittle. My mother seemed often on the edge of tears with tiredness, worry and irritation while my father was uncharacteristically sombre. He tried to ease the situation by suggesting that once Christmas and New Year were behind us, Helen should enquire of her sister Dot, who lived in Oldham, whether she might spend a week with her. The break would do her good and he would be able to manage the pub on his own; he expected the early weeks of January to be the low point of the commercial year during which customers would stay at* home to nurse their family finances, laid low by the season's prodigality, back to health. The visit was duly arranged and my mother went off to auntie Dot's early in the New Year.

I had secretly looked forward to the week alone with Dad, expecting to rediscover the freedom and pleasure in each other's company that we often achieved in the absence of my mother. In reality it was the start of a new and troubling phase of my time in Calcroft. He, who was normally so open and chatty with me, was subdued and preoccupied. I arrived home from school one day to find him pulling up outside the Railway Hotel in the family car. He said he had been out for a drive, he had things to think about. He did not explain why driving, an activity he normally avoided, had suddenly become necessary to his thinking processes. A few days later he took the bus into Doncaster to deposit the pub's takings at the bank, a task from which he usually returned before lunch. When I arrived back from school after four o'clock he was not at home. He appeared half an hour later mumbling vague explanations of having remained in town to look around the shops. Although I knew he hated shopping I never doubted the truth of what he said.

After the return of my mother our life resumed its normal course for a while. The only difference was Dad's newly acquired habit of taking excursions out in the car on mid-week afternoons when the demands of the pub were at their least intense. He said he needed time away from the premises and driving out into the countryside enabled him to relax; he must not let the pub take over his entire life. Mum accepted this with a good grace, recognising that Robert had always made great efforts to protect her own free time and that the main burdens of the business rested on him. She was less accepting when he returned home late on one occasion from his weekly trip to the bank, having left Helen in charge of the bar throughout the whole of an unusually busy lunchtime session.

109

*This happened while I was at school; I returned home to meet the backwash of what had obviously been a tempest of anger and recrimination, my mother tight-lipped with resentment buttering bread for my tea with quick, irritated strokes of the knife, my dad appearing at the sitting-room door, nodding at me to acknowledge my return from school, then disappearing again without speaking.*

*It must have been shortly after this that Harold and Rachel Davidson failed to turn up one Tuesday evening for the weekly trip to the Co-op ballroom. At first it was assumed that they were simply late. Alec and Miriam Bowen sat talking with Mum and Dad while I went to the bar for my lemonade and crisps and a chat with Joe Walker. When I returned to the sitting-room, Harold and Rachel had still not appeared and the atmosphere had changed. Alec Bowen and my father were debating whether to telephone the Davidsons or simply to assume that they were not intending to turn up. For some reason this simple question seemed to lock them in a mute but tense battle of wills, with my father eager to leave straightaway while Alec insisted they should make a quick call first, just to check that the Davidsons were not coming. In the end they left without phoning.*

*Later that night I woke in bed to hear my parents quarrelling downstairs. It must have been late for the pub was closed and everything was silent except for the sounds of muffled anger emanating from below. I lay there listening, appalled. What was happening to my parents? Why this fierce hostility to one another? For what I was hearing was different from their usual tiffs and squabbles. Although I could not make out the words, there was a harsh intensity to their speech that frightened me. Moments of relative quiet gave way to sudden surges of anger with my mother shouting and crying at the same time. At one point she stopped and gave out a sort of despairing, beseeching moan and began to sob. I could hardly recognise her in this torrent of despair. It was as though some strange wild creature had entered the house. I pulled my head under the blankets and put my fingers in my ears but could still hear her, until finally the sound subsided. For a while everything went still. I heard footsteps on the staircase. From the lightness of the tread I could tell it was my mother going to bed. I waited for my father to follow but he must have stayed downstairs for there was no further sound before I fell asleep.*

*My worry over my parents was intertwined with worry of a different sort. I had returned to school after the Christmas and New Year break to face a rapidly approaching nightmare called the eleven-plus examination. My grandparents had managed to provide a certain amount of money to fund my education in private schools but this had only covered my prep-school years. The hope was that, beyond this period, I would pass the eleven-plus examination and move on to a state Grammar School. Perhaps the hope was an expectation for I must admit that my grandfather was something of a snob whose pretensions often clouded his judgement. I don't think it occurred to him that people like us might fail to make the grade in competition with the great unwashed. The idea that I might go to a state Secondary-Modern School was simply unthinkable. Unfortunately, the reality was implacable: in order that some should succeed, many had to fail.*

*The week of the examination approached. Mrs Selhurst, the headmistress of Nightingale House, was confident of my ability. Miss Hopkins, my class-teacher who knew my work better, was less sure. She told my parents that since returning to school at the beginning of January I seemed to have lost concentration and let things slip. She wondered whether there was anything that might be worrying me. My mother assured her that this was not the case.*

*'Catherine is clever but erratic, she could pass on her day,' said Miss Hopkins.*

*My father tried to compensate for this feeble endorsement by much encouraging talk about my school performance the previous term. His attempts to boost my confidence, rather than reassuring me, made me more anxious for I knew the desperate hope that lay behind them.*

*In the event, it wasn't my day. I knew that I had performed badly and the news that I had failed came as no surprise. But this did not soften the blow. I felt that, in the midst of my growing worries about my parents, I had been set a challenge to save the family honour and had fallen short.*

# 15

## Child's Play

*The power of sudden revelation! A secret can explode in your face like a grenade. All it takes is a twitchy finger on the pin, a momentary loss of self-control by, say, a child consumed by anger and spite.*

*I hardly knew Neil Reckitt, or Recky as he was known in the village, and what I knew I did not like. A bully according to Stan. One to avoid. Stan had the evidence, a fading, yellowy-blue bruise on his shin from an assault on the football field that had been far from accidental* hopping with pain and falling to the ground clutching his shin, Recky standing above him, the others motionless, watching.

'What did you do that for?'

'Because.'

He is tall and broad with large hands and thick, bony wrists that protrude beyond the sleeves of a jumper which looks several sizes too small. His face shows no expression.

'Because of what?'

'Because.'

Recky doesn't need reasons. His sudden rages are a fact of life that Stan senses has something to do with his unhappy home with a violent father and a mother who always looks timid and sad. Stan feels sorry for Recky's mother and he sometimes feels sorry for Recky but mostly he just tries to keep out of his way. So he cannot remember how he came to be playing football with him or why, on this particular day, he was with Cathy and Recky on Lovatt's field. *It was a Sunday morning, of that I'm sure, for I was wearing a pair of new shoes that were a part of my Sunday-morning best clothes. They were pretty shoes, bright red with a single strap across the instep and stiff soles tipped with steel at the heel and toe to make them wear longer. I see us standing at the three points of a triangle, Stan, Recky and me, joined together by lines of tension and, on my part, growing nervousness. Between the thumb and forefinger of Recky's right hand is a small frog. One of its legs keeps stretching back in a slow convulsive movement as though it is feeling for firm ground.*

*I say: 'Be careful with it. You might hurt it. It's only little.'*

*Recky looks at me and then at Stan and says: 'I see you're still playing with lasses, Stan.' Stan smiles uneasily. I say: 'What are you going to do with the frog?'*

*'I'm going to blow it up and see if it'll bust. Have you never seen a frog blown up before? You're in for a treat.'*

*He bends down and snaps off a stem of hollow marsh-grass at his feet.*

*'You take a piece of grass like this. It's got to be hollow mind, and strong so it doesn't break. You nip the end off like this. Then you stick it down the frog's throat or up its arse and blow into it. The old frog blows up like a balloon.'*

*He looks at me and grins in anticipation of my shocked reaction.*

*'Why do you want to do that? It's cruel. You'll kill it.'*

*I am nervous but outraged. I do not understand this desire to hurt and torment, this cold aggression against a helpless creature.*

*'What's the matter with you. It's only a frog. There's hundreds of them round here. Anyway, mind your own bloody business.'*

*He is looking at me with an expression on his face that is somewhere between hurt and anger. The frog seems so soft and delicate between his finger and thumb that I feel he must squash it. I feel suddenly scared.* He is scared too. But he tries to control it, tries to ready himself for what is coming.

Recky says: 'Now then, this is how you do it. Just watch this.'

As he turns his hand to present the frog's behind to the stem of grass, Cathy's features harden into an expression of cold intent. She takes a quick step towards him and strikes her arm down hard on his wrist. The frog drops into the grass. Recky shouts out and bends to pick it up, then changes his mind and swings his body round, still half-bent, into Cathy's chest, knocking her off her feet. Stan, in a surge of outrage, strikes out at the side of Recky's head. Recky yelps with pain and turns to face him. Stan strikes again, hitting him on the mouth. A line of blood-flecked saliva flicks across Recky's cheek. *I feel the damp mud through my Sunday frock. I sit up. Recky is lurching forward to grab Stan round the head but Stan ducks and turns to run. Recky sets off after him; he half trips on one of the rough tussocks of the field and for several yards seems to be falling forward; then, against all the laws of mechanics and motion, he is running upright again and it is Stan who has slipped and fallen while trying to swerve out of his path. Recky trails his last stride along the ground and kicks into Stan's back. Stan hunches up, like a hedgehog in a ball, with his knees up to his chest and his arms around his head. Recky drops onto him knees first and starts thumping his exposed ribs. I get back on my feet and look wildly around Lovatt's field which suddenly seems vast and empty. The houses that stand across the field from the dog-track stand like a row of blind men with their closed doors and blank windows. Stan has rolled onto his front and is trying to push himself up onto his knees in an attempt to throw Recky off. Recky splays himself flat across Stan's back and forces him back down to the ground. He now lies across him, thrusting his elbow back and forth like a piston into Stan's ribs* holding himself tight, stiffening his muscles against the blows, Recky's hot, gasping breath in his ear, his elbow sharp and hard, the pain suddenly coming through. *I run over to them. I'm frightened but I'm thinking clearly, calculating what to do. I take off one of my shoes, the new bright-red shoes with the steel-tipped heels, and strike Recky* a blow on his back with the flat sole. He continues his pummelling of Stan who is now gasping with pain at each thrust of Recky's elbow. My fear gives way to rising anger. I turn the shoe round and strike again, harder, with the steel-tipped heel. Recky flails his arm behind him to ward me off and catches me a sharp blow on the cheek. He grabs a handful of grass and dirt and starts stuffing it into Stan's mouth. I'm engulfed by a wave of fury and disgust. I strike again with all my strength, then again and again. I'm sick of everything - of this bullying brute who torments frogs and people, of my quarrelling parents, of my whole collapsing world. I strike another blow, as hard as I can. Recky shouts with pain and screams out: 'You bastard. You fucking bastard' He pushes Stan away, leaps up and reaches out towards me but Stan grips him round his ankles and thrusts his shoulder into the back of his legs. Recky falls to his knees. I hear a shout: 'Hey, you lot, cut it out', and realise we are being watched by a woman who has come out of one of the houses. I recognise Mrs Cotterill, a regular of the Railway Hotel. She is a large and truculent woman who has reared four boys to live in fear for their lives. She puts down her basket of washing and walks down her garden path towards us.

'Neil Reckitt, are you fighting again? And you, Stan Walker, you should know better. Get yourselves home, the lot of you.'

She stands staring at us, waiting for us to leave. Recky is swearing under his breath but pulls himself to his feet and begins to move off. I sense that he's glad of this excuse to end the fight. Stan remains sitting on the ground spitting grass and dirt out of his mouth. I am desperately hoping that Mrs Cotterill will continue watching until Recky has gone. She turns back to her washing line but Recky keeps moving away. Suddenly he stops and spins round. He is looking directly at me. For a moment I fear he is going to come back. But he starts to speak.

*'You think you're better than us, you bloody stuck-up snob.
Just 'cos you go to a la-di-da school and your dad runs a pub.'*

*He pauses and attempts a smile, a disdainful curl of the lip
that seems intended to show his superiority to the assault he
has suffered at the hands of a girl. A bubble of blood-stained
spit emerges from the corner of his mouth and bursts, leaving
a scarlet trail across his cheek. But the failure of his effort to
appear cool and in control of the situation does not detract
from the force of the blow he delivers next.*

*'And you, Walker. You're the same. You think you and her are
better than the rest of us but you're not. Everybody knows
about her dad and your auntie Rachel. She's his fancy-woman.
My dad's seen 'em in a pub in Worlby.'*

*He stops abruptly as though realising the enormity of what
he has said but the poison is already infiltrating my mind*
spluttering and spitting, trying to clear his mouth of the filth Recky
has forced into it, trying to clear his mind too, as though spitting will
expel the words he has just heard *running alongside the fence of
the dog-track, across the road without stopping, arriving at
the back-gate of the Railway Hotel, my eyes stinging with tears,
my head bursting with the force of Recky's words. My dad! My
dad and Rachel Davidson! His fancy-woman! I feel assaulted
and abused* Recky moving off across Lovatt's field, stopping to
pick up a cigarette packet out of the grass, looking inside it and
throwing it away. Stan gets slowly to his feet. He wants to follow
Cathy but he doesn't want to attract the attention of her parents.
He must wash his mouth out and clean up the side of his face.

*I fiddle with the latch of the gate, blinded by tears, shaking.
I go into the outhouse and turn into the den. I stand holding
myself tight, seeing out the storm while staring at the old sofa
and the table with its candles rooted in their hardened wax. I
cannot risk meeting my father or especially my mother. My
new shoes, my knees and the side of one of my legs are scabbed*

*with drying mud. There is mud on my Sunday frock. I stand and wait, shivering with cold and grief.*

*Did I believe Recky? I don't think I knew. It was the idea itself, true or not, and the brutality with which it had been conveyed that seared me. It filled my mind like some seething, malignant force that left no room for reflection beyond itself. I finally began to get some order into my thoughts. What if Recky was lying? Stan Walker had told me he was a liar. I wanted Stan to come so that I could put the idea to him. I wanted him to say something that would relieve the pain I was feeling at the thought of my father with Rachel Davidson. I wanted him to come and say something to comfort me.*

He arrived home to find his mother in the kitchen cooking the Sunday dinner. 'Look at the sight of you, Stanley Walker. What have you been getting up to?' She did not wait for an answer but told him to go and get washed.

He was relieved by the ordinariness of what he found at home. In some obscure way he had feared things might be different, as though the knowledge he carried back from Lovatt's field had the power to change the world. But his mother was scrubbing potatoes and humming a tune to herself and Dad was sitting by the fire reading the *News of the World*. He wondered whether they knew what he knew. Nothing had happened in recent days and weeks to suggest they did; there had been no change in his parents' behaviour, no hint of a family secret. Is it possible to know such a thing and carry on as though life is just the same? Could his mother hide such a worry from him? It suddenly occurs to him that Recky might be lying. It would not be the first time, everybody knows he can't be trusted. Whereas his auntie Rachel, a member of his own family who everybody likes and admires, could she be anybody's fancy-woman let alone Robert Stapleton's, a friend of the family? But even as he thinks this he knows that his belief in Robert Stapleton has gone. He remembers Robert's expression that day returning

118

from the match, his faraway, captivated smile turning to a hard cold stare. Was it auntie Rachel he had seen by chance across the street? In the end he does not know what to think.

In subsequent days he met other members of his family – his cousins Keith and Frank, and some of his aunts and uncles. They all behaved in their usual way. On an errand to Morton's to buy slices of ham for Saturday tea he met auntie Rachel behind the counter. She smiled her rich, warm smile and called him 'Stanley' as usual. She was the only person he knew who used his full name.

At some point in this sequence of events Recky's revelation began to lose its sting. It passed imperceptibly from the realm of possible truth to the realm of probable falsehood. It could not be true that auntie Rachel was Robert Stapleton's fancy-woman because the world had remained the same and his family were their usual contented and congenial selves.

But somebody had changed. The one exception to all this ordinariness was Robert Stapleton. Stan came home from school one day to find him sitting in the Walkers' living-room. He was in Dad's favourite chair, his long legs straggled out in front of the fire and a cup of tea in his hands that he was raising to his lips as Stan came through the door. Mam and Dad were on the sofa, also holding cups of tea. His mother turned to smile at Stan while Robert reached down to place his cup on the carpet and said: 'There you are, Stan. We were just talking about you.'

Yet Stan has heard no sound of conversation before entering the room and he senses in their pleasure at his arrival a touch of relief, as though he has rescued them from an onerous silence. It is the first time that Robert has visited the Walkers in their home and the atmosphere is tense with the uncertainties of an abnormal social encounter. Dad is staring into the glowing coal-fire while Mam takes a sip of her tea and renews her smiling at Stan, glad to have this new object for her attention.

Robert continues: 'Your mother and father have been telling me you're worried about going to the Grammar School.'

Stan has not seen him for a few weeks and is struck by the change in his appearance and manner. His cheeks have a grey pallor of unshaved stubble and he is wearing a worn old cravat, stained with what looks like egg-yolk, tucked into the collar of his shirt. When he speaks, the liveliness of his tone is belied by the forced smile and the weary expressionless eyes.

Stan's mother says: 'He hasn't exactly said he doesn't want to go to Grammar School but he's not keen, are you, son?'

This issue of the Grammar School has been raised by Mr Holmes, the headmaster of Calcroft Juniors, who has let it be known that Stan and two or three of his classmates are 'racing certainties' to have passed the eleven-plus examination that they recently sat. Unfortunately, from Stan's point of view these chosen few will not include most of his best friends. The Grammar School is four miles away in the small rural town of Worlby and already in his mind he envisages the journey not simply as a physical displacement but as an enforced separation from the life and people he knows. At the same time, somewhere in the dark chamber of his fears and forebodings there is the faintest glimmer of a new awareness, a growing conviction that he will go to the Grammar School come what may. He feels the inevitability of it, the pull of the age like a wind tunnel sucking him towards a future that his parents have not known. Mr Holmes says the Grammar Schools have been set up precisely for people like Stan, whom he calls 'the nation's brightest children, the chosen few'. Uncle Harold thinks it would be a crying shame not to go, a scandal, a dereliction of duty. But for the moment Stan is digging his heels in out of loyalty to his friends and, beyond them, to the massed legions of those who will not go, the unchosen many.

There is something else he doesn't like about the Grammar School, and it is this that he mentions when he speaks.

'They don't play football at the Grammar School. They make you play rugby.'

He addresses the words directly to Robert, knowing that Robert shares his love of football and will understand the seriousness of the point he is making. But instead of responding with the sympathy Stan expects, Robert says: 'But rugby's a fine game. I played it myself at school. Once you get into it you'll enjoy it.' He passes his hand over his face and rubs the stubbled cheeks as though he is trying to disguise the inability of his features to confirm the enthusiasm of his words. He seems tired and distracted and Stan wonders for the first time what he has come to the house for.

Mam says: 'Did you go to the Grammar School, Mr Stapleton?'

Stan is surprised at the question. He knows from Cathy that Robert went to a private school and he has hitherto assumed that everybody else knew it too. But his mother sees little of Robert, and Dad - who doubtless does know - is an unreliable messenger with news of other people's lives.

'Well, no,' Robert says. 'I wasn't much of a scholar I'm afraid.'

He seems about to continue but stops short. Dad leans across from the sofa to poke the fire. They fill the silence by watching him attentively. He lays the poker down and eases himself back into the sofa.

Robert says: 'What do you think, Joe? Should he go?'

Dad ceases his silent contemplation of the fire and turns his head towards them. 'Oh, I don't know. None of us knows much about it. It's an opportunity right enough. It's an opportunity none of us had. But our Stan loves his football.'

'But he has to think of his future,' Mam says. 'Neither of us wants him working down the pit.'

She looks to Dad for confirmation of her point. He nods and says drily: 'Aye, I'm sure there are better ways of spending your working life.'

'I think you're right, Mrs Walker,' Robert says with sudden conviction: 'That's why I think he should go to the Grammar School. It's a great opportunity for children like Stan. He should make the most of his intelligence and get a good job. Something well paid and secure.'

He has been gazing down at the floor while speaking but he now raises his head and turns to Stan. 'All I can say is if I'd had his brain...' The sentence peters out. He smiles and shakes his head. He raises his hand again to rub his cheeks, then says: 'Ah well, no point regretting.' He looks at his watch and starts to raise himself out of the chair. Stan's mother accompanies him to the door. Stan hears them exchanging comments about the weather and saying goodbye. Through the window he sees Robert's stooped figure passing on the street.

When his mother returned to the sitting-room she gave Dad a strange look that was a mixture of worry and bemusement, but she did not speak. Stan got up and went into the back-kitchen for a glass of water. He heard Mam whispering behind him: 'Well. What was all that about?'

He never did discover what had brought Robert to the house that day. He knew from Cathy that he was worried by the declining custom of the Railway Hotel; perhaps he had wanted to discuss the problem with Dad. But in that case why were Mam and Dad themselves puzzled by his visit? He could think of no answer. What remained with him was the memory of Robert Stapleton passing by their window, the familiar stoop of his shoulders seeming to express a sadness that none of them understood.

# 16

## Into the Dark

*There had been a visit from Mr Gent.*

*Although I had not been in the house at the time, I picked up the particular atmospheric turbulence he habitually left in his wake, a cloud of dejection and anxiety that any comment from Dad could spark into lightning bolts of hysterical outrage from my mother. I did not know what tidings Mr Gent had brought but his words must have lacked the soothing tone of the speech I had heard him make before Christmas. Either that or the peculiar intensity of my mother's outbursts was due to her worsening relations with my father. For things were bad between my parents. The reasonableness with which Mum had accepted Dad's mid-week drives in the country had evaporated and his every absence was now the occasion for bad temper and resentful brooding. We would have meals during which they spoke to me but not to each other. Quarrels were frequent and sometimes of a stridency that would reach me even when they thought I was out of earshot.*

*I was anxious over my father's behaviour. The idea that he was 'having an affair', a phrase I had picked up in the playground gossip of Nightingale House, beset my every waking moment. I thought I saw changes in his facial expressions – a sudden flash of something like panic in his eyes, a weary, seemingly painful smile – that I surmised could be the reactions of a man who was 'having an affair'. With me he was often remote; his pale-blue eyes that had always had an abstracted quality, as though they were fixed on some inner rumination, now seemed like a disguise for his thoughts. I was taken by a nagging fear that he would one day leave the house and fail to return.*

*He was volatile. Sometimes, in a sudden rush of affection and perhaps guilt, he would take me in his arms and hug me. On one occasion he sang softly into my ear a few lines of a song, 'You are my sunshine, my only sunshine', that he used to sing to me when I was a child in Suffolk. I could feel the familiar, comforting tickle of his moustache against my cheek. Yet it felt wrong, an exaggerated attempt to comfort and reassure me that had the opposite effect. The bond between us had become twisted and knotted by feelings I barely understood.*

*For all my father's vagaries, it was my mother towards whom I felt resentful - for constantly being impatient and irritable with me and for starting quarrels with him for the pettiest of reasons or for no reason at all. When on one occasion he suggested he might attend an evening meeting of the Licensed Victuallers' Association she objected, though he had been to several such meetings before.*

*'It's not convenient.'*

*'But it's a chance to discuss things with other pub-managers, perhaps pick up a few useful tips. We need all the advice we can get.'*

*'And I'll need all the help I can get in the bar.'*

*This was a hollow claim for the pub was doing so little business in the middle of the week that my father was usually able to cover the bar entirely on his own. He said: 'I can get Joe in to help. I really think I should go to the meeting.' His voice was toneless and lacking in conviction.*

*'Oh, go on then, do what you like.'*

*She waved her hand in a gesture of disdain. She too seemed empty of conviction, her change of mind as mechanical as her initial objection. It was as though she was exhausted by her own deadlocked, jarring emotions.*

*I sat on the edge of this, ignored and feeling lonely. I could not believe the suddenness with which things had changed.*

*My new life of adventure and fun with Stan Walker seemed*
*surrounded by an impending doom. Our night-time encounters*
*were becoming less frequent for my mother was spending more*
*time in the sitting-room during the evenings. This was largely*
*because of lack of demand in the pub but there was also a new*
*insistence on her free time, which I sensed was a rebuke to my*
*father for his absences.* She is moody and bad-tempered when
they do meet, shrugging him off when he puts his arm round her,
starting quarrels for no good reason. She refuses to go to their den
to light fires and kiss and cuddle on the old sofa.

*The night of my father's meeting I asked Stan to come and*
*watch television with me while Dad was out of the house and*
*my mother in the bar. When Stan arrived I told him I'd changed*
*my mind, I fancied something more exciting. I wanted to climb*
*onto the Tap Room roof. He hesitated. I told him it wasn't*
*dangerous; the roof was flat, you could walk around on it and*
*look down through a big glass skylight at the customers below.*
He has two reasons to dislike this idea. The first is that he cannot
see that it is much fun. The second is that the only way onto the
Tap Room roof is by way of an outside drainpipe and Stan dislikes
climbing. Clinging to trees and drainpipes with large volumes of air
beneath his feet is an activity that makes him anxious, while the
experience of looking down from the heights so attained gives him
a mild feeling of vertigo. To have to do this in the dark of this
February evening, though he has brought his battery-torch, is an
idea whose appeal escapes him. At the same time he feels unable
to admit this weakness and the only objection he can muster – that
he would prefer to watch television – is swept aside with something
like contempt. Cathy is at her most impatient and domineering

*Why this crazy idea? What was driving me? Anger and hurt*
*I suppose. There were times when my parents, locked in their*
*separate miseries, hardly seemed to notice I was there. I wanted*
*to shock them, shake them out of this mood of cold resentment*
*against each other that had become the atmosphere of the*

*home. I felt careless but not in a good way; I was careless of myself and of others. I see myself climbing the drainpipe in the dark with Stan still standing at the bottom, shining his torch upwards, grumbling and protesting. It doesn't matter that he's scared. It doesn't matter if he falls. It doesn't matter if I fall. Serves them right. My anger gives me extra strength and a sort of reckless freedom. I grip the top of the wall and heave myself onto the roof. I shout down: 'Stop moaning. You're being pathetic.'* The contempt in her voice. He is stung. He stuffs the torch in his pocket and grips the drainpipe. It is easier than he expected. The drainpipe is narrow enough for him to get his hands round it and is pinned to the wall by metal brackets that provide firm toe-holds. He pulls himself onto the roof. Cathy is behaving oddly, waving her arms around and stamping her feet as though she is performing a war-dance. She goes over to the skylight, a square of thick glass set on a frame in the middle of the roof, and looks down through it pulling grotesque faces. Stan feels nervous – nervous at the thought that he will have to climb back down the drainpipe (going down, feeling for toe-holds, not being able to see what is below!) and nervous at Cathy's behaviour. He joins her at the skylight and looks down into the Tap Room. Several of the tables round the sides of the room are occupied by customers. It cannot be long before Cathy attracts their attention. He is relieved when she moves away. Outside the faint glow cast by the skylight the roof is in darkness. Cathy is a bent shadow as she walks, scrutinising the roof, searching for something.

'What are you looking for?' he says. 'There's nothing up here. I think we'd better go down now.'

'I'm looking for a brick or a big stone. Something heavy.'

'You won't find any bricks up here. Anyway what do you want a brick for?'

She walks towards him out of the darkness. 'I want to smash the glass and make them jump. Throw it through the glass.' She's grinning, showing all her white teeth; her eyes are wide and gleaming.

'You what! You can't do that. You might hit somebody. You must be mad.' The thought flashes through his mind as he says this that it might be true. It is only then that he sees she is carrying something in her hand. 'What's that?'

'It's what I was looking for. Half a house-brick.'

She holds it above her head and does a twirling, writhing dance-step while chanting a makeshift witch's spell. 'Oh, house-brick, wonderful house-brick, work your magic for me. Smash through the glass and frighten all the stupid, nasty people.' She laughs and turns to the skylight. He grabs her arm but she snatches it away with a force that surprises him. She reaches out towards the centre of the skylight with her hands gripping the brick. He takes her arm again, more gingerly this time, and tries to pull her back from the edge of the skylight. She turns on him spitting fury.

'Take your bloody hands off me.'

He has never heard her use even the mildest swear-word and is shocked out of all proportion.

'Go on, get off, leave me alone. I don't want you any more.'

He is stunned. She doesn't want him! He doesn't know whether to leave or stay. He is frightened by this wildness in her but feels that if he abandons her now it will be the end. And besides, lurking somewhere deep down inside him is a shaming, ignoble worm of a thought that defies his efforts to force it back into its hole: he needs her to guide him back down the drainpipe!

Then all of a sudden she begins to cry. She cries like a person who is alone, emitting little hiccups of grief, her head hanging down and her arms pulled back from the skylight still cradling the brick, as though seeking comfort from it. She seems unaware of his presence but though he does not know what to do he still cannot leave. He has the desperate hope that they will even now put all this behind them and take up the evening he thought they were going to have. He wants to be in the Stapletons' warm and comfortable sitting-room, laughing and joking with Cathy in front of the television; yet he knows that this simple pleasure is now far out of their reach.

He stands and waits for what seems an age until her weeping subsides, then he starts to walk back across the roof, wanting her to follow. She remains staring down through the skylight. He returns to her side and she looks up as though surprised to find him still with her. In the upward glare of the skylight her features are etched in shadow. Her mouth is twisted, though whether in grief or anger he cannot tell. She says: 'I want to go to the den.' Her tone is flat and sullen. The words, which would normally give him a glow of eager anticipation, disappoint him but he says: 'OK'. He knows that she wants to talk to him, tell him of her fear that her parents are splitting up and that her father will leave. She will rage and weep, and he will feel helpless and vaguely guilty, for Cathy has told him of her father's drives out into the countryside and he suspects they coincide with his auntie Rachel's time off from her work in Morton's store.

He says: 'Will you go down the drainpipe first? I don't like going down.'

She disappears over the side of the roof and he follows. As he slides his shoe down the wall, searching for his first toe-hold, he feels her hand take hold of his foot and place it on the top bracket of the drainpipe. She does the same for the next one and the third and the fourth, and then he is down on the ground. He is about to thank her but she speaks first: 'That was a bad thing to say…about not wanting you any more. I didn't mean it and I'm sorry.' Before he can reply, she has turned and is walking in the direction of the outhouse.

He is astonished that she can feel such concern for him in the midst of her unhappiness. He feels a rush of tenderness, a desire to put his arms round her and comfort her, which he has never experienced before for her or anyone else. It seems to come from somewhere inside him that he has only become aware of in recent weeks. Something has been happening to him that he feels but cannot understand. When he goes round to auntie Peggy's to borrow sugar or tea for his mother he notices the rich gravel-in-honey rumble of her voice and her shiny blouses that he would like to touch. One day in class he saw, down the top of Maggie Worrall's dress as she bent to pick a pencil off the floor, a delicate curve of white flesh. Something in him seemed to melt and the memory remained in his body for a while like a warming presence, faint, diffuse, everywhere and nowhere, unchannelled by a power of desire that was as yet beyond him. Chance happenings set him dreaming: a picture seen in the *Eagle* of some interplanetary princess tightly encased in a golden robe, a love-song heard on the radio.

As they walk across the yard to the outhouse it occurs to him that this feeling he has just had for Cathy may be what adults call being in love. The thought makes him feel solemn and important. He searches around in his head for an act of decorum that seems appropriate to the occasion. Catching her up, he takes a step ahead of her and switches on his torch in order to light her way into the outhouse. *I don't know how I come to be walking towards the outhouse with Stan. I have a memory of us on the roof of the Tap Room, my momentary madness, the brick in my hands, the blurred figures of the evening drinkers seen through the skylight. Then I am down in the yard. It is now pitch black apart from the thin beam of Stan's torch ahead of me. It is a purely visual image; I remember nothing of my thoughts and feelings, nothing of the strange turmoil that must have driven me to take Stan up onto the roof. It is my last memory of what I have come to think of as an old and impossibly remote self, the child Catherine Stapleton, a self that the events of the next few minutes were to destroy utterly* entering the main door of the outhouse and turning left into the den. As he swings his torch around, playing its circle of faint yellow light on the sofa and the old coffee table, he sees out of the corner of his eye, standing against the far wall of the den, the immensely tall figure of a man. His head is bent forward as though in prayer. Stan feels a thump inside his chest, his spine shrivels with fear. He turns to run. But even as he does so, with his heart banging hard and his whole body a tingling mesh of electrified nerves, the one thing he knows for sure, the one idea remaining in his mind that is otherwise obliterated by panic, is that the man is not standing!

And there was something else. A sound. The man was making a sound, a choking gurgle that seemed to be an attempt at speech!

Cathy is still at the door as he rushes out *bangs into me, grips my arm and pushes me back out into the yard. I wriggle to get free, he grips harder. 'Stop it, you're hurting me. What's the matter?' He continues pushing* putting distance between them and the figure in the outhouse, up the yard towards the back-door of the hotel. He still hasn't spoken, can't speak, gripped by a terror that has barely begun to subside.

'What's the matter?'

Her tone has changed; irritation has given way to a dawning awareness that something bad has happened. *He stops but keeps hold of me. When he speaks it is in a rasping whisper as though he is afraid of his own words. 'In there. There's somebody...hanging. Get my dad. He's in the bar.'*

*I dart to the backdoor of the hotel. Grasping at the latch, the door swinging open, the dark sitting-room. I bang my knee on the coffee-table as I run through. Along the corridor and into the brightness of the pub. Joe pulling a beer-pump behind the bar* stepping inside the house, slamming the door behind him and dropping the latch. He stands there panting, the uproar in his brain pierced by one clear thought. The man was trying to speak! He is still alive!

'Hurry up Dad, hurry up!'

The next thought is a dagger to his open wound. He should have stayed! He should have tried to free the man! Even now he could...But fear holds him rooted to the spot.

'Please Dad, hurry.'

*

*There is an ambulance by the back wall of the Railway Hotel. I can hear voices and footsteps in the yard. Joe Walker is out there with the ambulance men and the police. Stan Walker, white-faced and shaking with fright, has gone, taken home by one of the customers of the pub. I am on the sofa in the sitting-room, my mother is in the armchair facing me. She is leaning forward with her arms crossed over her stomach as though she is holding herself together. Her face is as pale and expressionless as stone.*

*We know nothing of what or who they have found out there in the outhouse. The waiting is a torture beyond anything I have experienced. My mother stands up and walks to the window that looks out onto the backyard. She stops without opening the curtains and returns to her seat. We sit again in silence. The air is heavy with an unspoken, suffocating dread that is barely lightened by hope. She glances at the clock on the mantelpiece, giving expression to my own desperate longing. I want my father to return from his meeting and walk through the door. I want him to be his old self, his voice brisk and cheerful: 'Well then, what's the state of play?' See his smile and feel the atmosphere warmed and quickened by his presence. But with every minute that passes the hope dwindles.*

*I hear the scrape of the backdoor opening. Joe Walker enters the sitting-room with a policeman. The policeman seems about to speak but, noticing me, gives a little cough instead. But I know from the expression on Joe's face and from his glance at my mother, who immediately rises from her chair and accompanies him and the policeman out of the sitting-room, that my father will not return.*

## 17

## *Lacrimae rerum*

*My father's death was a great crashing wave and I was the flotsam bobbing in its wake. I am still the flotsam. I have never fully recovered and I know I never will.*

*Within days the brewery had installed a relief manager in the Railway Hotel. One of the second-floor bedrooms was adapted for his use as a bed sitting-room for, as Mr Gent explained, it would be better if he were as self-sufficient as possible in order not to intrude on our grief. He took some of his meals at Calcroft's only café, the Smiling Milkmaid, and some of them he prepared himself in our kitchen before carrying them off to his room on a tray. When I bumped into him in the kitchen or on the stairs he would lower his eyes to the ground or give a tentative nod of condolence. I never spoke to him, never even acknowledged him; I cannot now remember his name. I was locked in a numbness so deep that it froze my responses to the world, including the simplest social courtesies. Only the spectacle of my mother – wreckage like me – pierced through the barrier to arouse something like normal human feelings.*

*I would find her sitting by the window staring emptily into the backyard, or standing in the kitchen, seared by sudden memory, swaying slightly, her eyes swimming with tears. I remember going up to her bedroom one morning to pass on a message from the relief manager; it must have been two or three weeks after my father's death; a bright spring daylight flooded the room. She was standing stock-still by the foot of the bed. I stopped in the doorway. Some superstition I'd come across in a book about the danger of breaking spells passed through my mind. Her face was turned away from me and* bent forward, staring into the corner of the room. I wanted to speak to her, pass on the message that I'd brought, but I was petrified by the silence and the notion of intruding on such rapt desperation. I heard her whisper: 'He's there.' A few seconds passed, then her whole body seemed to slump, as though it had been held upright by some electric current that had now been switched off. She sat down on the bed and crossed her arms over her stomach, whimpering and swaying back and forth.

'Oh Robert. What have you done to us? What have you done?'

She is hardly able to get the words out. I look on in horror at such utter abandon. I am consumed by pity, fear and repulsion in equal measure. I creep away.

My nights were a hell of nightmares and wrecked sleep. My mind played cruel tricks, drifting off, in moments of distraction, into a world where old habits and routines still held sway; I would be seized by the sudden wild conviction that Dad was still alive and that, as I entered the sitting-room, he would be there watching television. The sight of his chair, hollowed into a terrible emptiness by his absence, broke my heart.

The disarray in our feelings was reflected in our daily routines. I abandoned school until after my father's funeral while Mum kept out of the bar and left the running of the Railway Hotel to the relief manager and Joe Walker. She would sit for hours by the sitting-room fire, smoking cigarette after cigarette, locked in a cold, tearless misery broken by outbursts of rage and despair at my father's treachery. A few days before his death Robert and she had had a violent quarrel during which he had admitted what she had suspected for some months, that he had a secret relationship with Rachel Davidson.

'Can you imagine! All this was going on under our noses! He said it didn't amount to much. They hadn't...' She checks herself, sucks fiercely at her cigarette and throws it into the fire.

*'Didn't amount to much! And now this! What will we do? I can't run this place on my own. What will we do for a living?'*

*I sat silent through all this, absorbed in my grief, wishing she would spare me hers. In the evenings I was allowed to fall asleep on the sitting-room sofa until her bedtime, at which point she woke me and we went upstairs together. My fear of being left alone was such that I slept in her bed where we lay united as never before by our restless anguish.*

*There was a bleak and comfortless funeral, a dozen or so people in a cold, whitewashed crematorium chapel, among them my grandparents, frail and barely comprehending the disaster that had befallen them. There was an inquest at which Stan Walker described, with a courage and dignity beyond his years, his discovery of a hanging body.* The coroner peering over his glasses, speaking softly and kindly, asking him to describe what happened at the moment they entered the outhouse. When he has spoken, the coroner asks whether he saw or heard anything else. His reply is prompt and firm: 'No, sir.' The coroner thanks him, says he can go, smiling now, impressed by his calm and self-possession, wishing him well.

*Within two months we were gone from the Railway Hotel. Salvation came in the form of auntie Dot who insisted we should go to live with her until we managed, in her phrase, to sort ourselves out. I see us standing on auntie Dot's doorstep on that bright, raw day in April, a mother, a daughter and their suitcases. We had brought as many of our clothes and belongings as we could manage to lug between buses, stations and taxis on the tortuous journey from Calcroft to Oldham. Our furniture was still in the Railway Hotel doing service with the relief manager, a bachelor I seem to remember who was grateful to step into a ready-furnished home.*

*Auntie Dot was a long and pointed woman, a taller and more angular version of my mother, with trailing, bony fingers, prominent cheekbones and a sharp, narrow nose. Her odd appearance never seemed to trouble her; indeed she accentuated rather than disguised it by wearing her hair tucked up into a bun in a way that exposed her gaunt neck. She had a cheerful and self-mocking manner that contrasted strikingly with the querulousness of my mother. It was as though nature, on returning to the drawing-board, had smoothed away Dot's sharper points in order to produce Helen's slender elegance but in a scruple of even-handedness had given Dot the better temperament.*

*Her house was one of a row of neat bow-fronted semis that curved along a hillside. It felt small after the Railway Hotel but this was a relief to me, a welcome antidote to those empty corridors, rooms and staircases. Here, I told myself, the space is outside where it belongs. From my bedroom window I could see, beyond the streets and houses further down the slope, green hills rising to brown patches of moorland. Auntie Dot said they were the Pennines; she called them the backbone of England and told me that in her younger days she had often gone walking on them with friends. Even now, despite an arthritic knee, she would drive out occasionally with a woman friend who lived close by, and take short walks, supported by one of the collection of walking-sticks she kept in an umbrella stand by the front door of the house.*

*I would sit for hours in the bay of my bedroom window watching the distant hillsides change colour in the varying light, from a pale, powdery green, through shades of lowering darkness, to pure black when the clouds were thick and no sunlight penetrated. I watched the mist creep like a living thing along the summits, then lift and break into tendrils that thinned to nothingness against the leaden sky. As the evening light faded, the hills seemed to take on a heavier, more forceful presence that I found unnerving. I would go downstairs to join Dot and my mother for another evening of television or desultory gossip while Dot knitted and Mum and I played card games.*

*Auntie Dot was a woman of energy and character who had started her working life as a shop assistant and progressed to become a buyer for a large department store in Manchester. It was she who found me a place in a local prep school where I was to complete my school year. She urged my mother out of her torpor of shock and despair to arrange for the transfer of a portion of my fees from Nightingale House ('Tell them it's on compassionate grounds,' she insisted to a sceptical and reluctant Helen), and she made an agreement with my new school that absolved us from the obligation to spend large sums of money that we did not have on items of uniform that I would wear only for a part of that summer term.*

*In her robust, practical way Dot seemed to think that starting at my new school would help to take me out of myself and make a new beginning. The truth is I could not have been more indifferent. My failure to pass the eleven-plus examination had already sapped my commitment to school work. My father's death had now drained the whole world of interest and pleasure. I could see that people such as auntie Dot and Mrs Threlfall, my new headmistress at Truscott Preparatory School, were being kind to me but their kindness did not touch me. It was as though I experienced the world through an enveloping zone of dead air that muffled sound and blurred sight. At school I could not concentrate and my work suffered. I had always been good at arithmetic but now my brain seemed to baulk at the slightest difficulty, veering off into empty day-dreams that were soon filled by disturbing memories.*

*I missed my father terribly. My longing to have him physically beside me was sometimes so sharp I whimpered with the misery of it. He appeared to me in dreams of unutterable sadness from which I woke with my face streaming with tears. The worst thing was not being able to understand why he had done it.*

136

There was Rachel Davidson of course. There was his fear for his job. But could these things drive a man to abandon his wife and child? He had always said that he loved me, that I was the joy of his life. I could hear him singing to me: 'You are my sunshine, my only sunshine. You make me happy...' The memory got no further, obliterated by welling grief. How could he have left me if I meant all this to him? My grief gave way to a fierce, consuming anger.

There was no-one to put these questions to. My mother seemed out of reach, locked in the cell of her own unhappiness and still unable to talk of Dad without tears and hysteria. Auntie Dot's kindness was of a brisk, commonsensical sort that did not invite the sharing of intimate feelings. I thought of Stan Walker. He might not have understood such a terrible thing as my father's suicide but at least I could have talked to him and talking might have eased my pain.

I had had my last meeting with him on the morning we left for auntie Dot's. We stood on Station Road by the corner of the Railway Hotel, I still stunned with loss and the upheaval in my life, he staring down at the pavement, scraping pieces of grit into a heap with the toe of his shoe. When he looks up his eyes are blurred with tears. I don't know what to say and I want this to end. My idyll with Stan has been engulfed and swept away and I am already a different person. It is an old self that stands here trying to find something to say to him but failing to break out of the grey, frozen prison of my grief. In the end it is he who moves off, mumbling something about writing to me. I can still see the dejected slope of his shoulders and the slow walk as though he is waiting for me to call him back. Then he breaks into a run. He runs past Lovatt's stadium where we thrilled to the leaping greyhounds, and past the wall of the railway track where we hugged to keep ourselves warm. He runs up the sharp incline of Calcroft bridge. At the top he pauses briefly to look back. Then he is gone.

It wasn't his only cause for sorrow that day.

When he overheard Dad telling Mam that he had 'got the Railway', he didn't at first understand. It was only after several minutes' reflection that he realised it could mean only one thing. He knew that his father had wanted to leave the pit; he was forty-eight and had taken his first job on the pit-top at thirteen years of age. He was visibly wearying, spending long hours slumped in his chair in a dead sleep that neither Stan nor his mother dared disturb. His knees were painful from the constant kneeling and squatting in low seams. Stan arrived home from school one day to find him lying on his back on the living-room floor with his right leg in the air, twisting and bending it until it gave off the sharp whip-crack that told him his cartilage had slipped back into place.

It was now that his stubborn persistence in his second job at the Railway Hotel paid off. After much doubt and deliberation during the period of Robert Stapleton's management, the brewery had finally decided to maintain the pub as a going concern. When Mr Rodwell, the relief manager at the Railway - himself desperate for relief from a job that was being prolonged by the brewery's inability to find a suitable successor to Robert – suggested to Mr Gent that Joe Walker was the ideal candidate, the suggestion was taken up with alacrity. It was Mr Gent himself who encouraged Dad to apply and who, while muttering something about its being 'subject to the usual formalities', more or less told him the job was his. In retrospect it was surprising that it had taken Joe Walker the five years he had worked at the Railway to realise that he could do the job better than anybody else. Although a man of little education, he knew his own worth; a capacity for hard work, a head for figures and an ability to handle the pub's rough-and-ready clientele were the skills he had to offer. For Mr Gent and the brewery they were more than enough.

There was of course a problem, and the problem was Stan. To discover, at the tender age of eleven, a man hanging dead from a rope is not an experience to be forgotten overnight. To be asked within two months to live on the premises where the experience had occurred was a test of nerve for which Stan, two hours after his farewell meeting with Cathy Stapleton, was ill-prepared.

'How would you like to live at the Railway Hotel?'

Dad's expression was hard to read, though the fact that he had asked the question – he who was normally so lacking in questions – was proof that he realised what was at stake.

Mam said: 'You must tell us clearly what you want, son.'

He knew she disapproved of the idea. Although Mam and Dad were careful to hide their disagreements from him, he could tell they had been quarrelling.

How would he like to live at the Railway Hotel! He remembers his first tour of the building with Cathy, the hollow desolation of the rooms and staircases, her story of nights wrecked by restless anxiety. He remembers his entry into the outhouse that terrible night... How would he like to live at the Railway Hotel! His fear of disappointing his father is great but his fear of the Railway Hotel is greater.

'I don't want to.'

He is looking away, unable to meet his father's eye. He hears Dad say: 'Alright then, son. Your mam and me will have to talk about it again.'

It was his mother who told him a few days later that they had decided not to go ahead with 'the Railway idea'. She tried to make it sound as though it had never been a serious proposition but Stan was not taken in. He knew she was sparing his feelings and did not want him to feel guilty.

The ploy did not work. His failure to help his father escape the pit seemed an outgrowth of his earlier failure to help Robert Stapleton escape his death. He saw with brutal clarity the limits of his courage, and he felt them to be the limits of his worth.

# Part Three

# 2003: The Long and Winding Road
## 1957, 1968, 1975, 1986

# 18

## Native soil

The climb up the hillside of Jacob's Ladder is short but steep and he soon finds himself out of breath. He stops and stands, leaning forward slightly on his trekking poles. The day is bright and perfectly still. Silence seems to have been made visible in the steep hillside across the valley to his right and in the shining thread of water far below. The only sound is his own breathing, itself fading to silence as he recovers. He sets off again. As the incline eases he settles into his stride, walking at an even pace that is brisk yet within his physical resources, matching each footfall with a supporting, downward thrust of one of his poles. As he goes he makes small adjustments to his gear – removing his hat, unzipping his jacket – in order to maintain a stable body temperature. He is the maintenance engineer of his own body, presiding over the mechanisms of physical well-being that will ensure the completion of his task, which is to cover the sixteen miles that lie between Edale and the Youth Hostel of Crowden.

At Kinder Downfall he stops to eat a sandwich and drink a cup of coffee from his flask. Afterwards, he clambers carefully down a slope of tumbled boulders and jutting slabs of rock to the edge of the waterfall. The dry weather has reduced it to a thin column that breaks into spray and mist at a depth of twenty or thirty feet. He sits on a boulder, takes a map out of his rucksack and unfolds it across his knees. He runs his eye over the sinuous waves and whorls of the hill contours, the blue, spidery straggles of the streams, the roads, paths and boundary lines in green, red and brown. The names of the natural features are a poetic commentary on the terrain he will cover this day: Kinder Downfall, Featherbed Moss, Snake Pass, Bleaklow Head, Wildboar Grain. He picks out the line of green dots that mark the Pennine Way. They turn and twist from north-west to north-east, then back to north-west and down to the valley of Longdendale that contains the hostel of Crowden. This is how the path goes, in sideways shifts and detours but always edging towards his final destination in the north.

As he begins his descent from the Kinder plateau a voice begins to sing in his head: 'The Long and Winding Road'. He follows the stone-slabbed path over Featherbed Moss and crosses the Snake Road onto the lonely moorland of Bleaklow. The tap-tap of his trekking poles keeping perfect rhythm with his stride is like a ticking engine that carries him on. Thought has become movement and sensation: the regular stretch of his legs, the feel of the ground beneath his feet, the flick of his eyes from the near path to the distant horizon. Nothing troubles the serene vacancy of his embodied mind.

He leaves the path to find a place to eat his remaining sandwiches. He sits on a heather bank that slopes down to a wide channel of peat six or seven feet below. The rock at his back is at a comfortable angle for sitting, the heather pressing round is a snug fit. Beyond the far bank of the channel a hummocky landscape of bilberry, rough grass and heather stretches to the horizon where the rim of the fell-top appears zipped onto the sky. The day is warm. Above the tops of the heather little insects dart and buzz.

Cathy's book has left him reflective but calm, the emotions it aroused have receded with the night. Fifty years is a long time after all. Only the shadow cast by the hanging figure of Robert Stapleton still occasionally darkens his mind. The horrified thought that took hold of him in the moments after the discovery – that he might have saved Robert's life – has over the years lost its power to haunt, though it still sometimes recurs as an abstract possibility, no sooner contemplated than filed away in whatever part of his mind serves as a depository for nagging but insoluble questions. He told no-one what he heard that moment in the outhouse, not Cathy, not his mother, not the police who came to interview him at his home nor the coroner who gently questioned him at the hearing. He has told no-one to this day and although the thought of taking this small particle of the world's truth to his grave sometimes troubles him he knows that he never will.

The consequences for others were more severe. According to Cathy her father's death was responsible for what she called the 'dysfunctional' side of her personality: her periodic depressions and her insecurity. Then there was uncle Harold…

But he must not allow his mind to stray into such territory. He gazes down at the dark bottom of the peat channel seeking distraction. He likes peat, he thinks of it as his native soil, layer upon layer of rotted vegetation laid down over the centuries, trees, plants and grasses, their minute fibres preserved by the airless prehistoric bog. He has read somewhere that if you examine peat under a microscope you can identify the long-buried seed cases of ancient forests. It is a seam of the earth's memory, rich in traces of the pine and birch, the oak, elm and ash that once covered these hills.

He finishes his food and bends his head back to feel the sun full on his face. An airliner appears from the right, moving so slowly it seems impossible for it to remain aloft. He sees it before he hears it, surprisingly close and for a moment filling the sky directly above him like some stately prehistoric bird. He imagines its shadow over the land as it banks to gain height. The passengers will see the fell-top coming into view, a churned and pitted chaos of earth, rock and vegetation. What will they see of him? At most a speck of blue jacket shrinking to nothing as the aircraft climbs - microbial, invisible, one of those pollen husks that you need a microscope to see. Reduced to peat. Reduced to his native soil. The idea pleases him. He watches the aeroplane move away until it appears to hang motionless like a glinting shield of light pinned to the empty sky. He stands up, swings his sack onto his shoulder and threads his way through the deep heather to rejoin the path.

As he descends from Bleaklow Head the valley of Longdendale comes into view, a deep cleft through the hills into which industrial civilisation has squeezed the organs - reservoirs, roads and pylons - necessary for its survival. He is struck by the density of traffic on the road, a steadily moving stream glinting and flashing in the sunlight. He realises with a jolt of surprise that it is Monday! His usual walking-day is Sunday, and through the peace and quiet of these long hours in the hills a counterfeit Sunday has insinuated itself into his subliminal life. He has even felt in the last twenty minutes or so – an effect no doubt of the angle of the afternoon sun and the quality of the resulting light – a faint foreboding like a dark haze on the horizon of his pleasure. He understands now that this is a habitual reflex from his past as a Sunday walker, a recurrence of the melancholy he would often feel as his walk and his weekend of leisure neared their end. It dissipates immediately with his understanding of it, giving way to an almost giddy sense of relief. It is the first time he has felt so acutely his liberation from work. He glances at his watch. Ten minutes past four. Annie will have taught her last class and will be driving home from her school in the West End of Newcastle. His former colleagues will be at their Monday-afternoon meeting, sitting round the long polished table with their piles of papers, cups of tea and plates of biscuits. The Monday-afternoon meeting is a high-level one with the Vice-Chancellor and Registrar in regular attendance. The agenda will be future developments, the talk will be strategies, missions and vibrant universities for the twenty-first century, the infectious linguistic melodrama of the commercial world. He breathes a sigh of pleasure. Goodbye to all that! Goodbye and good riddance to all that!

He has to confess he is not keen on youth hostels. The problem is not their admirable principles of providing cheap accommodation and access to the countryside, nor the fact that their title offends his sense of linguistic precision (at a rough estimate the average age of this evening's intake at Crowden is sixty and rising). It is not the plain but serviceable furniture, the rows of dented tin tea-pots, the mix-and-match crockery: all these things appeal to his native thrift and sense of utility, his deep belief in wasting not and wanting not. No, the problem is that he dislikes sleeping with strange men. He hates being in a bedroom with people who have reached the day's finishing line before him and who have entered into their nocturnal other-life of grunting, sighing, and shouting to their drowning children or their parents returned from the shades to haunt them. He is a bad sleeper, and bad sleepers should not use the public dormitories of Youth Hostels.

Across the aisle that separates the two sets of double bunks lies Ernie (he introduced himself when he came in, red-faced and gleaming with sweat from a hot and tiring traverse of Bleaklow). Ernie is inflating and deflating with a slow and measured regularity - a deep intake of breath followed by a fluttering release like the emptying of a toy balloon - that drives Stan wild with envy. In the bunk above Ernie is the man who is doing the sponsored walk for cancer research. He himself has cancer, he told them, and has been given a year at most to live. Stan can just make out his silhouette in the dim light cast by the curtained window. He is lying on his back and gargling, and Stan wonders whether he should get out of bed and turn him onto his side. He has an irrational fear that the man will pass away in the night and he, Stan, will be the only one awake to know. The third man is in the bunk above Stan. He arrived late as Stan was closing his book and turning over to sleep, a Methuselah in khaki shorts and walking socks, with a grey moustache and narrow strip of grey hair surrounding a bald pate, his legs knotted with muscle and varicose veins. He is making his presence known in a modest, almost apologetic way, emitting a thin squeak that is barely audible, a wavering, ethereal, pathos-laden squeak that sounds as though he is strangling a mouse.

Stan tries to withdraw into himself, to dig back into the soundless burrow of the day's memories. Think of a journey his mother would say, it will journey you into sleep. He runs his mind back over the walk: Jacob's Ladder with the hills close and luminous in the morning sun, Kinder Downfall and its smoky downward spray, Featherbed Moss, Bleaklow Head...A bed creaks; the man with cancer is turning onto his side. His gargling subsides to a low steady breathing. Ernie has gone quiet too. Only the old man in the bunk above continues his squeaking, like a flute playing the final bars of some piece of chamber music easing to its close. For a split second Stan is pitched into utter blackness only for the flute to call him back. He tries to shut it out by thinking of the previous day's train journey with the fields and trees sliding past, the woman and her husband Bob, Durham, the Cleveland Hills, York. The names of the old city – Eboracum, Yorvik – flash in his mind, stirring some distant memory that flits bat-like in the twilit space between wakefulness and sleep. He tries to ignore it but suddenly it is there before him, stark and clear: a frosty January morning, uncle Harold struggling with the strange words as he reads the leaflet. His sad and weary eyes, his broken smile.

# 19

## Consequences

'Eboracum, Yorvik, York. That's the Romans, the Vikings and us, Stan. That's a lot of history.'

There are three of them - Stan, his mother and Harold – and it is their first trip out in Harold's new car. Harold has chosen York because he thought it might interest Stan. This desire to interest him is part of a more general concern that Harold has for Stan's well-being and education. Stan senses that it has something to do with the fact that, for some mysterious reason that people never refer to in his presence, Harold and Rachel were not able to have children.

Harold slips the leaflet back into his coat pocket.

'Well, what shall we visit next? What about the Minster?'

His smile is shadowed with sadness. Behind his glasses his eyes are bloodshot as though he has been rubbing them. Mam says it is because he has a heart condition that has got worse since his divorce. She worries about him constantly. She cooks dinners for him that she takes round to Morton's covered in a tea-cloth to keep them warm. On some evenings she goes to sit with him. They watch television and talk about their family and the past.

Harold's business has fallen on difficult times owing to the opening in Calcroft of a branch of the Co-op that has begun to take his trade. Already hit hard by the departure of auntie Rachel, he is finding it impossible to respond with the energy the situation requires. This much Stan has gathered from the conversation between his mother and Harold in the car. They return to the subject again as the three of them walk off in the direction of the Minster. Stan's mother is asking Harold what he thinks he can do to hold on to his customers but Harold seems unable to come up with any answers other than to say that he is tired of the whole thing.

'What I'd really like to do, Sally, is sell the shop and leave, get out of Calcroft altogether.'

'But what would you do for a living?'

'I wouldn't need to earn a lot of money. I've made a fair bit out of Morton's over the years and I'll still get a good price for it if I sell soon. I could buy a little business somewhere else, a smaller shop that I could run on my own, newspapers and sweets, that sort of thing.'

'That'd be a big wrench, Harold. You've lived all your life in Calcroft. You'd be leaving all your family behind.'

'There are some of them I'd like to leave behind, Sal. And they wouldn't be sorry to see the back of me either.'

'They'll get over it all.'

'I'm not sure about that, Sal. It's gone on for nearly three years now and these family quarrels have a way of lasting forever.'

They are approaching the Minster. Stan's eyes are drawn upwards to a great round window above the entrance but he keeps listening. Since Robert Stapleton's death divisions have arisen within his family that pain him but that he also finds interesting. Auntie Aggie, a loud and opinionated woman much given to moral outrage, objected to the fact that Stan and his parents attended Robert's funeral and has since refused to speak to them. His uncle Albert, a shy and amiable bachelor who was said to have harboured a secret fancy for auntie Rachel, was so shocked by the revelation of her affair that he insisted that the death of Robert Stapleton was a just reward for his behaviour. Oddly enough it was Harold who quarrelled with him over this, with the result that Albert and Harold have become estranged.

Inside the Minster Harold and Sally go quiet and stand still for a moment, wondering what to do. Harold removes his hat and gives a little cough. Mam smiles hesitantly at Stan as though waiting for him to make a move. Several people are sitting or kneeling at prayer. Sightseers drift around, stopping to gaze at wall-plaques, tombs and statues. Stan turns round to look up at the round window which he now sees is composed of richly coloured stained glass. A few feet away from him a man is pointing up at the window and speaking in a low voice to two young children. Stan moves closer to them and hears the man explaining that the window commemorates the ending of the Wars of the Roses.

'If you look closely you'll see the roses of York and Lancaster in the stained glass.'

Stan, who has recently been studying this period in class, stares up at the window, picking out the paired roses in white and red. He looks round for Harold and his mother but they have walked off down a side aisle. When they all meet up again he takes them to the window and tells them what he has heard. Mam remarks on the beauty of the window. Harold says: 'I wish I knew more about history. We were taught at school about the Wars of the Roses but I've forgotten everything about it except the battle of Bosworth Field. That was the one that ended it all wasn't it?'

Stan nods. Harold says: 'I'll bet you don't know the date.'

'1485.'

Harold laughs and calls him 'a right little know-all'. As they emerge from the Minster, he asks Stan whether he can remember the old names for York. When he hears them trip fluently off Stan's tongue he turns to Stan's mother and says: 'What a memory, Sally. Do you think he's one of them prodigies people are always talking about?'

Harold isn't to know that remembering words is the least of Stan's problems. Words in the head are an invading force, an obsession; he utters them repeatedly under his breath for the pleasure of their sound and feel. He likes the aggressive snap of 'Eboracum', he rolls the 'r' in Jorvik so that his tongue rattles against the roof of his mouth. It is the same with names that he hears in the cinema or on the radio: he relishes the trill and ripple of 'Geronimo', the springy rhythm of 'Mario Lanza', the squelchy 'sh' sound that makes the spit gather at the back of his mouth when he speaks the name of the Hungarian footballer, Puskás.

They sit on a bench outside the Minster and eat the sandwiches that Stan's mother has prepared that morning. Harold says: 'The thing is Sally, I've never had to make a decision like this before. What to do for a living and all that. Morton's just fell into my lap. It was an opportunity I couldn't refuse. I never asked myself whether I wanted to spend my life running a shop. And now that things have…gone off the rails you might say, I find it difficult to know what to do.'

He balances his sandwich on his knee, removes his glasses and gives his eyes a rub. He takes out a handkerchief and blows his nose. Stan's mother places her hand lightly on his arm and says: 'Maybe what you were saying earlier would be the best thing – a little newsagent's. But somewhere not too far from Calcroft.'

'Yes, that would be the best thing. But then, you see, it's not just a question of what I should do for a living. When something like this happens…the divorce and all that, you start asking yourself what you've done with your life. I sometimes think Morton's – coming into it the way I did - was a mixed blessing. It stopped me doing other things. I used to go to night classes. Do you remember? I was always keen on education. I stopped all that when I took over Morton's. I wonder what my life would have been like if I'd carried on with the classes and then gone on to choose a job instead of the job choosing me.'

He turns to Stan. 'Do you hear that, Stanley Walker? Don't neglect your studies.' His tone is jocular but his eyes drift away, unfocussed, his mind fixed on some inner thought. The conversation goes quiet. Stan's mother brushes the crumbs off her lap and into the path of a gaggle of strutting pigeons. She says to Stan: 'Have you told Harold your latest news from school?'

Stan says: 'What news?'

'The tests you had.'

Stan knows what she is referring to but feels a certain modesty is called for. 'Oh yes. We had some tests at the end of last term.'

'What sort of tests?' Harold says.

'Written tests on all the subjects we study.'

'And how did you do?'

'I came top overall in our class.'

Harold purses his lips in a 'phew' of astonishment. 'That's pretty smart, Stan. The first one of the family to get to the Grammar School and you're at the top of the class. What's your favourite subject?'

Stan hesitates; he doesn't know whether he has a favourite subject. School is a tide that washes over the beach of his mind once a day. Of the detritus it leaves, the thing that most pleases him, the exquisitely shaped and richly gleaming bottle that may contain some secret message, is poetry. Lines of verse sing and trumpet in his mind. A copy of *Paradise Lost* borrowed from the school library filled his head for weeks with the torrential clamour of Satan's fall: 'Hurled headlong flaming from the ethereal sky, With hideous ruin and combustion down To bottomless perdition'. He loves 'bottomless perdition'. He didn't get far with the poem, it was too difficult, but 'bottomless perdition' has stayed with him, lodging itself in his brain like a cuckoo in its clock, ready to spring forth at the most unexpected moments. When he heard on the radio of Mr Eden's humiliated resignation from the government, 'bottomless perdition' popped out to designate his fallen state. When Billy Grix was expelled from school for attacking a teacher it was 'bottomless perdition' that awaited him.

Harold's question embarrasses him. Love of poetry is not a thing that the fourteen-year-old sons of coal-miners proclaim to all and sundry. He says: 'I quite like English.'

Harold says: 'I liked English too.' He puts his handkerchief back in his pocket. 'Mind you, I wasn't much good at it. I was no scholar. But I used to like writing the stories that the teachers set. I remember my teacher once asked us to imagine we were doing some exciting job and I chose aircraft pilot. What's-his-name had just crossed the Atlantic. Do you remember, Sal? What was he called? Lindbergh. That's it. Charles Lindbergh. I imagined I was him. I got a good mark for that one. I remember our teacher used to tell us to aim high. Well, you couldn't aim higher than that in them days, could you?'

Stan says: 'I like rugby too.'

Harold says: 'I thought you liked football.'

'I do but I like rugby as well. I didn't at first but I do now.'

'And what do you like about it?'

Stan hesitates, then says simply: 'I like running and tackling.'

He finds it difficult to explain this growing attraction to the game of rugby. He thinks it is something to do with his father and with his own failure to help him escape his work down the pit. It is also something to do with the fact that, in their family of physical labourers, he is unusual and slightly odd, a scholar who it is assumed will work with his brain. Among his cousins destined for colliery jobs he is viewed with an affectionate protectiveness that he finds galling. What he is discovering on the rugby field, he understands, is a physical strength and courage that he feared he lacked. He remembers an incident that happened a year ago. He was playing in a house match and, being thin and wiry but quick ('The Whippet' his team-mates called him), he had been positioned on the wing. Ahead of him was a writhing, heaving mass of bodies from which, to his horror, there suddenly broke free, grasping the ball and running directly at him, a precociously gigantic thirteen-year-old called Frank Dobbs. Frank was slow but remorseless, a trundling, unstoppable barrel of flesh with bony joints like lumps of iron. Someone shouted: 'Get him, Stan.' The call rang in his head with an urgency that was morally compelling. Fourteen comrades-in-arms depended on the steeliness of his resolve. He held his ground, lowered his shoulder and drove forward into the stomach of Frank Dobbs. There was a gasp of escaping wind and a fat schoolboy on his bum in the mud. Stan felt a surge of pride, his team-mates cheered. To 'The

Whippet' was added 'The Demon Tackler'. It was only a nickname but it was the beginning of a new and more flattering view that he took of himself.

But Harold is not interested in rugby. He remarks on the chill in the air and suggests they find somewhere to have a cup of tea. They move off into the narrow streets by the Minster. Later, as they sit with their drinks Harold says that he has been to this café before. His tone is wistful. Stan's mother smiles at him but keeps silent. Stan stares down at his glass of lemonade. Harold has taken his handkerchief out again and is blowing his nose. 'Yes,' he says. 'How times change.'

It is the last memory Stan has of him. He died of heart failure later that year. The funeral gave rise to the usual fuss and bother. This time it was about the fact that auntie Rachel let it be known that she was going to attend. She had left the village shortly after Robert Stapleton's death and was living on her own in a flat in Scarborough, more or less abandoned by the rest of the family. It was generally felt that the separation had hastened Harold's end. Auntie Aggie was emphatic on this point, insisting to whoever would listen that Harold had died of a broken heart. It was only with great difficulty that she was persuaded not to confront Rachel at the funeral itself. Even so, when Stan entered the church he felt tense with the expectation of some embarrassing confrontation.

Rachel was the first person he saw. She was sitting alone at the back of the church, staring fixedly ahead. It was almost three years since he had seen her and she seemed smaller and less beautiful. Her magnificent hair had been cut short and was held up in a net beneath the black hat she wore. After the service he cast a glance round the mourners outside the church, fearing to see her, fearing some terrible uproar. But she had gone, having apparently booked a taxi to take her away immediately after the service. He heard later that no-one had spoken to her and he wondered if this included his mother. It seemed important for him to know but he dared not ask for fear she said yes.

He imagines auntie Rachel in her flat in Scarborough, lonely and rejected, and feels such pity that he cannot bear to think badly of her. He is tormented by the phrase 'bottomless perdition'. He wonders whether adult life is always sad and bitter like this.

## 20

## Getting Away From It All

'Do you mind if I join you?'

It is his dormitory companion from the night just gone, the old man. Stan is weary from his wrecked sleep and would prefer to eat breakfast alone. He says: 'Of course not. Take a seat.'

The man has cooked himself a full English breakfast which he is carrying on a tray with a pot of tea and several slices of bread. Stan smelled it immediately on entering the Members' Kitchen. He loves the smell of frying bacon, the instantaneous passage from richly infused nasal mucus to salivating tastebuds. He glances furtively at the lavish pile of twisted and crisped bacon, the two fried eggs, the thick curl of Cumberland sausage, then disconsolately down at his own muesli and yoghurt. Pallid usurpers of the native breakfast bowl! A mess of foreign potage!

'Fancy a piece of bacon? I've done far too much.'

'No thank you. I'm not much of a bacon fan.'

The words are out before he thinks. He is about to say: 'Well perhaps just a little piece…', but the man has carried on talking: 'Well I suppose I ought to go easy on it myself but you can't change the habits of a life-time. And at my age…' He offers all this without conviction, as a courtesy due to the devotee of low-fat food and healthy eating that he judges Stan to be. He is smiling broadly and Stan senses that his age isn't a burden to him. In the morning light he looks younger than he seemed the previous evening but still quite old – in his mid-seventies perhaps. The smartly trimmed strip of grey hair surrounding his copper-brown pate, the freshly shaven cheeks, the moustache clipped neatly in line with the upper lip suggest an ex-military man. Yet his clothes belie the air of overall competence and efficiency that he exudes. They are a vestimentary graveyard with corpses courtesy of army surplus: a pair of ancient khaki shorts, a khaki shirt, and a hairy wool sweater that looks as though it has been slept on by a moulting dog.

Stan is particular about his walking clothes; modern synthetic fibres – light, warm, and quick-drying – are what are required for these northern hills. To his surprise he feels slightly put out by the old man's indifference to such nostrums. It is as though one of his deeply held principles of hill-craft has been treated with disdain.

The man sits down and begins to stab at his bacon. He says: 'Are you doing the Way?' He chews while speaking, as though driven by the desire for economy in the use of his jaw muscle.

'That's the idea.'

'How long have you got?'

'Oh, as long as it takes but I'm aiming to finish it in three weeks.'

'Mm. That'll be…let me see…about thirteen miles a day. More if you take a few rest days. Sure you can do it?'

He is obviously a man who likes to get the essential information. Definitely ex-military.

'No but I'll try.'

'What if it takes longer?

'Oh, I can take a few extra days if I need them.'

The man nods, spears his last piece of bacon (Stan notices he's left his sausage intact) and raises it to his mouth. He holds it there as though waiting to synchronise speech with mastication.

'You…' – he pops it in and begins to chew – 'must be retired.'

Though Stan assumes he is retired too, he does not ask, merely nodding in confirmation of his guess. Nor does he ask whether he is walking the Pennine Way. He is reluctant to match the man's curiosity for fear he might suggest they team up together. Stan enjoys these chance encounters with other wayfarers and considers himself sociable enough, but to fall in with someone so early on his journey threatens his freedom. Getting away from it all is the name of the game, and for the moment 'all' includes other people.

The man still has his sausage to eat. Stan downs his last mouthful of muesli and stands up to carry his bowl to the sink. The important thing is to get out onto the Way ahead of him. Stan is fit for his age and with, he estimates, ten to fifteen years' advantage of him he should be able to keep ahead and pull away. The man takes a paper napkin out of his pocket and proceeds to wrap the sausage in it, remarking on the pleasure he derives from eating his sausage on the hills. Stan moves off with a haste he hopes is not indecent, wishing him joy of the sausage and suggesting, as non-committally as it is possible to be, that they might bump into each other again. The man waves his hand and laughs: 'Oh, I'm sure we will. I'm sure we will.' Then, seemingly as an afterthought he adds: 'Don Crick's the name.'

Stan hesitates, struck by the absurdity of introducing himself as he leaves. He says: 'Stan Walker. Nice to have met you.'

On the path above Crowden he stops to catch his breath. Looking back over recent months, he can see that he has become a poor starter, the first uphill work of the day often causing a weariness in his arms and a slight tightening of his chest that obliges him to stop and take a breather. This early-morning reluctance of the engine to slip into gear, he tells himself, is the first sign of ageing and is to be expected. It never lasts longer than a few minutes, the time it takes to get his pipes open and the old pump and bellows working full-blast.

Glancing back down the path he can see a figure with a walking stick, stooped under the weight of its rucksack. Don Crick! He must get a move on and shake the old boy off. In front of him the path crosses the flank of Black Tor. Above the ridge the sky is a cloudless steely blue and there is a sharp smack of autumn in the air that scours the throat and lungs. He makes good progress over Laddow Rocks and onto the side of Black Hill, glancing behind from time to time, expecting the distance to have widened between him and Don Crick. The old man is still there bent beneath his sack, losing ground perhaps but not by much, maintaining the same steady deliberate tread. Clearly a man Stan will have to cease patronising.

Black Hill, once one of the worst bogs on the Way, is a wound now stitched by the path of stone flags that bisects the hill ahead of him. The peat hags that used to sap the strength and will of hardened walkers stand like empty boasts on either side of the path, shrunken and almost benign against the bright stretched silk of the sky. Looking back down the path he can still see Don Crick; the distance between them hardly seems to have changed. He decides to take a break. A cairn of stones and boulders by the path offers the opportunity to fashion himself a seat. He sits and takes his flask out of his rucksack. The figure on the path gets closer; as he draws level with Stan he stops, rests on his walking stick and raises his free hand to the side of his head in a mock military salute. 'Beautiful weather.' Then, for the second time today: 'Mind if I join you?'

Stan sighs inwardly but the unwritten laws of the hills demand hospitality - a cheery welcome, a sharing of boulders. He says: 'Not at all. Pull up a rock.'

He is not a natural hypocrite and something in his tone must have suggested a reluctance to socialise.

'Are you sure? I can always move on a little way. It's sometimes nice to be on your own.'

'No, no. Please sit down.'

He is on his feet now, overcompensating. Don Crick seems to have the ability to put him in contradiction with himself. For a split second he wonders, absurdly, whether he should brush the dirt off one of the boulders.

Don sits down and starts rummaging in his rucksack. It is an old-fashioned frame sack, muddy yellow in colour, with a tightly rolled sleeping-mat attached to the outside. He eventually pulls out, like a conjuror from his hat, a tin mug followed by a small and battered tin stove and a miniature kettle, similarly battered. There follow two tea-bags and three plastic bottles of different sizes, containing methylated spirits, milk, and water.

'I like a cup of tea on the hills. Will you join me? The kettle takes just enough water for two cups.'

'No thank you. I'm drinking coffee.' Stan raises his cup to his lips by way of illustration.

'I'm not keen on vacuum flasks. They make the tea taste disgusting.'

Stan concurs with him that vacuum flasks are bad for tea but tolerable for instant coffee, which is what he is drinking.

'To each his own,' Don says, and proceeds to light his stove while continuing to sing the praises of tea on the hills. Stan wonders whether he's going to take out his sausage but it remains in his bag. Perhaps he likes to spread his treats out over the day and is keeping the sausage for later.

He is voluble and eager for conversation, launching into an account of his plans. He is not intending to walk the whole of the Way because he only has two weeks at his disposal. He will have to cherry-pick, he says, taking in the best bits – Malham, Pen-y-ghent, Swaledale and Upper Teesdale – and by-passing the rest on public transport. He thinks he might get as far as the Roman Wall before his time is up. He pats the rolled sleeping-mat and says that if the weather continues fine, he will spend the odd night sleeping out on the hill.

'Have you got a tent?' Stan asks.

'Oh no. I don't go in for the creature comforts. When I have a night in the open air I just pile all my warm clothes on. I like to lie and gaze at the night sky until I drop off.'

He places two tea bags into his kettle which is now hissing, and watches Stan drain his cup, as though anxious that he will move on before he has extracted sufficient pleasure from this moment of conviviality. Stan finds himself regretting his earlier failure to take an interest in the old man's doings. He is probably lonely, a retired bachelor with lots of time and little company. He decides it is time to ask.

'I take it you're retired like me.'

'Goodness no. Whatever gave you that idea?'

Stan looks at the figure sitting before him. He is obviously fit and strong; inside the open-necked shirt his upper body is a broad, tightly strung frame of muscle and bone. But he is old too, the leg muscles beaded with swollen veins, the hands flecked with liver spots, the skin of the face a good ten years further down the cracked and pitted road of decrepitude than Stan's own.

He tells Stan that he owns a fruit farm in Herefordshire. He runs it with the help of his two sons and it is they who are looking after it while he takes his annual holiday. He is a widower.

'When do you think you might retire?'

'Oh, probably never.' He laughs. 'I'm not the retiring sort. I'd die of boredom.'

Stan feels a brief flush of guilt at the earliness of his own retirement. Sixty years of age, sound in body and mind, and already withdrawn from the fray! He decides to give some thought to the idea of returning to part-time work or committing some effort to charity.

Don pours himself a mug of tea and sits holding it in front of him, waiting for it to cool while he gazes round the landscape, his eyes squinting against the white glare of the sky. Ahead of them the mast of the Holme Moss television transmitter rises above the moor.

Don says: 'There's a lot of junk on these hills when you think of it.'

'What do you mean?'

'Well, that!' He rests his tea on the rock beside him and waves his walking-stick at the transmitter.

'And this.' He points towards the slabbed path. 'Not exactly wilderness, is it?'

'Is wilderness what you want?'

'No, but I wouldn't mind something less cluttered.'

Stan has to admit there is much that is messy and intrusive in the country around them. They are passing to the east of the urban agglomeration of Manchester. It is a landscape in which nature long ago surrendered to the technological paraphernalia of modern life. He says: 'The price of progress I suppose.'

Don looks across at him and frowns as though offended by the glibness of the cliché. He says: 'Perhaps. Though I'm not sure I believe in progress.'

He is pouring the remainder of his tea from the kettle into his mug. He adds a drop of milk and raises the mug to his lips, blowing on the hot tea as he does so. After taking a sip he surveys the landscape again. Stan wonders whether he has forgotten what he has just said.

'How do you mean?' he says. 'You don't believe in progress?'

'I was born in India. My father was a missionary. I still go back there occasionally. It's a poor country, much of it untouched by what you call progress. But...' He hesitates. Stan interjects: 'People are poor but happy.'

Don Crick is either immune to the ironies of received liberal opinion or too bound up in his thought to notice. He continues: 'There's much misery. But joy too - vitality, optimism. People have a different perspective on life. It's still a religious country of course in a way that the West hasn't been since the Middle Ages. They don't have the despair and nihilism of secular societies.'

Stan's desire to object is checked by surprise and curiosity. He had not expected such talk from Don Crick, a man who wears clothes guaranteed to trap rainwater, weights his sack with antiquated ironmongery, and saves his sausage for eating on the hill. He feels like a spider whose pre-spun web of judgements has failed to catch the fly.

Don says: 'After all, just remember what happened over there forty years ago.' He flicks his hand in a roughly westward direction, then in answer to Stan's questioning look says: 'Saddleworth Moor. You remember the moors murderers, Brady and Hindley?'

Stan feels as though he's been struck a blow in the chest.

'They tortured and murdered children, then buried their defiled bodies in shallow soil. Not more than a few miles from where we sit. And for what? For their pleasure. And this happened in the enlightened West, in dear old Blighty, in the year of our Lord 1965.'

Stan gazes round at the hills that have lost their innocence, struggling to find a response. Finally he says: 'But you must believe in some sort of progress. Medical advances, a better standard of living, that sort of thing.'

Don laughs. 'Oh, of course. Everybody believes in *that*.'

He shakes the last drops of tea out of his mug and gets to his feet. 'But I fear I'm holding you up. We ought to be on our way.'

They walk in silence for a while. Faint swirls of white have appeared in the sky, a breeze has risen. Don points his stick accusingly at the slowly turning blades of a distant wind turbine. Stan spurns the invitation to discuss cluttered landscapes and says: 'How long did you live in India?'

'For the first ten years of my life. My father and mother returned to England in 1938. I remember it particularly because of the Munich business. It was the first time I'd heard anything about European politics, or indeed about any sort of politics. My father was very exercised by Chamberlain and Munich. He felt it was all a great betrayal and we were only putting off the day when we would have to take on Hitler.'

'Do you remember much about the War?'

'Not a great deal. We lived in the countryside and weren't much affected directly. And I was too young to be called up. I was conscripted in 1946 so I just missed the action.'

'A close call.'

'Indeed. Though I'm not sure it was a good thing.'

'How do you mean?'

'Well, it might have been a good thing for me personally, the war ending when it did, though I'm not even sure about that. I don't think a couple of years fighting for king and country would have done me any harm...'

'Unless you'd got killed. That would have been pretty harmful.'

Don laughs. 'True enough. But the point I was going to make is that I sometimes think the War should have continued. After defeating Hitler we should have turned on the Russians. Driven them out of Berlin and eastern Europe.'

'But surely that would have been unrealistic. The Russians had been our allies, and people were weary of the War.'

'In the long run it would have been very realistic. It would have spared a large chunk of humanity nearly half a century of Soviet tyranny.'

Stan feels irritation rising within him. He says: 'But within the short run, which is where most of us live our lives, it would have been totally unrealistic. People in Britain and America wouldn't have put up with a prolonging of the War. The Russians of course would have had no choice. And if their troops objected, they would have been bayoneted back into the front line. Stalin would have had no compunction. He was good at wasting lives.'

'That's exactly why we should have taken him on. Think of the wasted lives of Poles, Czechs, Hungarians. Even now the Wall's come down it will take their economies decades to recover from the dead hand of state control.'

'People didn't know all this in 1945. They were just weary of the War. They wanted to get on with their lives and build a better world at home. They preferred Atlee to Churchill...'

'Yes, and that was the second mistake.'

Stan's irritation gives way to puzzlement. Atlee a mistake? Although it is over twenty years since he left the Labour Party, he has retained a reverence for the post-war Labour government that is part political conviction, part gratitude for the social reforms from which he and his generation have benefited.

Don Crick continues: 'Britain was bankrupt. The last thing she could afford was the Welfare State and a government of do-gooding mandarins like Beveridge. People have placed too much faith in the state since the War, particularly in Europe. It's a European disease.'

'But that's absurd. Look at France. It was intelligent state planning that enabled her to recover from the War. The whole infrastructure was rebuilt by the state and the quality of it is acknowledged by everyone. Have you ever travelled on French railways?'

Don stops walking and holds his hand up as though in acknowledgement of some fault. He is suddenly all gracious and apologetic.

'You must forgive me, I get carried away. I'm afraid I'm out of sympathy with the age. It's to do with being born in India the son of a missionary. You can't imagine the strange things it does to a man.' He laughs out loud and gives Stan a friendly pat on the arm. Stan says: 'Well, we're all strange in one way or another.'

'You see, although I lost my faith as a young man I think I've retained a belief in original sin.' He laughs again and shakes his head in seeming acknowledgement of his own hopeless eccentricity. He then continues with the same dogmatic earnestness as before: 'We've replaced religion with politics and made the state our god. We think that a bit of social reform here and a bit of economic management there will bring us to some secular paradise. But there is so much in human nature that is out of the reach of politics, and so much of it is bad...'

'Hold on a minute! Who's talking of secular paradise? Not me. I'm no revolutionary. I'm a boring, middle-of-the-road, liberal sort of bloke who just happens to favour a transport system that works.'

They have arrived at the headwall of a reservoir which is where they must separate. Stan intends to make a detour into the village of Marsden where he has booked a room in a guesthouse while Don will seek a quiet and secluded place to spend a night out in the open. He says: 'I take your point. I do tend to see things in rather extreme terms. My sons say I'm a Christian fundamentalist but without the Christian bit.'

He takes Stan's hand and gives it a firm and hearty shake.

'We may run into each other again. And if we do, I promise you – no lectures on politics.'

'Not to worry. I enjoyed our conversation. And as for lectures on politics, well…I've always been interested in politics.'

Don shakes his hand again and turns to cross the dam of the reservoir. Stan watches him go, then takes his own path, reflecting on what he has just said. He reaches a small reservoir and sits by the waters to enjoy the late-afternoon sunshine. 'Always been interested in politics'. Not the literal truth of course. He remembers the surprise he felt at Marie Salasca's political awareness and commitment. At the age of seventeen he was still a political innocent. It was only at university that he found friends with similar concerns to Marie's. He accompanied them to debates and meetings, and began to read the literature on socialism and the working-class that they passed his way. He read bits of G.D.H. Cole and gobbets of R.H. Tawney, immersed himself in Orwell and dipped his toe in Marx. He began to take a view of his own class at the precise moment that he was beginning to leave it behind.

He is struck now by the oddness of it all. He pours out the last of the day's coffee and lies back with his head on his rucksack, trying to imagine himself into the mind of that stranger, the young man he was. What was it that drove him? There was youthful idealism, sure. There was the tide of history, the sense they all had of coming change, of the decay of those final Macmillan years. But there was something else. He wonders now whether joining the Labour Party was not some sort of atonement. He had always been prone to guilt at the hardships of his father's work. During his student years he experienced it as a faint, omnipresent sense of his own insubstantiality and the frivolity of his studies. Reading the poetry of Ronsard or translating a passage of Proust were activities that he found deeply absorbing but that left him asking whether this sort of thing could ever be considered work. He was acutely aware of his family's inability to see the point of what he was doing and felt diminished as a consequence. Political commitment to the party of labour was his way of making amends and putting on moral weight.

He received a letter from Marie Salasca. It arrived during the general election campaign of 1964. They had kept intermittently in touch since that summer of 1960 but it was now almost a year since he had heard from her. On returning to France she had become involved in the campaign against the Algerian War. Thus baptised she had entered into left-wing politics as into a new religion. For Marie the old certainties were still in place. Capitalism was exploitation and its latest incarnation as the consumer society was a hoax perpetrated on the workers. Since her last letter she had joined the French Communist Party which, whatever its faults (and there were few she was willing to admit), was still the best hope for a socialist alternative. As he trailed around council estates on cold October evenings knocking on doors to canvas support for a Labour government, he was conscious of the gulf between Marie's way of thinking and his own. The working people for whom the years of Conservative administration had been the most prosperous of their lives and whom he was struggling to bring back to the Labour fold were not the victims of a hoax. They were people like his parents who had a clear view of their interests and a desire to do the best for themselves and their families. The word 'socialism' formed no part of their vocabulary. Nor, while he was seeking their votes, did it form part of his. Marie's letter annoyed him for its demeaning view of his people while leaving him uneasily aware of his own want of socialist faith.

Their correspondence continued spasmodically for the next few years. Each letter of Marie's seemed to announce some new departure in her political odyssey, the most dramatic being her abandonment of the Communist Party because of its lack of revolutionary fervour. Stan was taken aback by this. There were, among his acquaintances, romantic souls who kept the revolutionary dream alive but the paucity of their numbers and the arcane nature of their debates condemned them to isolation and, from most of his Labour Party friends, amused condescension. It was a condescension that Stan shared and the fact that Marie Salasca (whom he still thought of with a tender admiration that was surprisingly strong) harboured notions similar to theirs dismayed him. He wondered from where she was getting her ideas. She had taken her first teaching post at a school in the Paris suburb of Nanterre and seemed to spend much of her time with students from the university campus there. He wondered whether these were the figures pulling her along the road to political unrealism.

After taking his degree he embarked on a course of postgraduate literary research. He wrote to Marie asking if she could help him find accommodation in Paris that would be conveniently placed for his work at the Bibliothèque Nationale. She replied that a student friend of hers was moving out of his room for a while but did not want to give the room up. He needed someone to occupy it and continue to pay the rent. She thought Stan and her student friend could come to some arrangement.

It was not only the solution to his accommodation problem that delighted Stan about this letter; it was the welcoming eagerness of Marie's tone. He began to entertain hopes of a renewal of their old relationship, this time in Paris, the city of romance.

It would be important to make sure that politics did not come between them.

# 21

## Spring-time in Paris

Jean-Louis speaks quietly in a tight-lipped, fast-talking, laying-down-the-chips sort of way. He is letting capitalism know that its days are numbered. He quotes Gramsci, Marcuse, Lenin while lightly tapping the table-top with a cigarette that he took out of its packet ten minutes ago and that has remained unlit. Stan has to concentrate hard because of the low, rapid flow of his speech. Every so often the roar of an accelerating vehicle on the rue de Richelieu swallows up whole sentences and he is left trying to connect the loose ends of a broken thread.

Jean-Louis is talking about the state, how it is just a front for the administration of the capitalist system. It has to be opposed, challenged, smashed. Smashing the state is his theme for today. Stan glances across the table at Marie who is taking a sip of her coffee. She continues to stare hard at Jean-Louis over the rim of the cup, nodding slightly as she draws it to her lips. It is as though Jean-Louis's words are some essential accompaniment to her coffee, a tasty ideological *croissant* to go with her *grand crème*. She lowers the cup to the table and continues to nod approvingly. Smashing the state's OK with her, she has no problem with smashing the state.

Jean-Louis is explaining that the bourgeois state is an excrescence, *une excroissance*, of the capitalist economy, and that those who manage the state and to whom we ascribe great power – Lyndon Johnson, De Gaulle, Wilson – are in fact the puppets of international capital.

'Ce sont des pantins, quoi. Des pantins.'

He utters this with the weary disgust of one who has seen the rottenness at the heart of things. He pauses and finally lights his cigarette. Stan waits for Marie to speak, hoping for some expression of dissent or, failing that, some indication that she shares the scepticism that he, Stan, feels but that for the moment he is struggling to articulate in a way that would trump Jean-Louis's self-confident dogmatism.

Marie keeps quiet and watches Jean-Louis as he lights his Gitanes. Stan feels let down. He is astonished by the changes that have come about in her. Her deference to Jean-Louis's every pronouncement is that of the humble concubine attentive to her master. Yet the transformation of her physical appearance - the lustreless hair that she has had cropped short, the sallow skin without a hint of make-up, the slight tobacco-staining of her teeth - seem like a deliberate attempt to abolish her sexuality, to be a man among men.

Not that it works! As she leans across the table to take a pull on the cigarette that Jean-Louis is sharing with her, Stan's eye catches the heavy sag of her breasts in the faded denim shirt. Desire stirs within his body's memory like the tail-flick of some coiled, dormant beast prodded into wakefulness. He can hardly believe it is almost eight years since the sexual passion that swept like a consuming fire through that summer of 1960. He has had other relationships since but none with the power to release this memorised longing deep within.

He feels one last urge to question Jean-Louis's argument but decides to let things go. He beckons to the waiter and pays for the coffees.

'Bon, je m'en vais travailler à la bibliothèque.'

He kisses Marie on both cheeks and takes Jean-Louis's limply offered hand. Jean-Louis asks him yet again what he is working on in the library. Stan has told him twice already but he either suffers from premature amnesia or considers Stan's research into the novels of Stendhal of so little relevance to the global struggle that it is not worth remembering. His own studies in sociology he views as valuable only in so far as they are useful, and useful only in so far as they serve his political ends. When Stan reminds him of the nature of his research, he utters a non-committal 'Ah', takes a pull on his

Gitanes, and launches a perfectly formed smoke-ring in the direction of the café ceiling.

Stan doesn't much like the reading room of the Bibliothèque Nationale but when he asks himself why, his answers are either trivial or irrational. The men who deliver books to the seated readers are often brusque and morose but since their job is to deliver books, not add to the gaiety of nations, why should it matter to him? The tenacious absorption of the readers themselves is as it should be; that is what they come to the library for – to give themselves to their intellectual passions. Why then does it fill him with such gloom? It is the same with the articles and books he reads for his research. The fact that some of them are dreary is only to be expected, even welcomed, for it means that he has *seen* the dreariness and can determine not to be dreary in his turn. Why then this intensity of dissatisfaction?

He is coming to the conclusion that the various, petty dislikes he experiences in the Bibliothèque Nationale add up to one great one, which is a dislike of what he himself is doing there. It seemed a good idea at the time – literary research leading to a PhD and a career in the academic world. With a keen brain and a good first-class degree he was told he had what was necessary to obtain a lectureship in an expanding university system. The prospect satisfied both his love of literature and a certain proselytising desire to communicate it to others. He took pleasure from his ability to express ideas clearly and articulately. What better profession then than that of university lecturer?

But he had reckoned without the long, slow grind of literary research and its capacity to turn cherished texts into quarries for the hacking-out of theses, articles and books. What has he to say about the novels of Stendhal that has not been said before, and more stylishly than he could manage? His research supervisor had advised him to choose a lesser writer, one whose obscurity guaranteed unworked seams ripe for excavation. But it wasn't the lesser writers who attracted him to literature in the first place. He had no desire to spend three years of his life in the presence of Octave Mirbeau or the Goncourt brothers. For he who craves the bracing air of the literary summits, the foothills will not do.

He is having a particularly bad afternoon, unable to concentrate on his books for half an hour without re-examining the contours of the ceiling or taking a walk to the catalogue-room or staring at the woman across from him whose finely chiselled features and almost vulgarly sensual mouth contrast interestingly with her absorption in the *Summa theologiae* of St Thomas Aquinas.

He is preoccupied by politics. His failure to respond to Jean-Louis's monologue has left him dissatisfied with himself, for his silence may well have been taken for assent. The basic problem, the thing that inhibits him from expressing his opinions, is his own uncertainty towards the matters that Jean-Louis expounds with such confidence. Back in England he and his Labour Party friends routinely disparage the capitalist system without asking themselves how seriously they take their own words. What they are expressing, he can now see, is not so much a firm belief as a form of therapeutic consolation; it is the homage they pay to a long-dead dream of revolutionary renewal. Meanwhile, the true activating force in their political lives, the force that brought them onto the streets two years ago to canvass for a return of the Labour government of Harold Wilson, is a modest reformism that is utterly bereft of romance. It is the apparent ineffectuality of the Wilson government, dissected by Jean-Louis in a passage of particularly incisive brilliance and derision, that has left Stan without the ammunition to defend his political stance.

He is both tempted and repelled by this rock-hard, anti-capitalist conviction that he has encountered in Jean-Louis and his student friends, tempted by its clarity and lack of debilitating doubt but repelled by its unreality and lack of proportion. Can it truly be the case that France - this nation that has risen, in little over two decades, from the devastation of war to the condition of prosperity he can see all around him - requires an upheaval on the scale they envisage? The idea seems crazy, self-indulgent, morally frivolous.

He begins to spend less time at the library. At first it is simply a question of finishing early on Friday afternoon but this quickly spreads to the other afternoons of the week. The retreat from five o'clock to four o'clock and then to half past three is a measure of his declining interest in his research. He sometimes takes whole afternoons off, which he spends walking the streets and boulevards of the city or sitting in his room reading detective stories and listening to French radio on the transistor set that his father bought him for his twenty-fourth birthday.

His room is the one provided by Marie's friend. Its position just off the rue Rambuteau is an ideal location for his daily walk to the library. The bad news on his arrival in Paris was that the friend in question was Jean-Louis and he was Marie's lover. He was giving up the room in order to move in temporarily with Marie whose flat was conveniently placed for the university campus of Nanterre where Jean-Louis was pursuing his studies.

He was initially surprised at the hold Jean-Louis had over her. On first meeting him Stan found him pompous and self-opinionated, a sub-Sartrean café bore intoxicated by politico-philosophical verbiage. He was a good five or six years younger than Marie and was much exercised by the living and working conditions of his fellow students at Nanterre, conditions that Stan could readily acknowledge were appalling but that he was less inclined than Jean-Louis to blame on the oppressive forces of technocratic capitalism. Nor could he agree that sexual relations between students – an issue that had caused much contention between them and the university authorities – were a manifestation of some revolutionary Eros that would loosen the deadening grip of the French state over the lives of its citizens. Such flights of utopian fancy offended Stan's stolid Anglo-Saxon pragmatism. They also exasperated him for the spell they seemed to exercise over Marie.

Yet gradually, and in spite of himself, he began to understand what had attracted her. Jean-Louis's knowledge and self-assurance in political matters were extraordinary for someone of his years. The son of highly political parents (both his mother and father were members of the Communist Party, the latter a trade union organiser at Renault-Billancourt), he had absorbed politics from an early age. He was now estranged both from his father and from a Communist Party he viewed as having lost its revolutionary zeal, but politics remained his absorbing passion. He was a regular and enthusiastic participant in the turbulence that swirled around the campus of Nanterre; meetings, sit-ins and demonstrations were his natural element. For Marie he seemed to represent some ideal of the militant intellectual for whom thinking and acting were indissoluble.

He was also, to Stan's jaundiced eye, depressingly handsome.

As Stan's interest in his research wanes, he begins to spend more time with Marie, Jean-Louis and their friends. A student like them and conscious of the manna that British higher education showers on its élite of beneficiaries, he takes to heart their complaints about the conditions obtaining in French universities: the overcrowding, the inadequate teaching, the absurd rules governing contact between the sexes in student residences. He becomes caught up in the passionate sweep of their debates about power structures, ideology and the repressive tolerance of the bourgeois state, debates in which everything is politics, from the sex lives of students to the pay of the workers, and in which Karl Marx, Arthur Rimbaud and the Beatles are all grist to the mill of revolution. The group refer to themselves, with more self-conceit than self-mockery, as 'les enragés'.

Stan feels he is being pulled out of his familiar political ground. What binds him to them, the passport that states their citizenship of a common land, is the notion of the Left, a notion that for Stan stretches to include Aneurin Bevan and Leon Trotsky, R H Tawney and Karl Marx. He does not reflect on such elasticity, imagining that all his political enemies are to the right. Of course there are embarrassments for one cannot always choose one's political friends. Stalin, the show trials, the Kulaks are scars that cannot be effaced or ignored. He has read Albert Camus's denunciation of Soviet totalitarianism in *L'Homme révolté* and studied the two sides of the quarrel it provoked between Camus and Sartre. On the whole he is inclined to think Sartre won the intellectual argument but temperamentally he knows he belongs with the decent, great-hearted Camus.

But the force that binds him most strongly to the 'enragés' is Marie. To be with Marie is inevitably to be with them, and being with Marie matters to him a great deal. Feelings he thought were long dead and buried are quickening into new life. Her manner towards him on his arrival in Paris was affectionate and welcoming beyond his expectations. A few weeks later she paid him an unexpected visit in his new accommodation. He, misreading both her motive and the warmth and vivacity of her manner, made a clumsy attempt to kiss her. Gently pushing him away she explained that she and Jean-Louis had been together for some time now and although she was sure Jean-Louis viewed sexual fidelity as no more than a bourgeois prejudice, she feared that he would nevertheless be hurt by any disloyalty on her part.

'Les hommes français, tu sais…'

She smiled and shook her head. For a moment she was the old Marie. He waited to hear that note of acerbic irony that he remembered from their first trip out together on their bicycles, but her tone was amused and affectionate. Jean-Louis had seemingly drawn the sting of her contempt for the vanities of the French male.

Despite this, the subsequent months have nourished rather than starved his early hopes. She is the only woman among Jean-Louis's friends and seems nervously unsure of her place in the group. More often than not she is a spectator at their debates rather than a participant. She has developed the habit of engaging Stan in half-whispered conversations in English on the edge of the group, and he feels that this establishes a special bond between them. There are times, as they talk, when her smile rests on him with a frank, unshadowed tenderness that surely denotes more than loyalty and affection towards an old lover.

He is beginning to relive the experience of his sixth-form year but in a more subdued and complicated mode. The erotic fervour that gripped him then is reborn as a constant tender ache that seems to bathe in the softening atmosphere of this early spring. The changes in her appearance and her subjection to the power of Jean-Louis have dimmed her glamour somewhat and he is less in awe of her. But he is drawn to her by something deeper, which is fellow-feeling for a vulnerability and lack of self-confidence that he does not remember having seen during their first acquaintance.

He accompanies her to a meeting in support of the Vietnamese people. On the way there they discuss the American presence in Vietnam and he recognises in her tone the generous indignation and uncomplicated moral candour with which she once recounted her father's abuse of the Arab servant. He feels the old tenderness welling inside him. They listen to debates in a cramped and uncomfortable lecture theatre. The fierce ideological divisions between the participants - Trotskyist and Maoist sects vying for occupancy of an ideological pinhead - leave him cold and unmoved. He is aware of Marie beside him; the warmth of her body and the faint smell of her skin carry him back to their summer of love. He finds it difficult to concentrate on the debate. He looks around at the faces taut with concentration, and wonders how many of them are a disguise for the boredom and discomfort he is feeling. Or is he an exception, an interloper, forcing himself to a commitment he cannot sustain for motives tainted by emotional self-interest?

Afterwards he asked her what she thought of the meeting.

'Ah, ces gens-là… They love to talk. They do not think of the Vietnamese people, they think only of themselves and their precious ideas.'

He objected, urging the importance of ideas and the need to think clearly about politics. But secretly he was pleased with her criticism for it was one that could apply equally to Jean-Louis and the 'enragés'. It seemed to strengthen her attachment to him.

Some time later he joined Jean-Louis on a demonstration outside an office of American Express. Stifling his doubts about the responsibility of American Express for the war in Vietnam and eager to display the seriousness of his commitment, he joined the chanting of 'FLN vaincra' while staring up at the flamboyant Second Empire backdrop of the Paris Opéra. An American flag was set on fire, windows were smashed. Before the police could respond the demonstrators dispersed and raced for the metro entrance. He veered off on his own into the Boulevard des Capucines and quickly got lost in the crowd. Within twenty seconds all sight and sound of the demonstration had been left behind and he was among people for whom it might never have taken place. He learned later that there had been arrests and the following day students occupied the administrative tower of Nanterre University in protest at the actions of the police.

He was beginning to inhabit a world that was exciting yet unreal. Reality was a research thesis waiting to be written, the nagging guilt of being unable to settle to it, and the looming prospect of a living to be earned. It was no use Jean-Louis's friends declaiming against the tyranny of the work ethic and extolling a politics of play, or Jean-Louis himself denouncing the academic profession's role in the legitimation of the capitalist system; the academic profession was the destination Stan had set his eyes on, and hard work was the vessel that would carry him to it. He knew that soon he would either have to return to the library and resume his research or inform the authorities that he had abandoned it. The fact that he was being paid a grant to do work that he had neglected for almost a month cast a veil of guilt and depression over all his days. He wondered what Jean-Louis would make of such a scruple, whether he would even acknowledge that one could have a sense of moral obligation to the capitalist state. He felt anew his difference from the people with whom he had spent so much of his time in Paris. The only one he cared for was Marie.

He returned to the library. On April mornings of glittering sunshine, he walked carrying his briefcase through the central market of Les Halles with the city springing to life around him. Leaving behind the meat porters in their blood-stained overalls, the café waiters sweeping the pavements, the cool, sooty smell of the freshly sluiced streets, he immures himself in the reading-room of the library. His mornings are industrious and productive, his afternoons less so. He takes his lunchtime sandwich in the gardens of the Palais Royal where he lingers, enjoying the spring warmth and the peace and elegance of his surroundings. The lingering lengthens; he muses and dozes in the sun, he reads the newspaper that was intended to accompany his evening meal. His afternoons are being swallowed up by the gaping maw of a whale of idleness until only the last hour of the working day remains, like a leg kicking outside the snapped jaws.

On a day of brief showers pierced by shafts of dazzling light he takes shelter in the arcades of the Palais. He wanders past shop windows in which the displays of furs, jewellery, and sumptuous knick-knacks have been fashioned into the luxurious dreams of consumer capitalism. He glances at his watch. It is after three o'clock! What is he doing here? Guilt and self-disgust rise within him, he turns and sets off back to the library. But before he arrives there he has made his decision.

Over the telephone her voice is light and clear as crystal. He feels a surge of tenderness and hope at the unfeigned pleasure with which she greets his name. He suggests they meet for a drink on Thursday evening. They can go on afterwards to the cinema or – he hesitates, making a quick mental calculation of the state of his finances - for a meal. She hesitates in her turn., explains that she had intended, after leaving work on Thursday, to attend a day of anti-imperialist events at Nanterre. Afterwards, she and Jean-Louis...

'What about Friday then?'

He tries to keep the note of bitter disappointment out of his voice but the brusqueness of the interruption has made her go quiet. In order to repair the situation he launches into a confused apology, the main burden of which is that he is rather on edge at the moment because he has decided to abandon his research. She responds with quick sympathy but he is annoyed with himself. He had intended to save this news until they met, and then move on to the question that follows from it: whether he should return home to England or remain in Paris. He doesn't want to raise these matters over the telephone because he would like to be in a position to judge her reaction. He wants to watch her expression for any hint that she might prefer him to stay.

She tells him that the anti-imperialist programme will continue throughout Thursday and into Friday but she does not think she will attend the second day.

'You know what these things are like. Lots of words and big abstract ideas. I have only promised to go in order to please Jean-Louis.'

His spirits rise. Her distaste for the theoretical joustings of the *groupuscules* seems to have become more insistent in recent weeks. Does it reflect a growing detachment from Jean-Louis himself? And if so, why would that be? Might it not reflect a growing attachment to one of those modest, unassuming Englishmen she once told him she preferred? They arrange to meet at seven-thirty in a small restaurant in the Saint-Paul area that is cheap and of good quality.

He arrives too early and takes a stroll through the Jewish quarter around the rue des Rosiers, stopping to read the restaurant menus and survey the exotic foods in the windows of the bakers. A notice in a tailor's shop denouncing a bad debtor gives him a slight pulse of anxiety: he wonders whether he will be asked to pay back the grant he has so far received for his aborted research. He tells himself that if he remains in Paris, he must set about searching for work immediately and refrain from spending any more of his grant money.

He returns to the restaurant just after seven-thirty and paces the pavement for a while. He goes in and orders a *demi* which he sips slowly while standing at the bar. The tables are beginning to fill up. At ten past eight he finishes his beer and steps back outside onto the street. The sky above the tops of the buildings is still golden with daylight but the street is beginning, at a distance, to dissolve into a blur of shadowy outlines and faded colours. He thinks he sees Marie approaching but when the figure gets closer it is a middle-aged woman dressed with the sort of chic and punctilious elegance that Marie disdains.

His assumption that she has been delayed gives way to a fear that she may not come. At eight-thirty this has become his near-certain conviction, and the hypothesis of delay is struggling to hold its ground; the idea that she has been held up by a breakdown on the metro system is his last flimsy shield against the thrusts of despair.

He decides to give up. Appetite has faded with hope and, instead of eating alone, he returns directly to his room.

He telephones her immediately on arriving and then again, at intervals, throughout the evening, his throat dry with anxiety. Finally, after midnight, as he is about to take to his bed, though hardly in expectation of sleep, the telephone rings and it is her. She tells him she is sorry to have missed their meeting but there has been a crisis during the day. She sounds breathless, though whether from physical exertion or some sort of nervous tension, he cannot tell. Her English, which is normally fluent, falters and she changes into French. She tells him that there has been a serious confrontation between students and the police in the area around the Sorbonne. Jean-Louis has been injured and taken to hospital. She had learnt all this just before setting off to meet Stan; one of Jean-Louis's comrades had telephoned her. He had assured her that Jean-Louis's injuries were

180

not serious, but she was mad with worry and felt she had to get to the hospital. In the circumstances it was the first priority.

The phrases emerge from the distant voice like poisoned darts: 'folle d'inquiétude', 'la priorité numéro un'. He sees with sudden and painful clarity his place in her scheme of things. She suggests that they arrange to meet in a week's time but she sounds tentative and distracted, her mind on other things. He replies with assumed nonchalance that he is unlikely to be in Paris in a week's time for he has decided to return home. He tells her - in a tone that is intended to imply the futility of the way of life of the 'enragés' – that it is time to be serious about life and find a way of earning a living.

His mother appears at the kitchen door and asks if he would like a cup of tea. He nods and smiles while continuing to watch the television pictures of milling crowds and waving banners. He scrutinises the faces of the leading rows of demonstrators on the off-chance of seeing someone he knows - Jean-Louis perhaps or even Marie herself – but the images are fleeting and confused. The camera shifts to the BBC reporter.

'Tonight the French state is rocking on its foundations. With nine million workers on strike and almost daily demonstrations in the capital city, a movement that began with the modest demands of protesting students has spread to all areas of French working life. The next few days may determine the future of President de Gaulle and perhaps of the Fifth Republic itself.'

His mother places the cup of tea on the low table before him and disappears back into the kitchen. He watches the news clip through to its end and switches off the television. He feels dissatisfied and restless. He drinks his tea and carries the cup through to the kitchen.

'Thanks for the tea, Ma. I think I'll take a walk.'

He goes out of the front gate and onto the street, past uncle Ted and auntie Kate's house, past Morton's which has changed hands several times since the death of uncle Harold, on each occasion falling back a step in its struggle to keep pace with the competition

181

of the Co-op. On top of the railway bridge he pauses to scan the line in both directions, a persisting reflex of his childhood; then he goes down into the Railway Hotel. He orders a pint of best and takes it to a corner table of the Tap Room. At this early stage of the evening the pub is almost empty apart from the woman behind the bar and a couple of railway workers, fresh off their shift, who are playing the Tap Room's one-armed bandit.

He likes this corner of the pub and often comes here in the early evening with a book or a newspaper. Since returning home a few weeks ago he has been surprised by his own contented state. The abandonment of his research has turned out to be a liberation. He has found temporary work on a building site that is reasonably well paid, and has returned with something like relief to the convivial world of his old school-friends. They drink in pubs and pursue girls in dance-halls. He has joined the village cricket team and plays every week in the local Sunday league.

But the biggest change is in his feelings for Marie Salasca which he can now see were inseparable from his situation in Paris: alone in a foreign city, marginal to the group into which she had introduced him, he had been drawn to her by a mixture of erotic memory and social need. Since leaving Paris he has missed neither her nor the life he left behind.

That is until this moment. The events he has witnessed on television have shaken him out of his self-satisfaction. Watching the street demonstrations in Paris, he has realised that the conversations he had with Jean-Louis and the *enragés* were more than the intellectual fumblings of the politically naïve; they were the prelude to great events. Indeed they were the germ from which those events have now sprung! He is painfully aware that he has turned his back on a larger thing than the life to which he has returned.

He sips at his pint of beer and watches the railwaymen playing the one-armed bandit. There is a whoop of delight followed by a rattle of coins as the machine yields up its bounty. One of the men smiles across at him. He nods and smiles back.

Of course he knows that had he remained in Paris his contribution would have been modest. He would have attended the occasional meeting, joined the odd demo for the causes he believed in: students' rights, the pay of the workers, that sort of thing. He would have been the proverbial flea on the elephant's back of history. But rather the elephant's back than his parents' sofa which is where he was sitting half an hour ago, flea-like, watching that history unfold on television.

He leaves the pub and hesitates about which way to go, finally heading off in the direction of the Recreation Ground. He will drop into the pavilion, see if there is anyone around to chat to and check the team-sheet for next Sunday's cricket match. Then he must remember to have a word with his mother when he gets home and make sure that his white shirt and flannels are in the wash. He is looking forward to the match and knows his name will be on the sheet for he is the young star of the side. Afterwards they will have a few drinks, perhaps more than a few. They will tell jokes and sing and talk sport. It should be fun.

**22**

**Making Progress**

As he approaches the ruined farmhouse of Top Withins a group of
Japanese tourists, standing in a rough circle, is being addressed by
a middle-aged woman. In the bright sunlight everything about them,
from their immaculate trainers, slacks and windcheaters to their
shiny cameras, seems neat and new. Once, after the abandonment
of his literary research, he had begun to study Japanese, intending
to apply for a post teaching English in Tokyo. In the end he settled
for places closer to home, France and Spain, and has retained little
of what he learned. He stands for a while on the edge of the
group, listening in but unable to make sense of anything beyond the
odd interjection of 'Heathcliff' and 'Cathy', and a strangulated
attempt at what he takes to be 'Thrushcross Grange'. The woman
is pointing to the derelict farmhouse and in various directions over
the surrounding moors.

The idea that these people from halfway across the world have
read and admired *Wuthering Heights,* a book so rooted in the
particularities of this place, gives him a little thrill of local pride,
though he fears they may be disappointed with the site of their
pilgrimage. The rectangle of reduced walls, solid and banal in the
bright sunlight and inhabited by nettles and strewn debris, repels
imagination. A plaque set into them disclaims any resemblance to
the Wuthering Heights of Emily Brontë's novel.

The woman pauses and gazes around as though unsure where
next to proceed. Stan briefly catches her eye and for a moment he
experiences a childish hope that she will speak to him, ask him for
some piece of information that would enable him to display his
knowledge of these parts, his native rootedness. But she turns back
to the group and begins to usher them round to the side of the ruin.
He follows, keeping his distance but listening hard. All he can grasp
from the woman's speech are the words 'Ponden Hall' and another

attempt at 'Thrushcross Grange'. He turns away and takes the path to Haworth where he has booked a room for the night.

The incident has set him thinking of *Wuthering Heights*. He remembers the first time he read the book and the mixed feelings it aroused. Mr Podmore, his English teacher, had asked the class a question: 'What do we think Thrushcross Grange and Edgar Linton represent in the novel?' It was always 'we' with Mr Podmore. He was inclusive, consensual, a nice man. He often arrived a few minutes late for class with a light dusting of cigarette ash on his coat sleeve or lapel, having lingered over his smoke in the staff-room. They liked him for this; together with the 'we' it seemed to make him one of them.

Stan knew what he was supposed to say in reply to Mr Podmore's question. It was obvious really. Edgar was soft and weak and... what was that word Mr Podmore had taught them? Effete. His house with its comfort and luxury, and his daughters squabbling over their lap-dog represented the decadence of the sophisticated life. The cold-eyed proletarian in Stan could see this and had adopted an attitude of appropriate disdain. Yet for some reason he could not quite fathom he felt a certain sympathy for Edgar and wanted him to win out over Heathcliff. When Mr Podmore talked of the tenacious passion of Cathy and Heathcliff he found himself thinking that Edgar's passion was tenacious enough.

He thinks now that it must have been a temperamental thing; his own accommodating nature gave him an affinity with Edgar that he did not have with the flinty, uncompromising Heathcliff. And somewhere in the background of these thoughts and feelings was perhaps a memory of his uncle Harold, a kind and gentle man whose wound was still raw and weeping three years after the departure of his wife. The mild-mannered have tenacious passions too.

On reaching the outskirts of the village he decides to visit the parsonage and church. By the Brontë chapel in a corner of the church stands a glass case containing documents. He stares down at the register of deaths for the month of December 1848, looking for Emily's name. There it is, written by her own father, Patrick, shortly after he had conducted her burial service. The strong, confident writing seems at odds with what it signifies: the death and burial of a daughter. In the parsonage museum the brute facts of Victorian Haworth shock: the average age at death 25, forty-one per cent of children dying before the age of 6, polluted water supplies, raw sewage standing in the streets, tuberculosis rampant. It was tuberculosis that killed her. He has read somewhere that at her death she was so wasted by consumption the local carpenter said her coffin was the narrowest he had ever made. She was thirty years of age and the fourth of the widowed Patrick's children to die. Anne and Charlotte would follow her within seven years. He tries to imagine the impact of such disasters on their father but Patrick is too elusive, his character clouded by controversy and competing representations. All he can do is fill the vacant space that is Patrick Brontë with the horror that he himself would feel in such a situation.

He steps outside into the late-afternoon sunshine. Modern Haworth, salubrious, prettified and commercially astute, awaits him. He makes his way onto the main street thronged with shoppers and sightseers. He takes a glass of ale in the pub where Branwell Brontë drank and buys cough lozenges in a nostalgically antique chemist's, feeling that a modest contribution to the local economy is in order.

The woman who answers the doorbell of the guesthouse is a trim and compact forty-something with short auburn hair. She wears a pale-blue fleece jacket and matching track-suit bottoms that are smart and stylish while suggestive of a passion for outdoor pursuits.

'Do come in. It's Mr Walker isn't it? You phoned yesterday from Hebden Bridge.'

Her accent is difficult to place but is probably some tributary of Estuary English. Inside, the house looks newly refurbished in a cool and minimalist way; skirting-boards and banisters have been stripped back to the bare wood and the pale mushroom-coloured walls are unadorned except for a print of the surrounding fells. The bedroom to which she takes him is a similar combination of plain wood and subdued colours. The attached bathroom is shiningly new.

He is pleased with the quality of his accommodation. A hot, deep bath eases his stiff limbs and the ache of an old neck injury that is aggravated by the weight of his sack. Later, as she serves him dinner, the woman tells him this is her second season in the guesthouse business; she and her husband have renovated the property from top to bottom.

'Well you've made a lovely job of it. I hope things are going well for you.'

'There's a steady trade in the summer, mainly tourists like yourself. We get all nationalities, what with the Brontë industry and all that.'

Tourists like yourself! The phrase surprises him. He is about to tell her he knows Haworth well but she continues: 'The trade's mainly seasonal of course, things are pretty quiet in the winter. But my husband does some consultancy work so we're not wholly dependent on the guesthouse.'

She tells him that her husband, Rik, is Dutch and she met him while they were both working for a firm of international management consultants in London. Two years ago they decided to change their lives and move north. Although Rik is an accountant by profession, his true passion is for cooking and he personally prepares all the evening meals.

Of course he understands perfectly well that for the woman who runs the guesthouse he is just another tourist, an item of 'the trade', a consumer of the products of the 'Brontë industry'. And of course, he has no objection on patriotic, gastronomic or any other grounds to eating *spaghetti Bolognese* cooked to savoury perfection by a

Dutchman who is a consultant in accountancy. For all that, he cannot help feeling that his home county is losing some of its homeliness. He takes a stroll along the surrounding streets feeling lonely and faintly oppressed. On returning to the guesthouse he lies on his bed and switches on the bedside radio. A man's voice is talking about literature, arguing that it should be subversive, transgressive, dangerous. The word 'dangerous' seems to give him a pleasurable *frisson* for he repeats it. Stan begins to drift into sleep. He is woken by the same voice deploring the state of English fiction, its insularity, its lack of engagement with the horrors of the twentieth century…. He yawns and switches off.

He telephones Annie. Her voice sounds strained and tired. She thinks she has picked up some bug or other during the first week back at school and intends to have an early night. Stan feels an apprehension that is out of proportion to her words. He says: 'Make sure you look after yourself and don't go in tomorrow if you feel worse. Get along to the doctor.'

Annie laughs and says: 'Don't be daft, Dad. If every teacher who had a bit of a cold stayed off work there'd be nobody to teach the kids. Schools are full of bugs and germs. Half the staff are sniffling and coughing.'

'I take it you're exaggerating.'

'Of course I am but you know what I mean. I can't just take time off in the first week of term because I feel a bit under the weather.'

'No, of course not. We'll just have to keep our fingers crossed and hope it's not consumption.'

'What? What are you talking about?'

'Just joking. I'm in Haworth. I went to the Brontë museum this afternoon so consumption's on my mind.'

'I think you'll find that's the only place it is, Dad. At least here in England, though there may be places where it's still rife.'

'OK. I'll try to stop worrying. What about the rest of your week? How are the little ones?'

'The little ones are fine. I've got a good class this year and there are not too many of them.'

'How many's not too many?'

'Twenty-nine, which is quite manageable. There are even fewer this week when you discount the two who have gone off on holiday with their parents and the one who was seen shopping with her mother in Newcastle city centre.' She laughs but she is dismayed by such fecklessness. 'Can you believe it! Taking your child shopping on the first day back at school!'

Stan reminds her of her own fraught relationship with school.

'But that was me, Dad, it wasn't my parents. You and Mum did everything you could to keep me on the rails.'

Everything but stay together! He feels a rush of gratitude towards his brave, forgiving daughter. He says: 'It's good of you to think it.'

'What do you mean Dad? Of course I think it. You and Mum were wild for education. You must have wondered what you'd done to deserve this little barbarian forever bunking off school.'

He begins to protest but chokes on his words, finally mumbling: 'Well, it's all over now.'

'Yes, I'm a pillar of the community nowadays. I'll soon be writing to the *Telegraph* complaining about the youth.'

'Why not? You'd speak from authority.'

'But what about you Dad? How far have you got? I don't really know where Haworth is.'

'I've done just over fifty miles and I'm purring along like the well-oiled machine that I am.'

'No breakdowns?'

'The odd bit of stiffness, nothing to worry about. Tomorrow's the first big test, over twenty miles to Malham.'

He tells her about the day he has just had, his visit to the church and museum, and the guesthouse with its Dutch-accountant chef. He would like to tell her more. He would like to tell her that the Haworth of imagination and the past is more real for him than the Haworth of the present, and that his experience of the Brontë parsonage and church, with its atmosphere of precarious life, has remained with him during the day and has turned into this dull, persistent ache of missing his daughter.

But this is not the moment. She sounds tired and he suddenly feels tired too. He wishes her goodnight and tells her he loves her. She says: 'I love you too, Dad.'

There is little traffic on the minor road out of Haworth and he is able to walk freely along the metalled surface. The weather is holding. The sky is bright blue with a stippling of white cloud; mist lies in the hollows of the fields like cupped milk. After a good night's sleep his reserves of energy are at their highest and the pleasure he takes in physical movement is at its most intense, but he knows that he must moderate his pace if he is to manage comfortably the long trek to Malham.

The road re-connects him with the Way. He passes Ponden Hall, crosses pastureland, walled and fenced fields, and a moor of flowering heather like soft purple dust stretching to the sky. For over two hours he sees no-one. Ruined barns and abandoned farmhouses stand like emanations of his solitude. A farmer erecting a fallen fencepost is the first, lone figure in his landscape. The thump of the hammer on the top of the post fades and he is left with the sounds of his own movement and the drift of his thoughts.

He feels grateful for a constitution that has given him sixty years without serious mishap. His professional life has spared him the bodily tribulations of his parents' generation. He tots up the damage so far: a touch of arthritis in the thumb joints and a troublesome vertebra in the neck from a minor car accident are his only persistent ailments. His legs and feet remain strong and unimpaired apart from an occasional twinge in his left knee that is the cry for help of an overworked ligament. The trekking poles are his response, a propitiatory offering to the god of complex, load-bearing joints.

He thinks of his father, the cartilage in his knees worn away by over thirty years of squatting and kneeling in low seams. He thinks of uncle Herbert crippled by his accident down the pit, and of auntie Brenda with her chronic back pain, girding herself for daily battle with poss-tub and mangle, with rugs that have to be shaken, mattresses turned, floors swept. He can still hear the mixture of excitement and mischief in her voice as she told him of her new labour-saving machine: 'Hang on, our Stanley. Don't leave yet. I've got something to show you.'

She goes through the door into the stairwell and emerges with the something.

'It's a Hoover. It sucks the muck up into this bag. Watch. I'll show you how it works.'

She uncoils the cable and plugs it in, then brushes a handful of bread crumbs from the tea-table onto the linoed floor. The machine roars into life and auntie Brenda pushes it over the crumbs leaving the lino bare behind it. She shouts above the noise: 'There, what do you think of that?' She switches off and repeats: 'What do you think of that?' She wears a clean, brightly flowered pinafore that stretches out over the bulge of her imminent fourth child. She begins to laugh. He tries to laugh with her but he doesn't grasp the importance of what has happened, the pleasure and relief she must feel at her lightened domestic burden. She laughs so hard she has to sit down. Stan is dismayed by such unbridled joy.

He stops on the open moorland to eat his lunch - cheese sandwiches, a Kit-Kat and an apple packed for him by the woman at the guesthouse. Thus replenished, it is mid-afternoon before he begins to feel the first creeping weariness in his legs. He rests and finishes his flask of coffee, then sets off again, ascending a gentle slope of heather and bracken. Ahead of him a fox breaks cover onto the path that runs diagonally across the hillside. It trots briskly as though on tiptoe with its head cocked to one side watching him as it goes. It stops by a large spread of bracken just below the line of the hilltop and turns round to get a better sight of him. Stan stops too, transfixed by its stare. The day is breathless, the hillside as still as death. The fox turns away and slips unhurriedly into the bracken.

He remains standing there, prolonging the moment, invaded by the deep calm of the hillside and the cool, measuring stare of the fox. What did it see he wonders? A figure of threat on the path, but at a distance; safety is close by, low thickets through which it can rapidly thread its way, then stop and listen for the footfalls of passing danger. He imagines it watching and listening in the depth of the bracken.

He resumes his walk, a regular loping stride matched by the regular muffled tapping of his poles on the sandy path. He slips into a rhythm that requires no conscious effort so that he can hold on to this stillness within him that is as deep and alien as the ocean floor. He wants to be without thought or feeling except for the sense of his own movement. He wants to be the figure on the path watched by the fox.

'Hello young man. Fancy meeting you again.'

He turns round from the display of post-cards. Don Crick is beaming with warmth and pleasure. With his mud-yellow rucksack clinging to his back like a baby chimpanzee to its parent, he seems to fill the small shop. He appears unsure how to continue and after a pause says, unnecessarily: 'Buying a few post-cards I see.'

'Yes, for my daughter and friends.'

Stan's mind is already running ahead to the implications of this chance encounter. He is reluctant to expose his solitude to a further invasion of Don's challenging opinions. He doesn't want to be challenged. He doesn't want this faint stirring of anxiety and unease that he feels in Don's company and that he knows is connected to the fact that he has withdrawn from the world of work at sixty while this great knobbly crag of a man is still labouring on his farm at seventy-five. He says: 'Are you staying in Gargrave?'

'No. I'm moving on to Malham. And yourself?'

The sinking feeling that Stan experiences is accompanied by resignation. Malham is six miles away, which is two and a half hours of walking at his present pace. Two and a half hours is bearable. Had they met earlier it could have been a whole day!

They cross the Leeds and Liverpool canal onto pastureland beside the river Aire. The declining sun casts their bobbing, hump-backed shadows to the side of the path. Cows stand still and silent in the shallow waters of the river. Stan soon finds himself regretting the meanness of his earlier thoughts. Don is garrulous but has a command of language and sharpness of mind that impress. He is knowledgeable too. A disquisition on the difficulties faced by dairy farmers in the current economic climate gives way to remarks on the type of vegetation favoured by the limestone soils. He points out the ancient agricultural terraces that have left their trace on the hillsides and explains how the old farmers built them in order to create flat strips that enabled them to plough straight furrows with their oxen.

'Such resourcefulness and determination. And all without subsidies from Europe.'

He laughs and gives a quick sideways glance to check that Stan has got the joke. Stan smiles and prepares himself for more political diatribe but Don goes quiet. The early-evening light is softening, the lowering sun has stretched their shadows. The raw croak of a pheasant breaks the silence; they hear it clattering out of a stand of trees and see it glide over a low hedgerow before landing and strutting to a halt. The path descends to a flat valley-bottom beyond which they can now see the Malham hills with, at their centre, the white and grey rock-wall of Malham Cove. Don begins to talk of his time in India and of the difficulties that he and his parents had in adapting to life in England.

'I'm not sure I ever have adapted. Not wholly. In India we lived within sight of the Himalayas and on clear days you could see faint peaks in the distance. Or at least that's my memory of it though it may simply be something I've been told. Whatever the truth, I've always found England... what's the word? Confining.'

'We can't help our geography.'

'No, of course not. But it's not just geography I'm talking about. It's everything. It's people's passions and concerns. It's difficult to describe. It's as though India has left some residue, some measure of grandeur and intensity from which England falls short. Do you think that sounds impossibly pompous?'

'Not really. And I'm sure similar things have been said before.'

'You mustn't misunderstand me. I'm proud of my Englishness. I'm quite patriotic really.'

'Identity's a complicated thing. There are people from the north of England who think Englishness is an invention of southerners. They prefer to call themselves British. But sit them in front of the telly when England are playing France at rugby and they're English to the core.'

Don laughs and says: 'Well I'm with them on that. Down with the French!'

'But if it's identity that concerns you the French have something to teach us. I'm sure you'll agree that the French are much more French than the English are English.'

'I might agree if I understood what you meant.'

'I mean that in their everyday life they do things that affirm their Frenchness. They drive French cars, they eat French food, they travel on railways that are a symbol of national pride. They hate the prospect of being swallowed up in some globalised nowhere in which everybody speaks English and feeds on burgers.' He thinks to himself: 'Or *spaghetti Bolognese* for that matter.'

Don says: 'That's very interesting. I can see I might have to revise my view of the French. And is that where you think we are heading? A globalised nowhere?'

'I don't know where we're heading. Though I know we've made it to Malham. And, God, am I grateful for that!'

He is weary; his legs are heavy and his familiar sore spots of thumb joints and neck vertebra have begun their slow crescendo of complaint. Don has booked a night at the Youth Hostel while Stan is taking bed and breakfast at a guesthouse. Later that evening they meet for a short stroll along the path by which they arrived earlier. From a rise in the path they turn to survey the scene, then set off back to the village. The light has faded, the hills stand black against a dark-blue sky. The good weather is coming to an end; a wind has risen and sudden gusts pick at their cheeks. A half-moon floats on rills of thickening cloud.

They are now on first-name terms, though Don maintains an element of formality by referring to Stan as Stanley. In reply to Stan's enquiry about his family and their life in Herefordshire, Don talks of the long illness and death of his wife ten years before and the gap it has left in his life. His tone is matter-of-fact and without despondency; it is as though for him these things are tragic yet commonplace. He says that both his parents were long-lived and he supposes he will be too. It is not a prospect that cheers him he claims, though he says this in a cheerful way, chuckling quietly in the dark and re-iterating the point.

'No, it doesn't cheer me at all.'

'But you are strong and fit,' says Stan. 'It's not everybody who tackles the Pennine Way…'

'At my age? No, of course you are right. I've a great deal to be thankful for, and I am thankful, believe me, I am. If there's one thing you learn through having a missionary for a father it's to be thankful for life's mercies. My point was a general one. Our obsession with staying alive is misplaced, ridiculous. Hardly a day goes by without some half-mad Californian professor, drunk on the blather of scientific progress, telling us we'll soon be living to a hundred. Can you imagine it? Living to a hundred!'

His raised voice echoes in the hollow night air. Stan says: 'I suppose it would test the truth of the phrase 'to die of boredom'.'

'Ah, you jest my friend but I've seen too many people going on into their eighties and nineties who *are* bored. They have outlived their zest for life. And, let's face it, they've outlived their usefulness too. They feel a burden to the young and to the earth itself. My father used to say that the world wasn't made for us, we were made for it. I never knew what he meant. I know now. We must obey its laws in the end.'

'True, but let's not be in a hurry. My parents did obey its laws, and earlier than either they or I would have liked. My mother was only my age when she died.'

'Oh no, don't misunderstand me. I hope I haven't offended you.'

He touches Stan's arm in a gesture of reassurance and goes silent for a while. Stan is getting used to these sudden fits of contrition and feels himself warming to this man in whom a natural courtesy does daily battle with exasperation at the vices of the world. Don is a stuttering volcano; for the moment he is quiescent but Stan senses serious explosions within.

They stop to say goodnight at the door of Stan's guesthouse. Don apologises once more for his earlier tactlessness and admits that he is inclined to be rather self-opinionated. He seems on the point of starting a new conversation about Stan's parents but Stan assures him that no offence is taken, and that it was all a long time ago. As he leaves, Don asks if they might walk together the following day and Stan agrees, stifling his misgivings.

## 23

## Son and Lover

He was working in Madrid when he heard of his mother's death. He received a telegram from his father informing him that she had had a heart attack. The brevity and baldness of the statement and the impersonal surroundings in which he read it – at the bottom of the stone staircase next to the mail boxes of the apartment block in which he rented a room - seemed to rob it of meaning.

Throughout the rush of the next thirty-six hours, during which he reported the matter to the head of his language school, obtained a late booking on a flight to England and arrived back in Calcroft, he seemed unable to bring his mind and feelings into alignment with the fact that his mother had gone from his world. It was only when he entered the house in Calcroft to find his father prostrate with grief in the bed that he and Sally had shared for over thirty years that he was stunned by the loss they had suffered.

The letter of condolence that his father received a week later from Catherine Stapleton almost escaped his notice. He found it by accident among a miscellany of everyday objects such as keys and bills that Mam and Dad kept in a sideboard drawer. In his mental and emotional disarray Dad had forgotten to mention it.

She said she had heard of Joe's bereavement and wished to send her deepest sympathy. She had always remembered the kindness of Joe and Sally during her period at the Railway Hotel and particularly at the time of her father's death. She also remembered with great affection her friend Stan. To him too she sent her sympathy. She ended by saying that if ever either of them was in her part of the world she hoped they would get in touch. There was a Manchester address on the letter.

He was moved almost to tears. To have written after all this time! To have remembered him and his father and to have remained true to the feelings she had for them twenty years ago! He folds the sheet of paper and places it in his trouser pocket, having decided that he will reply for both of them. He will let her know their gratitude and the fact that he remembers her with the same affection that she has for him. For the first time since hearing of his mother's death he feels comforted.

He returned to his work in Madrid to find that everything had changed. Where he had felt confident and free in his cosmopolitan life, he now felt rootless and insecure. Everything oppressed him: the apartment block in which he lived, the streets through which he walked to the Escuela Lope de Vega, the unrelenting heat of the Madrid summer. It was as though he had lost some essential balance between his own resistant self and the invasive world around him. The mere thought of the city's location in the middle of the baking Iberian peninsula made him feel desperate for escape. Sitting in his room reading, with the air wrapped around him like a warm poultice, his desire for hills, greenery and wind was overwhelming. Images of the landscapes of northern England mingled in his mind with memories of childhood and his mother. He lay on his bed, reversing in imagination his position and that of the cracked and dusty lampshade that hung from the ceiling. He held the Pennine chain in his mind, as though he was hovering above it, with its valleys and streams running off east and west into the villages and towns of Yorkshire and Lancashire. He had taken maps back to Madrid and would pore over them, planning walks for some future time and re-erecting in his mind the hilly landscapes that were flattened into the contours of the maps.

He decided there and then that this would be his last engagement abroad. At thirty-two years of age, the lightness of his life's baggage, that he had thought was freedom, was beginning to feel like purposelessness. At weddings he was one of a dwindling band of youngish bachelors, their thinning hair and pallid complexions gainsaying the impression they sought to create of free-spirited lives untrammelled by the burdens of marriage. To his surprise and dismay a recent christening that he attended struck some deeply embedded chord of paternal longing.

He wrote to Catherine Stapleton thanking her for her letter to him and his father. After some brief remarks on their childhood friendship and his life since, he tells her that he intends to return home to be with his father for a while. He has decided to study for a teaching qualification entitling him to work in the British school system and is in the process of deciding which universities he would prefer to study at. The University of Manchester has been recommended to him. Sometime in September, when he has fulfilled his contract in Madrid and returned home, he intends to visit Manchester in order to have a look around and decide whether it is the right place for him. He hopes that he and she will be able to meet and catch up on their lives of the last twenty or so years.

There was much in this letter that was true. He did intend to return home, he had decided to study for a teaching qualification, and he was trying to decide on a suitable university. There was even some truth in the statement that the University of Manchester had been recommended to him, though that was many years ago when Mr Derry, confronted by his reluctance to apply to Oxford and Cambridge to study French, had intimated that Manchester was one of the best of the 'redbricks'. Stan did not know whether Manchester was still judged to be one of the best of the redbricks but it suited him to think so.

Back in England he took temporary work in the administrative office of a small engineering company near Doncaster, Blackett's Bearings, that did much of its business with foreign buyers. A sudden and unexpected resignation had deprived the company of the only employee in the office with the ability to decipher correspondence in German and Spanish. Within a month, owing to the unexpected departure of the firm's office-manager, Stan found himself helping the company's beleaguered Managing Director, Tom Blackett, to run the office. It was Tom Blackett, impressed by Stan's organisational ability and quickness of mind, who first suggested he should think of a career in business or administration instead of teaching.

'Of course, Stan, it depends how committed you are to teaching. I wouldn't want to put you off a perfectly respectable career if that's your vocation. We need teachers. But we need good people in industry too – managers, people with brains who can run the show.'

Tom's words set him thinking. 'Vocation' wasn't the word he would use to describe his choice of teaching as a career; the phrase 'herd instinct' sprang more readily to mind. He was struck by the number of his contemporaries at university who had become teachers. Others, fewer in number, had gone into the civil service and the British Council or offered themselves for Voluntary Service Overseas. A career of worthy public service seemed to be the norm that had insinuated itself into the minds of bright, state-educated young people like himself possessed of degrees in the arts. The worlds of business, industry and banking were foreign territory, owing either to ignorance or to some vague ideological distrust of money and commerce. It was as though he had come to teaching at the end of a process of elimination that had been carried out in him independently of his will by his background and education. He decided to kick the habit.

But not just yet. He had arranged a trip to the School of Education of Manchester University and was reluctant to cancel it. He had written to Catherine Stapleton to let her know of his impending visit and to suggest they meet. She had written back expressing her pleasure at the prospect of seeing him again after all these years. His decision to turn his back on teaching must therefore be held in abeyance. No harm could be done by delaying a while, ruminating on the question and visiting the fine institution of Manchester University. He felt he ought to allow teaching a last chance to claim him.

*

In the crowd of people on the station concourse he doesn't see her until she is upon him.

'Stanley Walker I presume?'

He would not have recognised her. He was expecting someone slighter and blonder. It is her hair that strikes him first, light brown with a coppery sheen, falling straight to the shoulders of her cream-coloured raincoat. Her face is fuller than he remembers, the mouth and eyes that once seemed almost too large reduced to perfect proportion. He is surprised and somewhat daunted by her elegance.

She seems amused to have caught him unawares, with a rolled copy of the Guardian across his chest as agreed but looking in the direction opposite to the one she has come from. They shake hands and he wonders - while trying to decipher in this mature, attractive woman the slip of a girl who appeared in the sunlit glare of his father's shed door - whether he should kiss her on the cheek. She stands smiling, waiting. He decides to dispense with the kiss and says: 'Well, Catherine Stapleton. I wouldn't have known you. You're…different.'

She laughs and says: 'It must be those twenty years that have passed.'

'Do you know, you could be right.'

'You've changed a bit yourself. I wouldn't have known you without the Guardian.'

'I hope this isn't inconvenient for you, us meeting like this. I just thought…'

'Oh no. It's fine. I work close by and I finish at half past four on a Thursday. I thought we might have a coffee. I know a place a few minutes away.'

He is pleased and relieved. He had not known what to expect – mutual embarrassment perhaps and, on her part, coldness or even resentment at a meeting that she might feel had been forced on her. The warmth and humour of her greeting and now this brisk taking charge of events reassure him. On the short walk from Victoria Station he asks her about her work. She tells him she works in a law firm as secretary to one of the partners. He awaits further information but she says nothing more. He cannot tell whether this is from a reluctance to talk about her work or from the difficulty of maintaining conversation on the crowded pavement.

Sitting across from him at the café table certain fleeting expressions of her face – the widening of her mouth when she smiles, the slight, worried puckering of her forehead – arouse buried memories of the Catherine Stapleton he knew. They order coffee and, for her, a large piece of apple pie surmounted by a twirl of fluffy cream. She says, in a tone that is a mixture of explanation and apology: 'I missed lunch. We're busy at the moment and rather understaffed.'

'Do you like your work?'

'I don't actively dislike it but it's not a job I want to do for the rest of my life. What about you? You wrote from Spain. Tell me what you were doing there.'

He recounts his life of recent years: his university degree, the abandonment of his PhD and his subsequent years teaching abroad. She has removed her raincoat and sits listening, her spoon poised for the first strike at her apple pie. Everything about her is neat and clean and appealing: the soft-wool sweater that moulds to her shapely breasts, her smooth, unblemished skin, her even teeth. When she speaks it is with a faint Lancashire accent that makes her seem both homely and desirable at the same time.

He suddenly wonders what it is that has driven him to make a trip that has begun to seem irrelevant to his plans for the future. He is not without self-knowledge and has learnt to recognise the subtle intertwinings of need, desire and imagination that seem to predetermine his view of women. During his time abroad he met Latin males who had married effigies of their mothers, and he knows that he must be on guard against the emotional susceptibility left by his recent loss.

She says: 'I thought of applying to go to university as a mature student. After leaving school I attended evening classes at a local college, studying for A-levels – Art and English Literature. In the end I abandoned the university idea. What I really wanted to do was write.'

'What sort of writing did you want to do?'

'Fiction. Particularly stories for older children. It's still what I want to do. I've written various things and tried to get them published but it's a tough world out there. It's difficult to break into.'

'Why children's stories?'

'I'm not sure. I think it might have something to do with Calcroft – my father's death and all that. It marked me so deeply it seems to have fixed my imagination on that time of life.'

He is not yet ready for this. He says: 'I think you'd better have a go at that pie. And drink your coffee before it goes cold.'

He goes on to tell her more of his current circumstances, living with his father and working at Blackett's Bearings. The memory of his conversation with Tom Blackett returns and, with it, a sense of the falsity of his presence here. In order to dissipate the unease he feels he begins to tell her of his doubts about teaching while stopping short of admitting that he has more or less abandoned the idea of teaching altogether. Something in his words and tone must have given the game away for a look of puzzlement crosses her face and she says casually, as though it is a trivial afterthought: 'I didn't mention the reason why I didn't apply to go to university. I got married instead. I still am married.'

He is dumbfounded. 'But the name on your letters - Stapleton.'

'I've reverted to my maiden name. The marriage wasn't a success. We're separated.'

The relief he feels on hearing this surprises him almost as much as the original revelation of her married state.

She tells him that her husband's name is Rod Barnett. She had known him by sight and reputation at her secondary school where he was two years ahead of her and viewed by teachers as a prominent member of the school's 'awkward squad' - truculent, disaffected and ambitious only to leave school and begin work. When she met him again she was nineteen and still living with auntie Dot and her mother. Auntie Dot had called in a workman to replace tiles on her house that had been dislodged by gales. It was Cathy who opened the door to find Rod Barnett standing there. Over his shoulder she could see, parked at the gate, a battered old van with the words Rod the Roofer emblazoned on the side.

She was attracted by his good looks and breezy manner. The life he led seemed to her happy and free. He told her he loved his job and, being self-employed, could tailor his working week to suit his leisure activities which were three: rock-climbing, exploring caves and drinking with his mates. He persuaded her to join them; they were a mixed group he said, men and women, all with a passion for slithering through underground passages and hanging from vertical rock-faces. He made it seem both dangerous and hilarious at the same time.

He came to represent everything that was lacking in her life – excitement, companionship, and a rumbustious male presence that contrasted with the pinched gentility of home and the monotony of her job. At her school the message had gone forth that useful and rewarding employment for girls was to be had in nursing and office work. Her indifference to both these prospects had not prevented her from taking up her allotted role in the typing-pool of a major commercial company in the centre of Manchester and later as a secretary in a solicitors' practice. After meeting Rod, Saturday morning became the transforming moment of her week, when she would go off with him and his friends - half a dozen or more of them squatting on the floor of his van among their rucksacks and piles of equipment - to explore the potholes and rock routes of the Dales and the Lake District. She took to these pursuits with a skill and boldness that gained her the respect of a group that had initially been wary of her, finding her too refined and 'middle-class'. They would return from their expeditions, uproarious and drunk, infected by the wildness of the places they had visited, already making plans for the following weekend.

'Those were the good times. Being married to him was a different matter altogether.'

She pauses and jiggles her empty cup on its saucer. For a moment he wonders whether she is going to suggest they get up and leave but after a few seconds she continues: 'Until we set up house together I hadn't realised the scale of his drinking...that he drank during the day, even during working days. Can you imagine it! A man who earned his living clambering over people's roofs!'

She laughs and shakes her head, as though the memory arouses something of her old affection for Rod the roofer.

'There were other problems too. My favourite subject at school was English Literature. We had a good teacher, Mrs Mordue, who inspired a few of us to read regularly and even to try our own writing. That's how I first got started writing my own stuff. But Rod didn't like it. He didn't even like to see me reading a book. I suppose he felt excluded for he'd never read a book in his life and was uninterested in any of that sort of thing - anything cultural or artistic. If he caught me reading when he came home from the pub he would sulk or lose his temper.'

'Was he violent?'

'No, but he was a prey to his emotions. He was a big baby really. When we were splitting up I didn't know what mood he would be in from one day to the next. Sometimes he would be crying and feeling sorry for himself, other times he would be perfectly reasonable and sensible. At bottom he knew it couldn't work. I sometimes think he only married me because he said he would in a fit of sentimentality and he hadn't the heart to go back on it. He was a big baby really.'

She glances at her wristwatch. They have been sitting here for over an hour during which the Catherine Stapleton of his childhood, a first love wreathed in the golden veils of memory, has been replaced by a modern woman who has done the prosaic modern things of taking a dull job, marrying and separating from her husband. Yet she herself isn't prosaic. She is warm and funny and alluring, and Stan wants to keep her here, just as he wanted to keep that younger Catherine standing by the side of his parents' house in the sunshine of that late-summer day of 1953. At the very least he must set up another meeting with her. He says: 'I hope I'm not keeping you from anything.'

'No, I've nothing on tonight.'

'I was going to suggest we perhaps have a bite to eat somewhere. Unless you feel you've already eaten.' He nods towards the plate in front of her.

'No, that was just a stopgap. I'm a hearty eater. What's your preference? Italian, Chinese, Indian? Manchester has the lot. I think we even have English.'

He came back from Manchester to find his father lying sideways on the sofa with his head on a cushion watching television. When Stan returned to the sitting-room, having deposited his travel bag in his bedroom, the television was off but his father was lying in the same position as before. He began to speak as soon as Stan was in the room. He said that for some weeks he had been troubled by an ache between his shoulder blades that had now become so severe he was unable to continue the work he had been doing in his shed. Such a frank admission of physical frailty from his father was unusual. Stan said: 'When did you first notice the ache?'

'Soon after your mother died. I thought that was what had brought it on...the shock and all that. I thought it would go away. It did for a while but it keeps coming back. And it's got worse. It's more painful.'

His voice is toneless, the expression on his face a blank that could indicate either dejection or indifference. He rubs the corner of his eye with his index finger and Stan wonders whether he has been crying. The four months that have elapsed since Sally's death have done nothing to ease his grief.

'When I reach round with my hand I think I can feel a bit of a swelling on my back but it's hard to be sure. I can't twist round far enough to see it in the bathroom mirror.'

He pushes himself up into a sitting position and removes his pullover and shirt, an act of sudden and unaccustomed intimacy that makes Stan realise the urgency of his fear. His body is as spare and hard as a young man's, the skin a milky white with a constellation of small blue scars from his years underground. And there, a third of the way down his back, there is a slight hummock of flesh spanning the spine. Stan raises his hand to touch it but stops himself. Decades of silent self-containment stand between them, a taboo that cannot be breached.

Within a month the swelling is the size of a small orange and Dad's pain is so severe Stan hears him moaning in the night. His doctor has given him painkillers which he must take every four hours. The period between the fading power of one pill and the prescribed time for the next is one of growing discomfort. When Stan gets up and goes through to him he sends him back to bed, overcome with a sort of modesty and shame at his vulnerability.

Their life has become one of anxious waiting – for appointments with doctors and hospital consultants, for tests and the results of tests. It is Stan who makes the trip to Doncaster Infirmary for the result of the biopsy. The specialist tells him that Dad has cancer. It is already at the secondary stage and they cannot be sure where it started. It is now too far gone for surgery to be effective.

The day is Thursday and Stan is due, the following day after work, to travel to Manchester to spend the weekend with Catherine Stapleton. In the circumstances he feels he has to change his plan, unable to pass the sombre news on to his father and then leave him to a weekend of solitary despair. His pity for his father mingles with the bitter disappointment of having to cancel an event that has been the object of intense excitement and anticipation. Within a short time his relationship with Cathy has become the most important thing in his life. He has bought a second-hand car and drives to Manchester at weekends. They go to plays, concerts and films; they take trips out into the countryside; they eat and drink copiously; and they talk. Their twenty years apart are a bottomless well of stories and revelations about the journeys that have brought them from the children they were to the adults they are. And now – after a period of hesitancy and strange embarrassment - they make love.

One day while they are lying in bed together listening to the radio, the news is announced of the death of General Franco. He is pleased and interested but not excited as he would once have been. His life in Spain seems a long time ago and his passion for politics has been displaced by one that has become all-consuming and that leaves no room for rivals.

For three months his existence oscillates between this abundance of life and the impending death of his father. He has decided that Dad will remain at home for as long as possible. As his condition worsens Stan reduces his hours at Blackett's and sets up a complicated timetable of care, involving daily visits by nurses and periods of supervision by relatives. Auntie Kate prepares lunches which she sets on Joe's tray with a great fanfare of good cheer and injunctions to keep his strength up by eating. He is now permanently downstairs in the sitting-room in an orthopaedic bed that Stan has obtained from the hospital. Stan returns from his half days at work to find Dad attempting to consume auntie Kate's lunches in gratitude for her kindness while auntie Kate sits knitting in one of the armchairs or washing up in the kitchen. Radiotherapy has reduced the size of his tumour and his pain is controlled by heavy doses of a morphine-based medication that gives him fitful sleep ravaged by nightmares and waking hallucinations. When he sits on the side of the bed his feet beneath the pyjama bottoms are a fan of bones papered over with skin.

His grief at the death of Sally is engulfed by this new disaster of pain and fear. Stan saw it in his eyes when the men delivered the orthopaedic bed - a flash of wild uncomprehending panic as he lay on the sofa watching them edge it through the sitting-room door and set it on its legs by the window.

'That's my death-bed they're bringing, son.'

His eyes were swimming with tears, his voice querulous with misery. Stan went over to him. Down the pyjama collar that stood back from his father's wasted neck he could see the swell of the tumour. He put his hand out and stroked his head. But he could not find the words to set his fear at rest.

During his childhood and youth they had been distant from each other. For Stan his father was an object of admiration and fear, the admiration of the miner's child for his father's strength and toughness and the fear of offending such a paragon of the manly virtues. During his teenage years he felt anger at the tyranny of his father's moods and the unhappiness to which they condemned his mother but it was an anger held in check by the old fear and by the barrier – erected over the years and now impossible to cross – of their remoteness one from the other. To address words of anger to this man would have been as difficult as to address words of affection or intimate confession.

His father's sickness has burst this dam of silence and inhibition. The necessity of helping him fulfil his physical needs - holding his weak and shrunken frame as he sits on the edge of the bed to urinate or half-carrying him to the commode that must be kept close at hand – has made reticence redundant. Joe shakes his head in disbelieving sorrow at these humiliations but accepts the reversal of power and authority between him and his son with a resigned dignity that Stan finds all the more moving for being so unexpected.

It is only now that he tells Stan of the feeling he had at Sally's death that he could not continue to live without her. He tells him of his childhood blighted by poverty and of the redeeming pride he has always felt in Stan's talents and achievements. And on one occasion, in a sudden collapse of the courage he has struggled hard to maintain, he tells him of the fear he has of a painful and long drawn-out death.

Stan visits Cathy in Manchester every other weekend, departing on Friday and returning on Sunday for the start of his working week. Uncle Herbert spends Friday and Saturday nights in the Walker house, sitting up with Dad, talking to him in his waking moments, and snatching whatever rest he can during Dad's own restless sleep.

Towards the end of March, Stan returned one Sunday evening from Manchester to find the curtains of the house drawn closed. As he entered the sitting-room he saw that the bed was empty and neatly made up. Uncle Herbert was sitting on the sofa. He told Stan that Dad had fallen into a coma sometime during Saturday and had died during the early hours of that Sunday morning.

He had outlived his wife Sally by nine months.

**24**

## The Middle of the Journey

The weather has changed. Plumes of dark cloud move across a broken grey sky in which canyons of blue open and close like memories of the previous day's radiance. Stan tries to accelerate their pace, anxious to make progress before the onset of the rain that was promised by the morning's forecast. But Don is in no hurry. He seems immune to changes in the weather; his jacket is unzipped, his shirt-collar open. Only the woollen hat that he has put on for the first time that morning is a concession to the deteriorating conditions. He stops by Malham Tarn to emphasise a point he is making about the religious orders who once colonised these parts. The wind ruffles the surface of the lake flicking spume into the air and leaving little sequins of dew on his moustache and eyebrows.

'Do you know that the monks of Rievaulx and Fountains Abbey were pioneers in the breeding of sheep?'

Stan does; he nods and begins to move on. Don falls in beside him, discoursing on sheep and their role in the creation of the landscape.

'From wilderness to sheep pasture. That's the story of these fells.'

Stan knows this too but he keeps silent. He has to admit that Don also tells him things that he doesn't know. He is impressively well read on the history and way of life of the Dales. That and his experience of farming have given him an understanding of the area that makes Stan feel the tenuousness of his own connection with it. The hill-farmers of whose lives Don seems to have an intimate knowledge are for Stan figures in the landscape, their daily struggles lost in the unfolding vistas of hills, valleys and skies.

He is troubled by this. After over thirty years tramping these northern parts that he views as his home territory he should know more. He should be able to read the detail of a landscape which is the historical creation of centuries of human habitation and work. He should be able to recognise its underlying rock formations, its vegetation and its wildlife. But his plans to study geology and natural history have never been put into effect. Now and again he joins his friend and ex-colleague Jeff Birkett, a devoted observer of nature. They sit in hides and squat behind hedges, spying on bird and beast. Jeff delivers whispered observations on plumage, mating calls, nesting habits and the like. Knowing is seeing, he says; to be able to tell the difference between a tree sparrow and a house sparrow is to see both more clearly and in detail. Stan agrees but feels that such knowledge comes only to the observant and that he, Stan, is not very observant. Broad landscapes and the changing moods of weather and atmosphere are what please him; detail is not his strong point. Above all he cherishes those moments of sudden awe like his encounter the previous day with the fox, moments that catch him unawares and seem to touch some hidden depth of self-estrangement where all is still. He remembers other such moments: a herd of racing deer on a wind-torn flank of Ben Macdhui, a rim of dark forest glimpsed through the winter light of a late afternoon in north Northumberland…

'Yes, I'm fond of our woolly friends. Nothing would be the same without them.'

Don is smiling sideways at him.

'I beg your pardon?'

'Sheep, Stanley! I'm talking about sheep. You haven't been listening to a word I've said.'

For several days they walk and talk.

On Fountains Fell, the jostling wind plucks at their speech, carrying off words and phrases into the air, snaffling whole sentences with sudden sweeping gusts. As they cross the summit of the fell, with the long, hump-backed mass of Pen-y-ghent across the valley cleaving the gale-driven streamers of mist and cloud, they discuss the state of modern youth, bellowing their views on pop music and the legalisation of cannabis into the swirling air. By a pot-hole on the green road out of Horton-in-Ribblesdale, they ponder the geology of limestone while taking their morning drink. Don quotes *Kubla Khan*, one of the few poems he remembers from his schooldays. Coleridge's image of a river running through 'caverns measureless to man' is how he imagines the earth beneath their feet, a vast labyrinth of caves and passages full of rushing water - and everything completely black. Stan, who has been reading Auden, responds by quoting *In Praise of Limestone*. Don says it sounds an interesting piece but he cannot approve of a man who quit his country during the war; personally he prefers Kipling. Stan is tempted to object, feeling sure that in disputations about poetry he would have the edge. But he lets it pass.

In these divergences of will and inclination he tends to yield; such things don't matter he tells himself. But he sometimes wonders whether a person's tally of things that don't matter is a measure of some larger indifference towards things that do. He remembers again his conversation with Marie Salasca all those years ago. 'Sometimes nothing seems to matter because of the way things are.' Strange words for a youth of seventeen. Stranger still that they remain true for his sixty-year-old self.

Such thoughts make him want to recover his solitude and freedom. He did not embark on the Pennine Way in order to indulge in fits of self-analysis but self-analysis seems inseparable from his relations with Don Crick.

They spend the night in the village of Hawes. In a public house, over his 'nightcap' of whisky and water, Don expresses his firm belief that the world is entering into a new war of the faiths between Christianity and the Muslim world. This, he explains, is the significance of the attack on the Twin Towers; the war in Iraq is but a new phase of the conflict.

'We must hold to the alliance with America. It's served us well before and will do so again.'

Stan is tempted to try to change the subject but feels he must offer some resistance to Don's overbearing certainties. He is becoming irritated with his own tendency to appease. He says: 'Even if they drag us into unjustifiable wars?'

'In the long run we have no choice. The world is a dangerous place and increasingly polarised. It's us and them.'

'Them being Islam?'

'And others. The Chinese, the Russians. Whatever our differences with the Americans they are our people. We have a common history, a common language and religion. As I say, in the long run we have no choice.'

His manner is becoming peremptory. He finishes his drink and brings the glass down onto the table with a smack of finality. Stan feels himself getting cross.

'What about Europe? The Europeans take a different view of Iraq.'

'Europe is decadent, a refuge for crypto-pacifists. You would think a continent that has experienced two world wars would know a thing or two about the brutal truths of human history but Europe seems to have forgotten them. They even refuse to pay for their own defence. It's the Americans who have done that for them for the last half-century.'

'Maybe it's their experience of two world wars that makes them wary of invading other people's countries.'

Despite his anger he knows this is a facile gibe. Hypocritical too. Somewhere at the back of his mind he is reliving similar conversations with Annie but ones in which he argued a different case. She had asked him to join her on the demonstration against the invasion of Iraq and was disappointed by his refusal. Since then they have quarrelled frequently over the rights and wrongs of the war. He is dismayed by the venom of her attacks on America and her flattering view of Chirac (a wily old chancer in Stan's opinion) whom she sees as a statesman replete with the wisdom of old

Europe. He is now uncomfortably aware that if he takes one step further in his debate with Don he will be arguing the same himself. But the words that are already forming in his head engulf him in their wave of indignation and sweep away all thought of tact.

'I'm not an uncritical admirer of President Chirac.' Don begins to nod his agreement. 'But all things are relative. Compared with Bush he's a fount of political wisdom. I don't know what drives the Americans, whether it's half-baked idealism or naked self-interest, but with a President who's a Texan hick, ignorant of the world and up to his neck in oil interests, you have to be worried. Who knows whether Saddam's got the weapons and who the hell cares? Are you telling me some rust-bucket state in the Middle East is a serious threat to the most powerful nation in human history? And if we're engaged in a war of the faiths, God help us, because there's not much faith in anything over here – except money. We'll lose hands down.'

He stops, already regretting his drift into tirade, and reaches for his glass of beer. Don's expression is unchanged except for a slight pursing of the lips. After a pause of some moments he says stiffly: 'Well of course I don't agree with any of that.' He looks around the bar and glances at his watch. 'I wonder whether we shouldn't be getting back to the hostel.'

They climb the long curving flank of Great Shunner Fell enveloped in a mist so dense it seems to press on the lobes of Stan's brain, slowing speech and thought. Don is unusually quiet. The previous evening's dispute has left them both subdued. To have quarrelled seems to have given to their relationship a sudden and undue closeness that Stan finds embarrassing and oppressive. He had thought of suggesting that morning that they go their separate ways but was held back by the feeling that to do so would have been an admission of failure. They had smoothed things over. Don had apologised for what he called his 'tendency to pontificate', Stan had regretted the sharpness of his outburst. But their climb up into this world of thick, muffling greyness has renewed the uneasy silence between them, locking each into his private world.

Stan is having difficulty finding his rhythm. His breathing is an irregular panting, as though his chest cavity has shrunk and is squeezing the air from his lungs. His arms feel heavy with the effort of working his trekking poles. He puts it all down to the curious mental state he is in, in which the anxiety he feels over the previous night's quarrel seems locked in on itself and intensified by the damp, smothering shroud of mist.

Two Swaledale sheep appear by the path. For a moment their black faces seem to hover unattached before two grey fleeces loom into shape around them like coagulations of the fog. In order to give himself a rest and break the silence, Stan stops and says: 'Have you ever farmed sheep?'

He knows the question is absurd and that fruit-farming in Herefordshire has little in common with sheep-rearing in the Dales. But Don accepts the gesture; he stops and smiles and says that he had once been tempted by the idea of hill-farming but felt there was no future in it. Subsequent events - the outbreaks of disease, the declining demand for wool, the power of the supermarkets – have confirmed his view.

'Their glory days are past I'm afraid. It's astonishing when you think about it that such dull, modest creatures were once the engines of the nation's economy.'

He is suddenly back in full flow. 'These valleys would once have been full of people spinning, weaving and knitting wool.' He stops and stares at the Swaledales while continuing to talk. They stare back, their faces impassive, heedless of their historic achievement.

Stan joins in, eager to blow away the remaining vestiges of last night's disagreement and lighten his mood. He tells Don of his paternal grandfather who worked in a woollen mill in Huddersfield and who he feels gives him a family connection to this landscape. They begin to walk on. The conversation broadens to encompass the industrial revolution and the coming of the railways. Don extols the beauty of the Ribblehead Viaduct that stands a few miles away; Stan concurs while lamenting the deaths of the navvies who built it. They cross the sea to Ireland and beyond; they debate the Potato Famine, the Easter Rising, the pros and cons of the British Empire. In the interests of diplomacy Stan stills his misgivings as Don acclaims the imperial legacy in India.

The inn stands in isolation by a junction of moorland roads, an incongruous outpost of commerce in an empty landscape. A weak autumnal sun has forced its way through, thinning the morning mist to a nebulous glow that lightens the browns and purples of the surrounding fells. The countryside falls away to the north dissolving colours and shapes into blurred distances.

According to Don the inn's reputation as the highest in England requires them to stop and take a drink, perhaps even forego their sandwiches and have something to eat from the pub menu instead.

'I think we deserve a treat, don't you?' he says.

'Absolutely. Anything to give us a rest from cheese sandwiches.'

'And from vacuum-flask coffee?' Don grins in remembrance of their first meeting that is now ten days ago.

'And from vacuum-flask coffee.'

On the strip of ground between the road and the inn cars are parked. A few customers sit drinking at wooden tables. From somewhere out of sight the roar and whine of accelerating motorcycles pierces the air. As they approach the door of the inn Stan catches sight of them coming over the brow of a hill, three figures arched over their machines, swaying into a bend of the road like beetles in heavy flight.

He doesn't really want to eat at the Tan Hill Inn; cheese sandwiches suit him fine. As he works his way through the fish and chips and sherry trifle that he awards himself as a consolation prize for this latest acquiescence in Don's wishes, he decides that it is time for them to part. He will make the point that evening. He will offer no apology or justification, he will simply say that he would like to be on his own for a few days. He might suggest they meet up again further along the Way while relying on Don's tact and good sense to realise that he would prefer not to.

They are leaving the inn when they hear the commotion, a sudden burst of male laughter pierced by a female voice raised in protest. Stan looks round to see the motorcyclists he had glimpsed earlier forcing themselves onto a wooden bench already occupied by a young couple. One of them, his bulky frame given added menace by his black leathers and knee-high boots, is trying to put his arm around the girl of the couple. Stan feels a warning flush of apprehension. The girl is unattractive, thin and sharp-featured with sparse blond hair, and wearing a greyish walking fleece that flattens the outline of her already poorly shaped body. The attentions of the motorcyclist are a pitiless affront to her lack of beauty. He tries to turn her face towards him with his free hand. The girl stiffens her neck and stares straight ahead. Her companion – a pale and angular youth jammed like a prisoner between her and the two other motorcyclists – looks on with the weakly beseeching smile of the helpless.

Stan knows he must do something; he must intervene, as much for his own sake as for the couple's. He knows what will follow if he doesn't: the souring of his day by the memory of his little act of cowardice. The boyfriend of the girl is now sitting with his head bowed and his hands clasped together on his lap. Stan feels a wrench of pity for his humiliated state. He must act! But before he can move, perhaps before he has made up his mind to move, Don has stepped forward.

'Alright lad, you've had your fun. I think you ought to leave her alone now.'

He speaks calmly but with firm deliberation. The broad boney shoulders and square chest seem to render visible the authority in his voice. The biker looks up. He is young, barely of an age to have his motorcyclist's licence. He hesitates, weighing the balance of forces. His two companions are young too, and slighter than he. Stan cannot decide whether they are committed to the persecution of the couple; the one closest to the end of the bench has turned his head away from the action and is staring intently at the ground.

A small blue truck pulls onto the parking strip; in the front seat are two workmen in white overalls. They get out and stop to stare across for a moment. The biker says: 'OK, Pop. Take it easy. Just having a joke.' He removes his arm from the girl's shoulder with forced casualness. She immediately stands up and begins to walk quickly towards one of the parked cars, followed by her companion. As Don and Stan cross the parking strip to join the road they hear the bikers laughing; Stan catches the phrase 'fucking tourists'. Don smiles and shakes his head: 'Where would they be without the f-word? Ah well, boys will be boys. I suppose they'll grow out of it.'

Out on the road they walk single file along the edge. Don stops and mutters something about wanting to check the distance to Bowes. He removes his rucksack which he places on the road at his feet, and takes out a map. Stan stops further along the road to wait for him. The inn is now out of sight but he can hear the bikers revving their engines in the car-park. A few seconds later they swing into view, accelerating along the road towards Don and Stan with their headlights switched on though the morning mist has now completely cleared. Stan steps quickly off the road onto the verge of rough moor grass and shouts to Don to do the same. Don either doesn't hear or is too slow to make the move. As the bikers surge past him, whooping and shouting above the roar of their engines, the last of the three slows down and swings out a gauntleted fist that strikes Don a blow on the back of the neck. Don topples forward over his rucksack, reaching out a hand to break his fall. His head seems to bounce as it hits the hard surface of the road.

Stan rushes towards him. To his surprise and relief Don is already moving, trying to push himself up with his arm. He stops halfway. Stan drops his rucksack and trekking poles and bends to grip his arm and prevent him falling back onto the road. His eyes are glazed with concussion. From his temple to his cheekbone blood is seeping from the scraped and bruised flesh. As Stan fumbles in his pocket for a handkerchief the blue van that he had seen earlier in the car-park approaches along the road. He waves the handkerchief to flag it down. The workman in the passenger seat winds down the window and shouts: 'You alright mate?'

'I could do with some help.'

There is a brief exchange between the two workmen and they both get out. Stan asks them if they can get Don to a hospital or at least a doctor's surgery. He senses some reluctance on the part of the driver of the van but the one who has spoken to him, a young man in his twenties with an ear-ring and hair that trails in long greasy straggles down to his shoulders, bends down to examine Don's wound. He says: 'He needs to get that sorted. How did it happen?'

Stan explains. The young man shakes his head and takes another look at the wound. A thick worm of blood has descended Don's cheek and reached the edge of his moustache. Don hasn't yet spoken but his eyes are now focussed on the young man as he takes Stan's handkerchief, wipes away the trickle of blood and holds the handkerchief over the wound while talking over his shoulder to his colleague. It emerges that they are heading for Darlington to do some building work on a new housing estate. The young man says: 'We could drop him off on the way, at Reeth or Richmond. Mind you we've only got room for one of you in the cab. You'll have to jump onto the back of the truck. We'll shift our gear around so you can sit down.'

Don shows sudden signs of animation. 'No,' he says. 'I'll come on my own.' His voice is weak and strained with the effort of speaking. For the first time since they met he looks and sounds to Stan like an old man. He looks up at Stan and says: 'You carry on and finish the Way. I'll be fine.'

This is too expedient for Stan to resist. He and the young man help Don to his feet and into the cab of the truck. It is only when the truck has set off, with Don propped between the workmen holding Stan's handkerchief to the side of his head, that Stan realises that he has no way of contacting Don Crick again.

He hears the rain before he sees it, pattering on the heather behind him as it sweeps in from the north. Within minutes it is torrential and the hillside on the other side of the valley is obscured by downward-writhing veils that drift across it on the wind. Only the red signs of the military firing-range stand out at intervals on the moor, warning of the dangers of the shelled area. He is hungry and thirsty but reluctant to stop in such an exposed place. The rain eases as suddenly as it came; the cloud that carried it floats overhead, trailing ragged edges like thinning smoke. He presses on, uneasily aware of his isolation in the vast waste of Upper Teesdale. He imagines himself as he might appear to some rifleman on the distant hillside, a smudge of colour appearing and disappearing through the sheets of rain, caught in the sights of a gun. Such flights of paranoia he puts down to the anguished, self-judging frame of mind he has got into in the last few days.

He stops at the footbridge over the Maize Beck to eat the sandwiches he packed this morning. The beck is in spate after two days of rain. He stares at it as he chews, half-mesmerised by the sliding, roiling mass of peat-stained water. Deep, moving water fascinates him, drawing him into its elemental otherworld, dulling his sense of time and place. A sudden shiver brings him back to himself. The sweat inside his shirt is cooling on his body, he must move. He detaches his gaze from the flowing water and takes up his rucksack.

He has regained his solitude but not the peace of mind that went with it. He replays obsessively in his head the events on the road outside the inn. The approaching glare of the bikers' headlights and the cool deliberation of the blow that felled Don Crick have taken on a sinister, malign quality in his mind. He has brooded on his own failure to intervene in the earlier confrontation in the car-park and felt shame at his timidity and indecisiveness.

But *was* it timidity and indecisiveness? Surely he is being too hard on himself. He feels certain that he would have spoken given the chance; he was indeed on the point of doing so but Don's intervention trumped his own. Bad timing, that's all it was; the few seconds required to gather his thoughts and words were denied him by a man who, it has to be said, was decisive almost to a fault. Wasn't that the essential difference between them, the difference that underlay all their debates and disagreements? Don's abundant, some would say excessive, self-assurance versus Stan's more circumspect, perhaps more thoughtful, approach.

But he cannot convince himself. Nor can he change what happened by his repeated re-imagining of the event in the form of outcomes less demeaning to himself. The time to act was then, not now in memories adjusted to accommodate the actions that he might have taken had he been more…well…decisive.

He has arrived at the edge of a deep ravine. The rain has stopped but dark bellying clouds promise further downpours. For a few moments the name of the place escapes him; he sees only a chasm in the earth's crust gouged out by the savage power of ice. A rim of dark crags falls away through striations of rock and scree to a distant valley-bottom that is barely visible in the faltering light. He has a feeling of light-headedness that seems to spread downward through his limbs like a sudden loss of body weight. He presses down on his trekking poles in order to feel the solid, anchoring earth. Suddenly he remembers the name: High Cup! That he could have forgotten it, however briefly, is strange and unnerving for it is a place that he has visited several times before. He takes out his map and stares for a moment at the tightly drawn contours of the two sides of the valley. They have a sinuous grace that seems to endow the random effects of geology with artistic deliberation. The map itself is a work of art, a masterpiece of functional design that orders the chaotic landscape into a dense and intricate abstract of line and colour, symbol, name and number. He fits the contours of the map to the deep valley before him, noticing now the valley's elegance of symmetry and proportion, the smooth downward sweep of the two flanks that are like cupped hands, their meeting-point soldered by the stream that threads the valley bottom. High Cup indeed: a well-named place.

Order restored, he returns the map to his rucksack pocket and sets off to locate the path down to the village of Dufton. A sudden shower catches him before he can raise the hood of his jacket, sending a cold drip down the nape of his neck. He quickens his pace. It has been one of the hardest days of the whole walk. The familiar nodes of pain – neck, thumbs and knee – are but special cases of a general distress. His clothes are stuck to his skin with a gum of dried sweat and rain.

The path broadens into a rough cart-track leading sharply downhill. He can see the village in the distance, a blur of dark-grey buildings among trees beneath a lowering sky. Once, during the early years of his marriage, he spent a week in Dufton with Cathy and Annie, and the place holds happy memories for him. Tonight he will turn in early and tomorrow he will take a rest day there, potter around, and perhaps take a look at the place they rented all those years ago.

On the far horizon a strip of incandescent light is opening up beneath the base of the cloud. Within it he can see the faint outline of the mountains of the Lake District, transparent as glass in the blaze of the setting sun.

The cottage is as he remembers it except for an ivy plant that has spread up alongside the door and above the downstairs window. Its leaves rustle softly in the morning breeze. He tries to see into the sitting-room but the reflected sun flashes back at him from the window-panes. He wanders slowly away, turns round and passes again by the front of the house. He would like someone to emerge so that he can tell them that he stayed here over twenty years ago, and perhaps get himself invited in to look around. There is a path that runs alongside the house to the garden at the back. He is tempted to go along it and take a look. It is the garden that he remembers best, a lawn enclosed by flower-beds and a hedge of matted thorn bushes. Here they sat and sunbathed, ate and drank and read their books while Annie pottered around with her toy watering-can and spade. As the week progressed it became a haven from which they were reluctant to move.

It must have been 1979 for Margaret Thatcher had recently won her first General Election. He remembers Cathy calling him from the door that led into the garden; the report of the new government's first budget was coming through on the radio, was he interested? He shook his head and sank back into the depths of his deck-chair. Through his eyelids half-closed against the glare of the sun he could see Annie waddling away from him towards the edge of the lawn. Beneath the bulge of her nappy her legs are podgy and pinky-brown. She stops at the flower-bed, swaying like a drunk, as though trying to decide whether to launch herself into it. He calls to her softly. She turns and falls down, picks herself up and staggers stiff-legged back across the lawn to her father, her hands outstretched to receive his welcome. As he sweeps her into his lap he glimpses Cathy watching and smiling at the door.

It was a moment of the purest fulfilment, his love for his daughter a bubbling spring of tenderness and delight, his love for his wife a passion that he thought would never die. Indeed he wonders whether it ever has, whether the obscure sense of loss and yearning he still feels when he thinks of Cathy is not the smouldering vestige of a love that even now would burst into flames if she were to return to him. If she were to return to him! After seventeen years apart! The fact that he can still entertain such a fantasy is evidence enough that his condition is incurable.

He steps onto the path beside the cottage, treading lightly and feeling shifty and foolish. He is drawn on by curiosity rather than nostalgia. He knows the garden is bound to have changed, and the mild disappointment he feels on discovering the soulless makeover that confronts him – an oblong of pink paving-slabs where the lawn had been, surrounded by a fence of bare wooden boards - is purely aesthetic. His dominant feeling is one of curiosity satisfied. He returns to the street and resumes his walk around the village, limping slightly from his sore knee.

Of course their relationship was unequal; he always knew that. There was something in her that he could not satisfy, a recklessness and a love of recklessness in others that had found a fellow spirit in Rod Barnett. After her separation from Rod she missed her expeditions with his gang, and tried to interest Stan in rock-climbing. Stan, remembering his difficult childhood relationship with trees and drainpipes, demurred. She insisted; she borrowed ropes, harnesses and hardware. He, fearing to disappoint her, forced himself to the task and discovered that the reassurance given by Cathy fixing the rope above him as they climbed, calm and competent in everything she did, was sufficient to enable him to tackle routes of modest difficulty. Nevertheless, it was a relief to him that her pregnancy intervened before she asked him to take the decisive step and lead a climb for the first time.

It was the pregnancy that hastened their marriage, though of course it didn't cause it. They had more or less decided that once her divorce came through they would marry. Any slight hesitancy on her part sprang from her wariness of stepping too hastily from one marriage into another. It was understandable really.

He walks out along the minor road beyond the end of the village in order to take a look at the hills he will traverse tomorrow. The sky is overcast. To his right a ruff of grey cloud encircles the summit of Dufton Pike and cloud lies thick like fur in the folds and gullies of the hills to the north. He turns round and heads back to the village. He takes an early lunch: slices of stringy beef and a Yorkshire pudding whose rapid transit from deep-freeze through microwave to his plate has left it dry of sap and flavour. He lingers over his coffee, feeling morose, half-regretting that he has taken a day of rest in this place that kindles sobering memories.

Annie's birth was difficult for her, both physically and mentally. The depression that had stalked her since the death of her father returned; it was six months before she could interest herself in her child. Later, the delight she took in the flowering of Annie's intelligence, wit and energy was tinged with a sort of bewilderment at the fate that had befallen her. She was never what you might call motherly. Not cut out for it she said. She returned to part-time work as soon after the birth as was possible but the combination of secretarial work with the role of housewife and mother failed to satisfy her. She was becoming frustrated with her life; the years were passing and she would soon be into her forties; her ambition to write seemed a dream fading ever further out of sight.

His attitude to his own work fed her frustration. Soon after the death of his father he had left Blackett's Bearings to live and work in Manchester. The first post that came his way, and that he viewed as a stop-gap pending his move to higher and more lucrative things, was as an administrator in a small technical college. The gap thus stopped grew into a period of time, the period of time stretched to several years. By the time he stirred himself to look for work elsewhere, the widespread business closures of the early eighties had narrowed his opportunities.

Screwed by Thatcher and his own lack of ambition was how Cathy put it. It was one of the recurring themes of the scratchy discussions they had on matters ranging from the state of their finances to the state of the nation itself. The spirit of that angry and contentious time seemed to have settled over their household. Although of no very strong political persuasion, Cathy was a devout critic of Margaret Thatcher in whom she claimed to see what she called 'the petty-bourgeois myopia' of her mother. Helen was still living with Dot in Oldham and the two of them formed a worshipful Thatcherite sect, thrilled by the coming to power of a figure who gave such downright expression to their view of the world. Cathy would return from her visits to Oldham fuming over the inanities she had heard and cursing her fate that the Prime Minister of the

United Kingdom had turned out to be her mother in a blond wig and bright-blue suit. When Stan wondered aloud whether such emotional identification made for very sensible politics she accused him of being priggish. Too detached, a cold fish.

He remembers the aftermath of one of Annie's birthday parties that took place during their time in Newcastle. Stan's friend and colleague, Jeff Birkett, had arrived to pick up his son Alex, the last remaining member of the clamorous mob who had wreaked havoc through the Walkers' house for the previous three hours. Jeff, Cathy and Stan sat drinking beer while Alex and Annie were off-stage, scuffling and laughing in one of the upstairs rooms. Cathy was recounting her latest visit to Oldham during which she had quarrelled with Dot and Helen over their purchase of a modest but profitable handful of shares in one of the privatised utilities.

'I hadn't given the matter much thought before, but to see them calculating their gains brought it home to me. We're flogging off the family silver as Macmillan said.'

'But the fact that your mother's benefited from privatisation doesn't mean you have to be against it. You bring too much family baggage to your politics.'

'I could argue that you don't bring enough.'

'What do you mean by that?'

He knows well enough what she means for they have been here before. She goes silent and casts a quick glance at Jeff who decides to take a tactical pull at his beer. Stan continues: 'If you mean the miners' strike you couldn't be more wrong. I didn't like Scargill but I was with the miners one hundred percent. How could you think otherwise?'

'I thought you dithered rather. I was surprised that's all, given your family background.'

'I didn't dither. I was divided, as many people were. I thought Scargill was a political adventurer who was leading the miners to disaster. No amount of emoting over my family background could

227

get round that awkward fact. And when you look at what happened you can hardly say I was wrong.'

He can see from her hesitation that she feels wrong-footed and is struggling to find a response. Though low blows are not her stock-in-trade they are not to be spurned *in extremis*.

'It's people like you who brought Thatcher in.'

This stings. His voice rises to a yelp of incredulity. 'What? How do you make that out? I never voted for Thatcher. I've never voted Tory in my life.'

'No but you voted for the Liberals in elections she won. You split the vote and let her in. You were a part of the swing to the right.'

Jeff has drained his glass and is smiling at them.

'Now you two. Don't spoil the party.'

Cathy smiles back at him, grateful for the chance to cool the temperature. Stan shifts into facetious mode.

'I was part of the movement of history, a fleck of foam on the ideological wave that brought Thatcher to power. A mere fleck of foam. A little man in a big crowd.'

Cathy gets up and goes to check on the children. Jeff says: 'You're just spreading the blame, Stan. But there's no need. You're allowed to vote for whoever you like.'

He is smiling in a way that may be conspiratorial. In this middle-class suburb of Newcastle, the Walkers and their friends are an enclave of the left-leaning public sector. Jeff alone is suspected of being a closet Tory. His insistence on the privacy of his own voting record is widely taken to be incontrovertible evidence of reactionary tendencies.

Stan says: 'I'm not spreading the blame. There is no blame to spread. Voting Labour is neither an obligation nor a virtue. I'm just saying that, along with lots of other people, I moved on. We were disillusioned by the events of the seventies. The bitterness entered our collective soul.'

He feels anxious for reasons he cannot identify but that seem to have little to do with the conversation he has just had. He is breathing heavily and can feel a prickle of sweat on his forehead. Cathy returns with Alex clutching his party-bag and balloon. Jeff reminds Stan that they are going to the match the next evening. He will pick him up after tea. They must not be late or he will be unable to find a parking space. Stan accompanies him to the door and returns to the sitting-room. The carpet is covered in wrapping paper, burst balloon-skins and fragments of food. As he bends to start clearing the mess he can hear Cathy and Annie talking in the kitchen. Their voices fade suddenly as though the sound is being sucked out of the air. The light dims in his head and he pitches forward into utter blackness.

# 25

## Matters of the Heart

The man on the screen is an enthusiast. Stan can tell he is an enthusiast because he cannot keep still. He is striding around the television studio, pointing to charts and diagrams, and emitting astonishing pieces of information in a loud and enthusiastic voice. Apparently the space-craft in question rivals in complexity the human body itself. It contains a zillion microchips and a tangle of wiring and tubes that would put a barrel of spaghetti to shame, the whole thing being geared to one sole purpose – to challenge the mysteries of outer space. That, he informs the viewers, is why it is called Challenger.

Stan looks sideways to Eddie, gingerly, taking care not to disturb the pads on his chest. There are just the two of them, Stan and Eddie, in this narrow annexe of the main ward, with two empty beds between them. Eddie is asleep and completely still. He's like that, Eddie, one minute awake and watching the television, which is all he can do at the moment, the next minute flat out like a baby, his bottle the drip.

The shuttle is on the launch pad, strapped to its booster rockets. It looks like a temple with a soaring central dome flanked by slender minarets. Someone is speaking in voice-over. His tone is hushed and solemn, almost reverential. A group of astronauts in shiny light-blue space-suits are climbing onto the bus that will take them to the launch pad. They have broad American smiles on their faces, and one of them is a woman. She is pretty in a homely, girl-next-door sort of way and she waves energetically at the camera. She seems bursting with the anticipated pleasure and excitement of what she is about to experience. The voice-over says that she has won a competition for a place on the mission. She is a teacher, someone with whom ordinary Americans can identify.

He looks sideways again, gingerly. The light outside fades as a dark cloud crosses the sun. In the sudden gloom Eddie is so still he appears sculpted in the rock of his bed. He stirs some distant memory but Stan cannot pin it down. He can make out the needle of Eddie's drip like a blood-sucking tick on his forearm. There is something up his nose as well, held on by a bit of plaster like insulating tape across his cheek.

The presenter is speaking again. He explains that during take-off the astronauts will be lying rather than sitting in their seats. Stan realises what it is Eddie reminds him of – the statue of a knight on a slab seen during a visit to a church with Cathy some years previously. He remembers the shaft of light from a high window catching the foot of pitted stone. Further up, the stone of the legs and body shone like dark, polished metal. It was the head that had suffered the worst damage, so badly chipped and eroded that it appeared little more than a shapeless excrescence of the tomb itself. Stone on stone, the body's continuity with the mineral world, the perfect stillness of stone.

The screen is showing the control-centre, a line of men and women staring into monitors. The presenter announces that, barring last-minute hitches, it will soon be all-systems-go for Challenger. He repeats the phrase. All systems go.

Stan looks across at Eddie. Immobile, set in stone, his trailing tubes barely visible in the gloom. All systems gone.

Except that it was the other way about. It was the shuttle that wouldn't go. It was some problem with the weather that caused them to put it off for another day. Meanwhile Eddie struggled back to the surface again. Stan hears him groan and start sucking his dry mouth. He mumbles something Stan can't catch, then mumbles it again, this time more clearly. He needs a drink. Stan presses the attention button above the head of his bed. The nurse who appears at the door is the very young one, Donna. Some of the nurses look as though they have been poured into their uniforms, their plump arms tight against the short sleeves, the uniform a supple second skin. Donna is different. Hers seems to have been slotted over her like the outside part of an empty match-box. You feel that her skinny arms and legs might rub themselves sore on the stiff edges. She has short bubbly hair and a nice young girl's smile that shows all her teeth. She pours Eddie's juice and holds his head forward so that he can drink. Her movements are awkward and lack the confidence of the older nurses that enables them to be quick and protective at the same time. As Eddie drinks, she chats to him about how well he is doing and how pleased his visitors will be when they arrive. She talks comfortably as though she is gossiping with a neighbour. Eddie finishes his drink. Donna takes the glass away and places it on the side table while continuing to hold his head with her other arm. Then she gently lowers him to the pillow, leaving him propped at an angle sufficient to enable him to view the television.

'There now. I'll pop back in half an hour to see how you are, and then it'll nearly be tea-time. We'll see if you can manage a bit more than you did at lunch.'

Eddie moves his hand out from the centre of the bed to touch hers which is resting on the edge. She smiles down at him, pats the back of his hand and goes off. Within seconds Eddie is snoring gently through his tube.

Stan is worried. His blackout may not in itself have been serious (in fact the word 'blackout' seems too dramatic for the brief loss of consciousness – no more than a few seconds – that pitched him onto the sitting-room carpet as he was clearing up after Annie's birthday party) but there had been worrying signs for some time: sudden fluctuations in the rhythm of his heart-beat and, at moments of stress, a prickling sensation across the shoulders accompanied by sweating and a tightening of his chest. These were the symptoms he had awoken to after his faint. Convinced he was having a heart attack he had asked Cathy to get an ambulance. The fact that he is now sitting in a hospital bed has shifted the event into a different and more sombre key. Matters are not helped by Eddie. Not good for morale, Eddie: four hours having surgery, then groaning into consciousness as Stan was putting his pyjamas on. Stan feels anxious and lonely, and finds himself looking forward to Cathy's evening visit.

When she arrives it is nearly eight o'clock and she appears tense beneath her smile. She says it is because there is an evening match on in the city and she's been trapped in the traffic, but he wonders whether she simply cannot see the point of coming in tonight for the consultant has said that he will be discharged tomorrow unless the tests uncover something much more serious than he expects. Stan wants to say something to mollify her but seems unable to find the words. They talk desultorily about family matters - repairs to the house, her visit to see her mother in Oldham -, then make last-minute arrangements for the next day. Stan expects to see the consultant with the results of the tests immediately after lunch. He will phone Cathy and she will drive in to pick him up. They kiss awkwardly and she leaves.

After lunch next day his anxiety increases. It would help if he could do something, walk around, look out of the window. They've taken the pads off his chest so he's free, but he hesitates to get out of bed. He should have asked the nurse before she left. Fear of medics, strange at his age. They've got him by the short and curlies: nurses, doctors, and consultants in ascending order of tightness of grip.

Then suddenly he is there standing at the foot of the bed, Mr Borthwick, the consultant. He is younger and more diffident than a consultant should be. He seems to hesitate over whether to disturb Stan's thoughts. It's the ward sister who brings him back to reality.

'Mr Walker. Mr Borthwick would like a few words with you.'

It is all so quick and casual that it takes a few seconds for it to sink in. They can find nothing wrong with him. The heart seems to be in excellent condition. The occasional rhythmic abnormality is due to the electrical impulses that govern the beat. It's a common enough phenomenon and, in Stan's case, not serious enough to require any action. His blackout may have been due to the acute anxiety he has been undergoing in his personal and professional life. He was right to get himself brought in, especially in the light of his family history, but really there's nothing he should be worrying about unduly. He turns and moves on to Eddie. The ward sister draws the curtains around Eddie's bed.

Stan swings his legs over the side of the bed and feels the cool solid floor for the first time for two days, an astronaut touching *terra firma*. He glances at the ward clock – five to two – and makes a mental note to watch the launch of the rocket while waiting for Cathy. He is full of a sudden indulgence towards things. He wonders whether to get dressed first or go and phone Cathy. He hasn't been in hospital long enough to get used to the idea of wandering around in his pyjamas so he gets dressed and goes off to find the public telephone.

She is relieved when he tells her. She starts laughing and tells him how anxious she has been. He feels a rush of tenderness and guilt and says he's sorry he's been so much trouble. They'll make up for it he tells her. They'll really celebrate. When he has put the phone down he takes a walk along the hospital corridor to the main entrance. Outside, the weather is bright and crisp. The remains of the previous night's frost sparkle in the drive-way that runs in front of the building. He screws up his eyes against the glare and breathes in deeply the air of his liberation. To the right of the entrance there stands a middle-aged man in a dressing-gown and slippers. Stan smiles at him and says: 'Lovely day. Looks as though there was a fair old freeze last night.'

'Aye. It's a nice day, right enough. Makes a change from what we've been having.'

Stan wants to tell him that he's going out of the hospital, he's going home. He wants to tell him that he has been weighed down by anxiety but now it is all over and he is going home with his wife. They are going to celebrate and start afresh. Things haven't been going too well recently but they will make a new start now that

234

they have got this worry off their minds. Stan is about to speak when the man starts to cough, a deep retching cough that makes him purple with the effort. He turns away to spit into a drain by the side of the doors, supporting himself with one hand against the wall while holding the other firmly into his ribs. Stan turns back into the building, lifting his hand in a vague gesture of goodbye.

Back in the ward Eddie's curtains have been drawn back. The tube has been removed from his nose and he is propped up higher than usual on his pillows watching the television. As Stan arrives, Eddie smiles at him and nods in the direction of the screen. Stan sits on his bed to watch. The shuttle and its booster rockets stand on the pad dwarfed by the launch-tower, like a temple attached to a skyscraper. Beyond it the horizon is edged by a scarlet and orange sky that shades upwards into yellow, white and pale blue. The camera switches to a grandstand where the relations and friends of the astronauts await the launch. It picks out the mother and father of the woman astronaut. The voice-over talks of their pride in their daughter's achievement.

Stan turns to Eddie. 'You're looking much better today.'

'Yes. I feel a hundred-per-cent better.' His speech is clearer and the colour is returning to his face.

Stan remembers the visit of Eddie's wife and son the previous evening, and realises that during his strained conversation with Cathy some portion of his mind must have been registering their behaviour. He recalls the son's inability to look down at his father, his eyes flicking round the walls of the room as though seeking escape, or resting in studied absorption on the patterned quilt of the bed. He recalls Eddie's wife sitting close by the head of the bed talking quietly to Eddie, then, when he falls asleep, holding his hand until the end of the visiting period.

He says: 'Your wife and son will be pleased to see you looking so well.'

'Yes, they'll be here tonight. I'll look a different man.'

'It helps that they've taken your tube out.'

'The one from my nose, yes. Though the other's still there.' He looks down at his arm, then up at Stan, smiling. 'You've got to be grateful though, haven't you? It all helps to get you better.'

He suddenly seems weary with the effort of speaking. His eyes slide sideways to watch the television, signalling the end of the conversation.

The shuttle and its rockets stand upright against the bright sky. The voice-over is now that of the control-centre itself, calm and matter-of-fact. There are two minutes and twenty seconds to lift-off. Eddie starts to speak again, slowly and abstractedly, as if he's talking to himself.

'It's marvellous what they can do nowadays. All this progress.'

Stan isn't sure whether he is referring to the space-craft on the screen or the treatment that has given him the prospect of life. Perhaps both. Science is one and indivisible.

The countdown has begun. Stan concentrates his attention on the television. Five, four, three, two, one. Lift-off. Flowers of violent flame spill from the bottom of the craft. It seems to rise slowly, almost decorously, then tilts away from the camera and moves off. Stan looks round at Eddie. He is asleep. Donna appears at the doorway and glances in Eddie's direction. As she turns to leave she says to Stan: 'I think your wife's just arrived.'

Stan turns back to the television just in time to see the space-craft explode in a ball of fire and white smoke. Glowing pieces of debris shoot out from either side trailing white fleecy arms like stretched cotton wool. The voice-over talks of a major malfunction. Stan looks around the room at Eddie asleep and the two empty beds. Nothing has changed. He looks back at the screen, at the arms of smoke slowing and spreading as they reach out across the vast ice-blue sky. He feels shocked and agitated. At that moment Cathy enters the annexe. She is smiling and he notices she is wearing make-up and her best suit. She puts down the hand-bag she is carrying and steps quickly over to him.

'Are you alright, Stan?'

'Yes. But something bad has happened.'

Her face tightens with concern.

'No. Not to me. It's not me. Look.'

He takes her arm and turns her to face the television. The pictures are being played again in slow motion, juddering from frame to frame, and then freezing at the moment of the craft's explosion. He tries to fit this white, fleecy cloud on the screen to the enormity of what it contains: the screaming mayhem, the split-second terror of people becoming insensate, flung matter. His mind flashes to the woman and her happy, confident smile. Erased, scattered on the air. Or hurled at accelerating speed towards the ocean below. He suddenly remembers a remark the presenter made about the woman's children. She has children! They will be watching! He feels something rise within him like a wave of fever, an old pain that feels familiar but that he cannot yet name.

They are still watching! At this very moment, an ocean away, wishing back the minutes to before their lives were destroyed.

The wave reaches his throat and erupts into a sob. Cathy takes hold of him by the shoulders and stares anxiously into his face.

'What is it Stan? What's the matter? You're going to be alright now.'

He shakes his head but is unable to speak. She takes him in her arms, placing his head on her shoulder.

'Poor dear. You've had a bad few months. You're a bit overwrought. The good news hasn't had time to sink in. But you needn't worry any more. It's all over now, it's all over.'

She was right of course; he was overwrought. The previous months had been difficult, with their move to Newcastle and the start of his new job; two attempts to purchase a house had fallen through and he had been almost overwhelmed by the size of his workload. Then there were the symptoms that had preceded his blackout and the blackout itself. She was right, it had been a difficult time.

But that was not the whole story, and when he told her about the woman astronaut and her watching children, she put her hand to her mouth in a sudden, shocked realisation of what it was that had moved him. For a brief moment they were children again themselves, bound together by a flash of remembered horror.

The death of her father had been much on her mind in recent times. For over a year she had been involved in the writing of her novel, *Missing Dad*, and for the past six months she had tried in vain to find a publisher. It was Pip Slaley who suggested that she might try to work through an agent; he himself had a 'contact' who, he was pretty confident, would be willing to look at Cathy's work. Since their move to Newcastle Pip had become a lively if intermittent presence in their social world. In the diary of contacts and commitments that seemed to rule his life, meetings with the Walkers had figured a number of times since their arrival the previous September. It was now February and they had invited him and a friend for dinner.

The friend was a woman whom he introduced as Lola, though her comfortable local accent and English-rose appearance – blond hair, pale-to-pink skin without make-up and flawless except for a faint freckling round her nose and cheeks - belied the exotic promise of her name. She looked a good fifteen years younger than Pip and was chatty in a droll and self-deprecating way that Stan found appealing. When he remarked on her unusual name she explained that her mother - who ran a public house in Gateshead - had named her after Lola Montez, a nineteenth-century dancer and courtesan whom she had come across in a romantic novel she was reading during her pregnancy.

'My mother thought a courtesan was a lady of the court, so for her the name combined artistic talent with social distinction. Unfortunately I have neither.'

She turns the corners of her mouth down in a comic display of despondency. Stan says: 'Well she wasn't any old courtesan. At least the beds she slept in were high-class ones.'

'Including some king or other I believe.'

'That's right. Ludwig of Bavaria.'

'You're the first person I've met who knows anything about her.'

She seems impressed. Stan feels pleased with himself. She is further impressed to learn that he has a language degree and has worked in France and Spain. When he goes to check on the roast that he is preparing for their meal she accompanies him out of the room.

'I would love to speak foreign languages. Particularly Spanish. It must be the Lola thing. I'm attending classes in Spanish.'

'I must confess I don't speak my foreign languages much nowadays. They're rather rusty. I don't get over to the continent as often as I should, and with languages it's a question of 'use 'em or lose 'em'.'

She seems disappointed with this, as though it sullies the image she has of him as a free-wheeling cosmopolitan. He adds quickly: 'Of course it wouldn't take much to get them back into working order. We might have a longish spell abroad this summer.' (It is Cathy who has suggested this; he has made clear his preference for a walking holiday in the Yorkshire Dales.) 'I also do a fair bit of reading in French and Spanish.'

'I hardly read at all, even in English. Pip says I'm a philistine. I sometimes wonder what he sees in me.'

'What about beauty, lack of vanity and a great sense of humour!'

'What a nice thing to say.'

She seems genuinely surprised, as though she is not used to nice things being said to her. On a sudden impulse she gives him a quick kiss on the cheek and says he is a lovely man.

They returned to the sitting-room to find Pip and Cathy discussing publishing. Their visit to the kitchen seemed to have drawn some boundary line between them and Pip and Cathy that held firm throughout the evening. Stan was struck by Cathy's animation. Her speech and gestures had an edge of enthusiasm that he realised he had not seen for some time. Their recent upheavals had made her subdued and moody, and she sometimes complained at the lack of fun in their lives. Her inability to get her novel published added to her dissatisfaction.

It turned out that Pip's 'contact' in the publishing world was his first wife, Patricia, with whom he had maintained an amicable and, on occasion, commercially fruitful relationship.

'You see, our friendship always had a business side to it. We met in the late sixties. I was trying to get a foothold in journalism, she was interested in publishing. We set up our own little publishing company but it went bust within a year.'

Cathy says: 'Did you try any other business ventures?'

'No. The marriage went bust six months later. That was a sixties venture too.'

He is in high spirits and already seems slightly drunk, as though he has been drinking before his arrival.

'My wife was into all that sixties stuff. She believed in something she called cultural radicalism. It made for interesting politics but bad business. We had a catalogue made up almost exclusively of obscure erotic fiction and sex guides for advanced people. Our sales went from poor to worse than poor. I remember we published a booklet for young boys that we thought would appeal to sixties-type parents keen to give their sons a guilt-free puberty. We called it *Getting to Grips with Willies*. It sold not a single copy.'

Cathy bursts out laughing and Stan can see that she too, although a modest drinker, is already onto her second glass of wine. Her cheeks are flushed and her eyes are liquid-bright. He is surprised at her air of excitement. On sexual matters she is discreet to the point of primness. In the conversations they had after their reunion, when they filled in for each other the empty canvas of their years apart, she insisted that the sixties had passed her by. She said she had no regrets about that for she suspected it had passed most people by and was largely an invention of metropolitan hucksters.

He says in reply to Pip's story: 'Perhaps there weren't as many advanced people around in the sixties as the myth would have us believe.'

He looks to her for support, trying to draw her back to his side of the boundary, but she remains silent. Pip says: 'Oh but I'm sure there were. In my neck of the woods you hardly knew who you'd be sleeping with from one day to the next.'

Stan says: 'Ah! The acid test of sixties enlightenment.'

Cathy says: 'Well, it broke some pretty stifling taboos.'

He is astonished at the glibness of this. He is about to say: 'Including fidelity to your spouse?' but stops himself, not wishing to appear prudish and entrench further the division he feels opening up between him and them.

Months later, when suspicion first pierced his mind like an adder's sting, he remembered that moment as the point at which she began to seem a stranger to him. On the phone to Pip two days after the dinner-party (he had contacted her to confirm that Patricia had agreed to look at her manuscript) her responses were warm and familiar to a degree that contrasted with the reserve she normally displayed to acquaintances outside her immediate circle. Later she returned from a 'business' lunch with Pip flushed both with excitement at the prospect of the publication of her book and with unaccustomed daytime drinking.

Stan himself saw nothing of Pip for several weeks after the February dinner but he felt his growing presence in their life. Cathy announced one day that she was abandoning her part-time secretarial work in order to devote herself to her writing. She had not discussed the matter with Stan and he suspected Pip's influence for he had taken upon himself the role of mentor and adviser in her pursuit of a literary career. It was only during the next working day, as Stan's thoughts wandered from the papers of some meeting he was attending, that it occurred to him that if she gave up her job her days would be free for activities other than writing, once she had dropped Annie off at her junior school. He was shocked by the crudity and disloyalty of the idea. He tried to stifle it but once born it recurred throughout his working day, taking on ever more expansive and lurid forms. It was as if his mind had spawned some leering, cynical goblin that he was unable to control and that was feeding him fantasies of betrayal and deceit.

During a weekend when Cathy was visiting her mother in Oldham, he ran into Lola while shopping with Annie in the centre of Newcastle. Their intimate moment in the kitchen seemed to have left no trace for she appeared flustered and in a hurry to move on. In reply to his enquiry about Pip - a casually delivered 'How is he? I haven't seen him since that evening *chez nous*' - she replied that she thought he was away for the weekend; she wasn't sure where for she was seeing less of him nowadays. She looked embarrassed and glum. He sensed that 'less' meant 'nothing'.

The encounter left him anxious throughout the remainder of the day. On going to bed he replayed it incessantly in his mind. Away for the weekend she had said. Not sure where. He slips into a light and agitated sleep only to wake with a sudden start. He is possessed by the certainty that Cathy and Pip are together. His suspicion is fed by his own most intimate knowledge of his wife. He sees Cathy's body pale and soft in the half-light of their love-making, the curve of her breast, the swell of her abdomen that he loves to stroke. The thought of another man touching this cherished flesh is a torture beyond endurance. He tries to hold off the image, throwing himself bolt upright and staring wildly into the dark. He passes the remainder of the night in an agony of virulent imagining.

In the morning he phoned Oldham. It was Cathy who answered the phone. The familiar voice, light and innocent, almost girlish, dispersed the lingering fumes of the previous night's atmosphere. He felt faint with the relief that flooded through him.

Her book was accepted for publication. At the small party they held to celebrate Cathy's success, Pip announced that he too had achieved a long-held ambition and would soon be leaving to work for a national newspaper in London. Stan heard this news with a thrill of pleasure such as he had not felt for some time. While assuring Pip that he would be sorely missed, he could hardly contain his satisfaction at the further news that Pip's departure would take place within two weeks.

He did not yet know that within three months thereafter his wife would leave to join him. For the goblin had got it right. With his nose for the decay of love and the treacheries it breeds, he had played out through Stan's diseased imagination a fantasia on the truth. The truth itself therefore, when she confessed it, came as little surprise. What surprised and devastated him was the fact that things between her and Pip had gone so far that she had decided to join him in London. He felt the life-blood drain from him.

'But what about Annie? What about your daughter?'

She remains silent. Her face is grey and haggard with tension.

'Don't you remember the effect it had on you as a child, your father and Rachel…'

A look of such horror takes hold of her features that he stops, horrified himself.

'Don't, Stan. Please don't. I must do this. I only have one life to live.'

'But what about our life? What about me and Annie?'

She goes silent again. She knows she cannot answer. That there is no answer.

In the strained and bitter talks of those final months they spent together, the defects she pointed to in their marriage were none of them beyond repair. Stan was in favour of renovation, a new start. She had wanted to travel abroad: they would travel abroad. She had wanted to write full-time: she had begun to do so, having given up her part-time work. But her complaints were pretexts. They were soon abandoned for the harsher truth that their love and commitment had always been unequal. He had known this and

243

had assumed that it was true of most marriages. But most marriages had never played host to someone like Pip Slaley. She and he were planning a life together that, far from the passing infatuation Stan at first believed it to be, was to endure. Has endured.

# 26

## Disorientations

The arrow has got it wrong! He feels sure the arrow has got it wrong. He stops and gazes around him into the mist. A light drizzle is falling, relentless, penetrating, cold. His every instinct tells him to continue straight ahead but the arrow tells him to pull to the left. Since taking his gloves off to get what he hopes is a reliable bearing on the summit, his fingers have gone numb. His right boot is wet inside from a rash attempt to cross waterlogged peat. He sets off again, walking slowly west, his eyes fixed on the compass, resisting the pull of his mind and body to the north-west.

The summit of Cross Fell: the highest point of his walk, the lowest point of his morale. With still a hundred miles to go he feels a weakening of his resolve. For the first time he thinks he might give up, find his way off this god-forsaken waste of squelching bog and impenetrable mist and take the quickest route home. What is he doing here anyway, a sixty-year-old man, alone in one of the most exposed and hostile places in the land? He feels a wave of disgust and irritation. He has always hated the stories in his local newspaper of feisty geriatrics performing feats of improbable vitality: sky-diving grannies, global circumnavigators with multiple by-passes, potent old gigolos siring their broods of wretched offspring. The vanity of it all! The sheer pointless vanity of it all! Yet what he is doing is no different. Equally pointless, equally vain.

To the east lies the valley of the river South Tyne from where he could take buses – warm, comfortable buses - that would carry him home in a few hours. He could take up his normal, sensible life with his books and CDs, his gardening, his friends. A fitting life for a man of his years. The thought barely has time to take hold when he spots the summit shelter, a dark rectangle of shadow on the veil of grey fog. It is straight ahead, skewered with perfect precision by the arrow of his compass. His relief is accompanied by pleasure in his feat of navigation. The appearance of the shelter is like the solution to a mathematical problem, brought about by a combination of long-acquired skill with a willed submission to the laws of physics.

From the shelter, he takes a new bearing on the track that will take him downhill. He sets off briskly, compass in hand and whistling, and arrives there within minutes. The track is wide and welcoming, his direction-finding problems are over. As he loses height the drizzle stops and the mist thins. Spoil heaps of old lead mines loom into view through the dusky haze. He stops at the refuge of Greg's Hut to drink the last of his coffee and change his socks. Replenished and dry-footed he resumes the long descent to the tiny hamlet of Garrigill, beginning to take pleasure in the rhythm and efficiency of his movement. At moments like this he is impressed by his own rude health. Apart from the occasional tension in his chest (which he experienced briefly this morning on the climb out of Dufton) he is aware of no deterioration of his walking performance in recent times. His doctor has told him that he can look forward to ten or twenty years of what he called 'physical and mental vigour'. Though he is reluctant to tempt fate, Stan believes this to be a reasonable judgement. There will be the walks he has planned, the books he has never had time to read, the hobbies he has neglected. He will enjoy it, this Californian dream of cheated mortality while knowing that, in the end, it is only a dream. But what else should drive us on? Reality will have its way with us. But not yet. Not just yet.

The valley of the South Tyne feels like home. He was here less than a month ago with Jeff Birkett whom he had joined on a tour of the region's industrial relics. They visited old mine buildings on the open moor and walked a stretch of the disused railway line that was built to carry lead ore along the valley from Alston to Haltwhistle. They witnessed eye-pleasers and eyesores: chimneys elegantly poised on lonely hilltops, desolate heaps of waste, spruced-up railway stations inhabited by refugees from the town.

At the viaduct that carried the railway line over the river they descended to the riverbank by the foot of one of the pillars and ate their sandwiches with their backs against the rough stonework. It was a hot day; the bright, cloudless sky and the river swirling close by gladdened their hearts. A narrow strand of pebbles shelved gently down. Jeff walked to the water's edge with his cup of coffee and looked back up at the arches above them.

'I love this spot. When I die, Stan, I want you to bury my heart at the Lambley Viaduct.'

'You'd better put it in writing.'

'You must admit, the Victorians got it right. What a heritage!'

'I'm not sure they got this right,' says Stan, flicking his thumb upwards. 'Didn't the railway fail? A slump in the production of lead if I remember correctly.'

He too loves this spot, but he dislikes the word 'heritage' and enjoys throwing a spanner into the works of Jeff's Tory nostalgia. He knows Jeff will enjoy throwing it back.

'Oh, Walker. You vulgar materialist.'

'But it's true isn't it? That's what they built it for. Not for the delectation of twentieth-century suburbanites out on a Sunday picnic.'

'But, my dear Stanley, we are permitted to delight in it. And you've got to hand it to the Victorians; architecturally speaking we're still living off the legacy they left us. Just look at the centre of almost any of our northern cities.'

'I'll grant you that.'

'I'll go further. Their superiority was more than architectural, it was intellectual. Think of Darwin. Even moral. Think of Florence Nightingale...'

'What about child labour?'

'Good point, Stanley. A blot on the record. One cannot approve of child labour.'

'What about imperialism? Marching into other people's countries, carving out meaningless borders, telling them you've come to save their souls while filching their wealth.'

'True. A dodgy business, imperialism. Though it had its upside. We gave them parliamentary institutions, the English language, cricket.'

Stan laughed. Jeff grinned and finished his coffee. The moment was too precious and the weather too hot for serious debate. Stan took off his boots and paddled in the shallow edge of the river. Through the sunlit peaty water the stones of the river-bed appeared cast in bronze. Above him the arches with their rough, dark-grey stone curved into the trees on the far bank of the river, reaching back over the decades into a past that was his. Railways and mining had run through his life. The engine works at Doncaster, the pithead machinery of Calcroft Main, his father and his uncles - a generation now dead - were receding into a history that embraced the Lambley viaduct and the lead miners of Garrigill and Alston.

'You're right, Jeff. It's a great spot. It makes you feel ...connected, plugged in.'

'To what?'

Stan sweeps his arm round the enclosing vista of viaduct, trees and river.

'All this. A landscape that you feel is your own history.'

Jeff nodded and smiled, feeling vindicated.

He remembers that moment now as he passes through the village of Slaggyford. From here he could deviate from the official route of the Way and follow the railway line to the viaduct, returning to the Way a few miles further on. But he fears disappointment. Epiphanies are not made to order. The weather is cool and overcast, and he is alone. He decides to stick to the Way.

From Hadrian's Wall he gazes out over a landscape of low hills covered in conifer plantations. He tries to imagine how it would have looked to the legionnaires who guarded the Empire's northern frontier almost two thousand years ago for he knows that these border forests have reversed the clearances of prehistoric and Roman times. The tree cover is dense and uniform, its edges slicing in dogged linearity across the hills and heathlands of north Northumberland. It appears not so much sprung from the earth as rolled out and pinned down like pieces of carpet. Directly ahead of him stand two rectangular plantations with, between them, a single field that has been left clear. The green of the field is of an almost luminescent brightness against the darker green of the trees. It claims attention, like a symbolic remnant of a once-free land that has been invaded by some occupying arboreal force.

The weather is grey and still as he crosses the stretch of moor and rough pasture that lies between the Wall and the first line of trees. The day started bright but a thin gauze of cloud has thickened until the sun is now a pale blue disc blurring at the edges into the general greyness of the sky. To his right the lough beneath Sewingshields Crag is the colour of dark pewter. Suddenly, above the crag, a military aircraft appears like a rapidly widening slit in the sky. It swings round in a sharp arc, trailing engine smoke. The noise builds so quickly he can hardly get his hands to his ears before it is above him, then gone, leaving a corridor of raging air that he can feel reverberating inside the pit of his stomach.

Once on the forest road he makes good progress. The hard surface permits quick walking and he is immediately into his stride. The trees on either side of the road block out all landmarks. The effect is to enclose him in the experience of walking: the rhythmic counterpoint of breathing and striding, the regular tap-tap of his trekking poles on the hard surface of the road, the fixity of his gaze which rests, undistracted by scenery and horizons, on the near and middle distance of road and trees.

He reaches a turning area for forestry vehicles, a sideways bulge of the road with, round its edges, broom and heather re-colonising the ground. He stops for a drink of coffee then pushes his way through the vegetation into the forest to urinate. It is an irrational reflex he knows, for here if anywhere his privacy is assured. Inside the trees the silence is absolute, the peculiar, unnerving silence of absent birdsong. Over the years dense planting has caused the canopy to close so that the grey light of the overcast sky scarcely penetrates and he can see a mere thirty feet or so beyond where he stands. The colonnaded uniformity of the trees is a bar not only to sight but to imagination and thought. He longs for the crookedness of oak, the spreading crown of a beech tree, the light and freedom of a glade. He knows that the bulk of these trees are Sitka spruce but what is Sitka spruce to him or he to Sitka spruce? The spiky foreign name has no resonance whereas oak and ash, willow and yew, the broad-leaves of the native woodland have nourished his inner life. He remembers the dark spread of the yew in Worlby churchyard at dusk, the twirling sycamore seeds, conkers and cricket bats of his childhood. He thinks of willows that weep and willows that 'grow aslant the brook where poor Ophelia died'. His fancy takes the high road of national glory to the long-bows of Crécy and the oak-timbered men-of-war of Trafalgar. What has Sitka spruce to do with such a lineage? It is a visitor who has arrived too late for the defining moments of the nation's sylvan imagination. The heroic age of wood is over. The bulk of the product of these forests goes into packing crates, construction timber, fence-posts - worthy uses all, but unlikely to add further lustre to the rich symbolism of trees.

He gives his penis a shake, adjusts his walking-trousers, and returns to the road which is beginning a long curve to the right. The wide, hard surface gives way to a narrower track, the trees close in. Although he knows he is changing direction from north to north-east, the knowledge remains abstract for it is unaccompanied by any change in his surroundings or in the position of the sun which has now disappeared completely behind the thickened cloud. A firebreak through the conifers reveals a rounded hill in the distance that has been harvested by some process of industrial barbering, reducing its crew-cut of regimented trees to a shaven skull, pimpled with the dark stumps of those same trees now felled. He feels suddenly oppressed. He wants to get to the end of these columns of still and silent mourners, and onto the high Cheviot Hills that are the last leg of his journey. Ahead of him the tall figure of a man appears, standing to the side of the path and gazing into the trees, but when he looks up again after glancing at his watch the figure has gone and the road ahead is empty.

He emerges from the forest to see two people approaching across the open moorland ahead, a young couple carrying large packs of camping gear. Their talk and laughter precede them, piercing the still air. They stop to exchange pleasantries about the weather and the route. He is surprised at the relief he feels at the sound of human voices.

The daily distances are taking their toll. The fifteen miles from Bellingham to the village of Byrness that he covers on the next day leave him empty of energy and enthusiasm. The village is a half-hour's drive from his home in the Tyne valley. Though he has booked a room for the night he is briefly tempted to phone Annie and ask her to take him home so that he can re-gather his strength. The final stretch of his journey, from here to Kirk Yetholm, is the hardest part of the Way, twenty-five miles of rough high-level walking that are beyond his strength in one day and that offer few places of overnight shelter. A remote farmhouse is his best chance of breaking the journey but even that is fifteen miles away, the same distance as the walk that has exhausted him today and over more rugged ground. He stops on the edge of the village square while deciding what to do. Would a night or two at home infringe the ethics of the long-distance walk? He decides that it would and goes to find the house at which he is to spend the night.

The woman who meets him at the door is polite but uncommunicative. Having shown him to his room, she disappears into her living quarters. He can hear a radio or television playing. A door opens somewhere and the noise spills into the corridor outside his room. Someone is speaking about China; he can make out a few phrases about the Communist Party's dilemma…the acceptance of capitalism…industrial dominance…global ambitions. The door closes and the sound retreats into the distance. He feels a passing unease at what he has heard. China, India, the Asian Tigers, these things worry him. The world is tilting; the sun of power and prosperity will set on his time and place.

He must try to dispel this gloom that has settled on him. He goes out for his evening meal in a nearby pub and afterwards returns to his room, intending to phone Annie on his mobile. He wants to let her know that he will be home in two days' time, though she already knows this from his previous phone-call which was only a few days ago. The phone rings several times, then stops. Annie's voice asks him to leave a message on her answering machine. He rings off without speaking.

The house is completely silent yet it is only half-past nine, too early to go to bed. He looks around for something to read. On a set of shelves he finds a book on the natural history of Northumberland. His attention is caught by a chapter on the planting of the border forests and the creation of the great Kielder reservoir in the valley of the River North Tyne. According to the writer these two developments transformed the landscape of North Northumberland in just over fifty years, obliterating ancestral fields, villages and heaths, and changing the face of a nature that we like to think of as eternal and immutable. He quotes the story of a previous inhabitant of the valley who, during the construction of the reservoir, returned to watch bulldozers destroy the house in which she had been born and had lived her childhood. Close by, a tower was being built. Her father told her that the tower would control the flow of water from the reservoir into the River North Tyne, from where it would supply the homes and industries of the north-east of England. It was a great work of progress that would benefit them all. Later, after the completion of the reservoir, the sight of the tower emerging out of its dark waters aroused in her strange feelings of fascination and unease. In a dream that recurred on several occasions she would descend into the tower and walk out from its base into the depths of the reservoir, breathing freely and walking with a slowly bouncing stride, buoyed by the water. On reaching her old home she would find it still standing. Looking in through the window she saw the floating bodies of her family, including her own.

The story disturbs him. He is reminded of Cathy's book and goes to retrieve it from his rucksack. He reads the opening pages with their imagery of flooded valleys and the drowned world of childhood memories. He continues to read, skimming forward, stopping at passages that catch his eye. In the last chapter he reads: *My father's death was the defining event of my life. I believe it was the source of the dark and dysfunctional side of my personality, my periodic depressions and my insecurity. I believe it taught me to fear failure.*

The first time he read this, on the eve of his walk, he was sceptical. It was a story too often told, the early event that shapes a subsequent inner life. Something in him resisted the dramatic simplicity of it, the determinism, the recasting of fate as childhood trauma. He asked himself what that terrible moment in the outhouse had done to him. What mark had it left on him? What lesson had it taught him? Surely no more than later happenings such as the death of his mother, Harold's bleak and loveless final years, his father's illness. There was no defining, traumatic event, there was just life unfolding, yielding up its inevitable, banal secret: men suffer and die, it is the way things are.

But he knows this will not do. It is not a question of lessons learned or of ideas consciously held. The terror of that moment in the outhouse was more like a nuclear flash that burnt the hanging shadow of Robert Stapleton into the mind and feelings of the vulnerable child that he was. He can sense it, this shadow-self, in the dimly lit alleyways of his innermost life; it is the apathy and indifference that stalk his easy-going nature, the sense of futility that is his lack of ambition. And he sometimes wonders whether his want of courage that night has spawned that squirming, hypocritical beast his modesty that confesses inadequacy to the world for fear the world will judge him inadequate.

But such questions are beyond solving. He is becoming morbid. Solitude and apprehension at the thought of the next day's walk are undermining his morale. Fifteen miles of hard going in his present state of fatigue seems unwise, perhaps foolhardy. The tension in his chest has been more troublesome in recent days, lasting longer into his walk and, two days ago, coming upon him as he ate his evening meal. Indigestion he told himself, the result of his disrupted dietary habits. But now he is not so sure. He thinks again of going home for a few days or at least of taking a rest day in Byrness but decides against it. He feels he is being weak-minded, giving in to a familiar reflex of fear and renunciation that is close to cowardice. Yes, he will struggle tomorrow, he will arrive at the farmhouse of Uswayford exhausted, probably wet and cold, but he will have risen to the challenge, and he will be one day from his final goal. He must not weaken now that he is within sight of home.

He decides to have an early night. He falls asleep almost immediately on going to bed but is woken after several hours by a tightening of his chest. He turns from side to side trying to find the most comfortable way to lie but in the end has to sit on the side of the bed and wait for it to pass. Outside he can hear the steady, heavy thrum of falling rain.

The tree-clad hillside above Byrness makes for a hard start. The path that cuts through the sodden, encroaching vegetation is steep and thick with mud. He has to stop twice to recover his breath before he emerges from the trees onto less steep ground. The rain has stopped but the grey cloud of recent days persists. Ahead of him lies a broad ridge of low hillocks swinging away to the north that provides easier walking. On the farthest summit he can make out a group of people but at such a distance that he cannot tell in which direction they are moving or whether they are moving at all. He is dismayed to find his chest beginning to tighten, this time on a downward slope. For the first time it occurs to him seriously to ask whether he has misread his symptoms. Weariness, anxiety, indigestion: are these the lesser evils he has invoked in order to disguise a more brutal truth? When were those hospital tests? Seventeen years ago! And the relief they gave him is the balm he still applies to soothe away his worries!

He stops and waits for the discomfort to pass. He has arrived at a flat area that accumulated rainwater has turned into a patchwork of dark, peaty bogs and shallow pools separated by islands of reeds and bright-green moss. In a sudden mental slippage that wipes his mind clean of memory and understanding, he finds himself wondering why he is in this place. The moment passes but leaves him shaken. He decides to give himself another mile or so to get into his usual rhythm of breathing and movement. He will then take stock and, if necessary, turn back. He picks his way slowly across the swamp, steadying himself with his trekking poles, disheartened by the brute indifference of nature to his need to make progress. A phrase flashes through his mind: the world was not made for us. Who said that? Don Crick. Too true, old man, too true.

He is descending into a depression between two hilltops. His way is barred by a wide channel of peat and dark water that runs off down the hillside to his right. Crossing the channel to his left is a line of posts supporting a wire fence. He stops to assess the best way of getting to the other side. On the hilltop ahead of him, the group that he saw earlier are still standing. He can make out now that they are soldiers on a training exercise. As he contemplates them they set off down the hill in his direction. He can hear somewhere above and behind him the roar of a helicopter engine and the rhythmic swishing of its blade.

He begins to ease his way carefully down the bank of the peat channel. As he reaches forward to place his foot on a half-submerged rock he feels a stab of pain in the middle of his chest. He makes a grab for the nearest fence-post. His chest is tightening, his arms feel leaden, he is gasping for breath. He realises with the clarity of long-postponed conviction that he is having a heart attack.

'You bloody fool, Stan Walker. You bloody fool.'

He has dropped his trekking poles and is leaning with his left forearm on the top of the fence-post, his right hand gripping the wire. Beneath him is the peat with its skin of darkly glistening water. The tightening of his chest is now a sensation of being crushed; he feels as though the air is being sucked out of him, leaving a vacuum into which his ribcage is buckling. If the pain doesn't stop he will surely die.

The strength that holds him upright seeps from his arms and legs. As his mind begins to close down a dream flashes on the screen of his brain: he is being flung sideways and downwards beneath an ice-blue sky; the sky rapidly darkens and in a split second of electrifying terror he sees the myriad stars wheeling above him as he falls.

His last sensation is of a cool, easeful sinking. A bed of soft earth. A lapping of waters.

## 27

## Sightings

As they ascend from the valley the tree-covered hillside wheels and tilts, the trees fall away and the sky rushes to meet them. They are now flying over open ground, hills of bleached-green grass flecked with white rock and purple stains of heather. The co-pilot can see the unit of a dozen soldiers directly ahead, descending from the far hilltop. Away to his left he catches sight of a walker, his blue jacket bright against the green of the hillside. The helicopter banks and circles; the dark line of a peat channel below rotates like the hand of a clock, coming to a halt as they begin to hover. The co-pilot checks their position and reports the sighting of the troops. As they lift away he sees the walker stretched out against the peat and thinks it odd. He feels a fleeting unease. But they are climbing quickly and from up here so much is odd - foreshortened, shrunken and deceptive to the eye. Already against the blue smudge of the walker's jacket the white face is a featureless speck that could be a rock or a stone. Within a few seconds more the blue itself is difficult to make out. He watches it shrink and fade to nothing against the dark of the peat.

Part Four

2008: Afterwards…

I turn over to look at my travel clock but even before I open my eyes I'm ambushed by weariness and slip back into sleep. I am with Phil on a hill somewhere. There are other people around but none that I recognise; I can only sense them somewhere outside the line of my vision. I'm watching Phil who is walking uphill and waving to me. I want to go with him but I know that I must turn round and go down the hill; there's something I have to do, some obligation to fulfil. Perhaps it's my work. Is it a working day? I must go down to find out. When I look back up the hill, Phil is almost out of sight. I wonder again whether to follow him but the pull of the other thing, the thing at the bottom of the hill, is strong. I stand indecisive, not knowing what to do.

My anxiety wakes me up. The travel clock says 8.03. It is Saturday. I turn over and try to hold on to the mist in my head that might yet thicken into an extra half hour of sleep. But it's no use. I can hear movement in the kitchen next door, the hiss of a kettle beginning to boil. Then I remember: 'Eight o'clock', she said. 'I'll bring you a cup of tea.' I protested: 'I'll bring you one.' We left it unsettled. It seemed to typify the evening, the quiet drive back from the train station along the Tyne valley, the slight awkwardness during the meal, the inability to resolve our feelings into the usual easy, affectionate flow.

I get out of bed. I have a sudden vivid memory of the Railway Hotel, me reaching for the light-switch of my bedroom, the cold linoleum beneath my feet. This is my first time in Annie's new flat and strange bedrooms do this to me; every one strikes a splinter off the rotting stump of old memories. I take a quick peek through the curtains. The flats are a new development on the edge of the village. Across the minor road that we came along last night is a stand of Scots Pine. In the gaps between the trees I can make out white flecks of the River Tyne.

I swallow my pills quickly, put on my dressing-gown and go through to the kitchen. She is standing at the sink with her back to me. I hear a quiet 'Fuck. This bloody plug.' I say: 'Good morning, sweetheart.' She turns round, already smiling, wipes her hands quickly on a towel and steps across the room. We hug as though our lives depend on it, which in my case is perhaps not far from the truth. We stand rocking gently from side to side. I can feel her cheek warm against mine. She whispers: 'Welcome back, Mum.'

The situation is new to me. I feel its oddness like a quirk of vision that alters my perspective on things. Of course it is good to be here joining my daughter for breakfast. And such a daughter! The infrequency of our meetings has sharpened my awareness of the changes that have come about in her over the years, the step-by-step transformation from fractious teenager to this smart, humorous, loving woman. But the feeling of oddness is still there. It is as though I'm standing outside myself looking at the monuments of a life completed: the published books, the broken marriages, the daughter who will carry life forward. I have to keep telling myself that this is a beginning, not an end.

It is the suddenness of the dislocation of course; the separation from Phil and the sale of the house – so unexpectedly quick in the present climate - have left me feeling adrift. My freedom is both heady and terrifying. I am a sixty-five year-old woman with a pile of cash in the bank, a new life to create and, I sense, some expectations to live up to. Or destroy.

I go to work on the jammed plug, winkling it out with the sharp end of a knife. She says: 'Brilliant! That's just what mothers are for,' and gives me another hug. It's been a good start, I feel suddenly full of anticipation of the day ahead. I sit down at the table and say: 'So. What's the plan?'

'The plan, mother, is not to worry about the plan. For the moment just enjoy your breakfast and bring me up to date with your news.'

'I have no news. I phoned a couple of days ago with my news such as it was. Nothing much has happened since. What sort of a life do you think I live?'

'The life of a successful writer. Fan mail, parties, bibulous lunches with louche young men from publishing houses. You know the sort of thing we provincials fantasise about.'

'Well it's not quite like that. Days in front of my computer followed by evenings in front of the telly are more like it.'

She is having trouble getting the toaster to work. I suggest she tries switching it on at the wall-socket. She says: 'Good God, woman, is there nothing you don't know how to do?'

'Stay married?'

I immediately regret my words. It's too soon for all that and I'm still nervous of her possible reaction. Twice is just about understandable, even when one of the husbands was her much-loved father. Three times stretches indulgence.

She says: 'Ah yes, of course. Well, I suppose practice doesn't always make perfect.'

'Well, it's never the same the second and third time round, so you don't know exactly what it is you're practising for. However, we'll talk about it all later.'

'No, go on. You've got me interested.'

She reaches for the toast that has just popped up. As she spreads her butter she watches me, smiling, letting me know that it's all alright, I can tell my story and she will understand.

I say: 'Well, whatever went wrong with Stan, it had nothing to do with other women. That was the difference between him and Phil, the thing I hadn't practised for.'

I don't know how much she knows or has guessed about Phil. Over the years Stan must have told her something but discretion and decency might have held him back from giving the full picture. She says: 'Ah, I see.'

'Even with Rod Barnett that wasn't a problem. Rod was attractive to women and had affairs before he met me but I'm pretty sure he stayed faithful during our marriage.'

She waits for me to continue but there is nothing more to tell; it's one of the oldest stories in the world. Finally she says: 'How old is Pip... Phil?'

I laugh and say: 'The same age as me but if you think that makes any difference, you couldn't be more wrong. If anything it made matters worse. The older he got that more anxious he became to... how shall I put it? ... display his credentials. And the women seemed to get younger.'

'I remember Dad told me he was a womaniser.'

'Did he tell you about the Marie Salasca episode?'

'No.'

I don't know why I'm telling her this but it seems somehow to be part of the story.

'Marie Salasca was some French teacher at the Grammar School Stan and Phil attended. They both fancied her like hell but in the end it was Stan she went for. I get the impression it was one of the few occasions Phil came off second-best.'

She frowns and says: 'You don't think that is why he...'

I realise with horror what she is thinking. I say: 'Oh no. You mustn't think he bore some long-term grudge against your father. Goodness no. It was a story he told against himself. It amused him, it was all part of the game. The thing about Phil that it took me years to realise is that he's a sort of moral dilettante and he expects others to be the same. The upside of it is that he doesn't bear grudges. No more than if you'd beaten him at a game of cards. The trouble is he viewed marriage that way too. He took advantage... as though it was a game he was playing.'

I'm getting deeper in. I'm talking too much and too early. All this should come later when we've had time to gossip about things that don't matter, go shopping together, meet for lunches. But she sits attentive and expectant. She says: 'What do you mean?'

'Your father and I quarrelled often. We had difficult times. The funny thing was that even when Stan had right on his side, he would sometimes still give in. You see he didn't like me to feel defeated

263

and resentful. What he wanted was peace and quiet and some acknowledgement of the fairness of his position. Phil was different. Peace and quiet bored him and fairness was for suckers. Arguments were to be won. He took advantage of every weakness and pressed his advantage home. And now I think more clearly about it, it wasn't a game. It was about power and at bottom it was deadly serious. Phil always had to have his way. Always and with everyone.'

I realise I've contradicted my previous view of him but she either doesn't notice or chooses not to pick me up on it. She says: 'What about Rod? Where does he fit into this?'

'I think it was a power thing with Rod too. He was happy in the early months of our marriage when I still looked up to him as the great mountaineer, the dominant stag who had chosen me from among his willing hinds. Later on when he saw my view of him change because of his drinking and all that, it was the loss of power he couldn't cope with.'

'So Dad was the odd one out?'

'My feminist prejudices tell me there must have been a power struggle going on somewhere, even with Stan, but it was hard to detect. Power wasn't his thing.'

'What was?'

I hardly dare say it but it feels too late to go back. I say: 'Love.'

'Sounds like you had a good deal with Dad.'

She's smiling again, trying to take the sting out of the comment. I'm trapped between what I've said and what I cannot say. I cannot tell her that there was a problem with Stan that no amount of love from him could overcome, namely that I had never wanted to marry him; I had half-wanted it at most, and the lack in my conviction was made up for by her, Annie, who at the time was an as yet unnamed ball of cells in my womb. Later there was the depression and the other mothers with their disapproving glances and their smug absorption in their precious ones, there was the sense of my life slipping away, the thing I really wanted to do being put off, constantly being put off.

I say limply: 'That's not all there was to it.'

Then she says something astonishing: 'I know Mum, I know. Women don't always get what they need. And sometimes love isn't enough.'

We get into the car and drive out west along the Tyne valley. The long flat ridge of the far riverbank is black beneath stacked, charcoal-grey clouds. Streaks of rain claw the distant horizon. I say: 'The weather doesn't look too promising.'

'It has time to clear. The forecast was good for this afternoon.'

She begins to tell me about her new boy-friend, the latest in a longish line. I remember her teenage worries about her body; she thought she was too short and too fat, unable to see her own burgeoning shapeliness. Now nearing thirty she hardly seems to have changed except for the fullness of her breasts and hips, and a softening of her facial expression into that grave and earnest calm, lit up by frequent smiles, that I have seen over the breakfast table.

She jokes about her relationships with men. A colleague at work has told her she is 'hungry for love'. She finds the phrase hilarious, a warmed-up Hollywood cliché. I say: 'And are you?'

'Am I what? Hungry for love? Not really. Peckish at most. But the fact is I like being on my own and men can't understand that. The fact that a woman might prefer curling up with a good book to curling up with them is beyond their imagination.'

Does she really mean what she says? I find it difficult to understand this blithe independence of spirit, for I have always disliked being on my own. Nothing horrifies me more than the thought of a lonely old age, which for me, it goes without saying, means old age without a man. I wonder again what future I am going to choose. I know that she hopes I will return permanently, and I want to please her. In fact I am in danger of being engulfed by this desire to please her which fits so neatly with my desire to escape the wreckage of my marriage that I cannot tell the one from the other.

From a rise in the road the valley opens out ahead of us. The widening prospect of hills and sky is like a beckoning freedom. During my time in London I longed for this easy access to the countryside. I missed living in a city that knows its limits and hands you over unbegrudgingly to spacious landscapes within half an hour of leaving its crowded centre. But what I feel now is something different; it is an old dream of living in the countryside itself. What better use for my flourishing bank-balance than a cottage in Northumberland, with my computer and my cat and my daughter close at hand. During our time in Newcastle Stan and I planned just such a move. We spent hours poring over the property columns of the region's newspapers. We drove out to view crumbling farmhouses in improbably remote locations. It became an activity in and for itself, combining our family walks and picnics with the pursuit of a dream. Later, when we separated, Stan was left to pursue the dream alone, by which time it had come to seem more like therapy. He once told Annie, who told me, that it was the need to get away from the associations of our marriage that led him to move into the Tyne Valley. I know now how he felt. I ask myself whether history is about to repeat itself.

As we pull into the driveway of the bungalow, he is already waiting for us at the front gate, smiling broadly. I haven't seen him for almost a year and I am struck by his flourishing appearance; with his close-cropped hair, tanned features and his fleece jacket open at the neck, he looks like one of those ads for a fit and healthy old age or a pin-up boy for Saga magazine. But then he always seemed in good shape; he was the last person I would have expected to have a heart attack at sixty. He springs forward to my side of the car and opens the door.

'Welcome Cathy. And thank you for agreeing to join us.'

'It's a pleasure and an honour, Stan. I just hope you know what you're doing.'

He plants a diffident kiss on my cheek. He and Annie hug. He invites us to have coffee but we sense his eagerness to move off.

We set foot in the house, compliment him on his newly decorated sitting-room, and re-emerge five minutes later. In the car he sits in the back seat and leans forward to take part in the conversation. It is the first time the three of us have been together since my separation from Phil and I feel again the sense of oddness and unreality that I experienced earlier in the morning. We are a pretend family waiting for some magic spark to turn us into the real thing. Conversation is strained; unable for the moment to ask the question that preoccupies us, we fill the silence with whatever comes to mind. Stan asks me what I think of Annie's new flat, Annie reports to Stan on my skill with sink-plugs. We are like moths circling a flame; the first to fly close is Annie.

'I must say, Mum, you did well to sell your house so quickly.'

'Yes we were lucky. And we got the asking price too.'

Stan says: 'Have you started looking for a new place down there?'

He gives no hint that he hopes I might return to the north; he seems eager not to presume, and I am grateful for this. Annie is less tactful.

'Don't forget that Mum only has a half share of the sale of the London house.'

I know what she is getting at and I'm sure Stan does too: property prices are lower in the north, my money will go further up here. But he refuses to take the hint and diverts the conversation onto wider matters. He has been listening to the morning news of the collapse of the American mortgage companies and wonders whether any of us are safe from the growing financial crisis. Annie accepts the change of topic but I know she will return to the matter later.

We discuss the state of the economy in a desultory, slapdash sort of way for none of us understands very well what is happening. Annie is characteristically fierce, wishing death and destruction on the City of London. Her politics seem to have escaped the mellowing of her general approach to life and it suddenly occurs to me that this is where her anger has gone.

Stan says to her, provokingly: 'What do you think we should do with these bankers then?'

'Hang a few I say.'

'*Pour encourager les autres?*'

'Exactly.'

He laughs delightedly. Annie grins at him in the rear-view mirror. I feel like an intruder on some intimate ritual of playfulness forged during the years of my absence.

'I thought you were against capital punishment,' he says.

'I'd bring it back it for financiers on obscenely high salaries. Then I'd distribute their loot to school teachers.'

Stan says: 'What about pensioners?'

Annie accepts that some of the loot could go to pensioners.

I say: 'Struggling writers?'

It is agreed that struggling writers could have their modest share.

We go silent for a few moments, pondering this new and better world. The road climbs steeply. From the top of the rise the land falls away revealing a horizon of moorland and hills beneath a sky of immense clouds like floating continents. I whistle and say: 'Just look at that view.'

Annie nods and smiles. 'Dad'll be tripping along those hilltops like a mountain goat in a couple of hours, won't you Dad?'

I say: 'Are you sure you're up to this, Stan?'

'Absolutely. A man can't leave the Pennine Way unfinished. I've done plenty training over the last few months and the fact that I'm taking two days over this last stretch makes it fairly straightforward.'

'What do your doctors say?'

'Oh, they think I'm in great shape for a man returned from the dead. It's amazing what they can do with angioplasty.'

'I can swear to that,' says Annie. 'He's a bundle of energy.'

Stan says: 'But what about your own health, Cathy? I must say you look well.'

'I am well, apart from the odd bit of wear and tear, mainly in the memory department.'

'Well, we all have that.'

'I'm sure we do.'

He hesitates, then says: 'And what about the depressions?'

'Oh, the depressions come and go. I've been on an even keel for some time now. Things are not too good at the moment for obvious reasons. But that's just old-fashioned unhappiness.'

'I know. It's hard for you. Desperately hard.'

As it was for him no doubt! Yet there is no hint of false commiseration in his voice, no apparent consciousness of the fact that I may be reaping what I've sowed. Nor am I surprised by this. Our relations since we separated have gone from warfare to truce to a friendship rekindled by passing time and Annie's diplomatic manoeuvrings. Somewhere along the way I have come to realise that for Stan hope has never died. Annie, who is not given to fantasy, once told me he will always love me. Always love me! The idea left me, a professional purveyor of fantasy, speechless with astonishment and incomprehension.

He says: 'By the way, how is Helen?'

I say: 'Surviving.'

'How old is she now?'

'She will be ninety-five in a week's time. She's the oldest person in the home according to the care-assistants.'

I visited Oldham before coming to stay with Annie. It was Nicola, the tall pasty-faced one with the ponytail, who mentioned the birthday. I let her believe I'd remembered it while inwardly cursing my increasingly wayward memory and wondering yet again whether this dreadful condition that has ravaged my mother's mind and identity might run in families. We were standing in the corridor outside Helen's room. Nicola had stopped to speak to me though she was clearly in a rush; I could smell sweat through her nylon overall. She asked if I would be coming to Helen's party. I was surprised at this for my mother has barely spoken since Dot died and hardly seems to be aware of what is going on around her. Recently she has spent much of her time in bed, a shrunken, withered figure beyond communication. I looked into Nicola's face, trying to detect a hint of a reservation, any suggestion that she might see the pointlessness of such an event. Her expression was one of frank, unqualified sincerity. She said: 'We think she can't hear us but you never know, do you? You never know what they're thinking and feeling in there. Sometimes a little party perks them up. You see it in their eyes. They know they haven't been forgotten.'

I suppose I was already feeling guilty about not having visited for almost a year. I said I would be back for the party and thanked her for arranging it.

I say to Annie and Stan: 'I'll be going back to Oldham in a week's time for the birthday. They're having a little do.'

Annie says: 'I'll come with you. I'll drive you over. I haven't seen Gran for donkey's years.'

'That's kind of you, Annie, but it seems a bit excessive. Are you sure?'

'Of course. It might be my last chance to see her.'

We used to visit her and auntie Dot when we lived in Glossop. This was not very often, perhaps once every few months, but it was still too often for Annie who would complain noisily about this theft of an occasional one of her precious Saturdays. She and Helen didn't get on; Annie found her grandmother bossy and interfering while Helen lamented Annie's failure to live up to her notion of the ideal grand-daughter who was quiet, polite and 'biddable'. After my divorce from Stan I believe he and Annie made the journey from Newcastle once or twice but then, over the years, they lost touch.

It wasn't the only thread that was broken during that period for none of my Newcastle friends maintained contact with me. Not that they were numerous. Friendships come in waves, and the major life-events that produce them – going to university, entering the world of work, becoming a parent – had either passed me by or failed to operate in the customary way. University remained out of my reach, while the possibilities offered by the secretarial pool or the gaggle of mothers I used to join at the school-gate (hanging around on the edge, waiting to be spoken to rather than speaking) were not to my taste. I was a misfit and I paid the price. Then of course the circumstances of the divorce did not help my case. An errant wife and mother is not going to be at the top of anyone's visiting list, especially when the husband is decent, lovable old Stan.

He is joking now with Annie about his coming walk. I gather that at some point during the first few miles he will climb onto the ridge where he suffered his heart-attack. He refers to it as 'cardiac arête' and says he will be glad when he has got past it. Annie giggles and tells him to take care, the British Army might not be around this time to save him. I try to hang on to my line of thought, knowing its importance for the decision I have to make. I must not forget the fact that it was only when I moved to London that I thrived socially. Phil was an excellent cook and loved to entertain. Our guests were mainly from the worlds of publishing and the media, and initially I found them intimidating. It was my own success at getting my books published that gave me the confidence to feel their equal. I blossomed in the warmth of their respect and admiration. I made friends, good friends who supported me when Phil began to stray and who have remained strong and loyal since the break-up.

I wanted Annie to see my life in London. I wanted her to understand what it was that I had sought in going there. But her visits were rare, awkward events and she preferred me to make the journey north. With Phil she was reserved and wary like an animal guarding her lair. She found his flamboyance suspect and responded to his attempts to win her over with a sort of tactical doling out of bits of herself in the interest of courtesy and peaceful relations. As for my friends, she hardly knew them. My London life - all twenty years of it, the most exciting and productive of my life - was for her a wrong turning, a development to be borne in the hope, I believe, that it might turn into an intermission. I think of her words this morning at the breakfast table. 'Women don't always get what they need. And sometimes love isn't enough.' Such understanding. But it was rarely in evidence during those twenty years. Is it simply that she feels she can afford to be understanding now that it is all over? I hate myself for the thought. I am beginning to feel confused and resentful.

They are still talking. She is telling Stan he is lucky, the weather is clearing, he will have a lovely day. He replies: 'It's not too late to join me. We can go back and pick up your walking gear.'

I think he is teasing her but I'm not sure. I feel left out again, anxious to the point of alarm.

Annie says: 'You're joking. Mum and I have serious business on hand.'

'What's that?'

'Oh, you know. Morning coffee, lots of gossip and shopping. Women's stuff. It wouldn't interest you.'

I say: 'Are you sure you wouldn't like to join your dad?'

Stan says: 'No, Cathy. I wasn't being serious. You and Annie have some catching up to do.'

Annie gives my hand a quick squeeze. I am reassured, but I am also dismayed by my volatile feelings. The break-up has left me flapping like a rag in the wind, insecure and divided against myself. I want my friends and I want my daughter. I want the peace of the countryside and the convenience of the town. Above all I want love. I need love. An old wound of loss and abandonment has split its scars. There have been times recently when I have felt the wild panic of someone on the edge of an abyss of loneliness and rejection. Only my friends have kept me sane, my friends and a renewal of the medication I thought I had left behind during the happy times. I like to think that I will leave it behind again, for the pain will not last forever. This is the thing I must hang onto. The pain will not last forever. I will cease to need pills and consolation. I will take up my life, a new life with old friends, those who have stood by me. I will write books. Who knows, I will perhaps love again and be loved.

Stan must sense something of my brooding state for he places his hand on my shoulder and says: 'Are you alright, Cathy?'

'I'm fine, Stan.'

'Bearing up?'

'Bearing up.'

I place my hand briefly on his.

The car is slowing down. I catch sight of a sign that says 'Byrness'. We pull off the road into a parking area by a small church. On either side of the road are the conifer slopes of the border forests. Stan goes through the plan he has agreed with Annie. We will leave him here, from where he will join the Pennine Way. He has arranged to spend the night at a farmhouse that is about halfway to the end-point of the walk at Kirk Yetholm. We will meet him in the pub at Kirk Yetholm tomorrow late in the afternoon.

He says: 'Right. Time for a photograph. This is a solemn moment, the beginning of the last lap. It must be commemorated.'

We all get out of the car and Stan goes round to the boot to find his camera. He gives it to Annie who takes a snap of him in full walking regalia of boots, rucksack and trekking poles. She hands the camera to me and asks me to take the two of them together. As she stands beside him he tweaks the lobe of her ear in a gesture I remember from way back when she was a child. She pretended to hate it then and would yelp with forced outrage at the liberties adults take with children. Now a faint smile plays around her lips and she reaches her arm round his waist.

I realise that my decision has been taken. It has grown within me as the day has progressed, beginning as a vague mood, barely discernible. Now, like some cloud of interstellar gas, it has cohered into the solid matter of certainty.

'Let's have one of you and Dad now.'

She takes the camera and I join Stan. He places his arm round my shoulder and pulls me close. When the photograph is taken he kisses me on the cheek, a more lingering, tender kiss than before. He says: 'Going back to what you said in the car, Cathy, that comment about old-fashioned unhappiness. I know there's nothing much we can do about it, Annie and I, but I want you to know we will always be there for you if you need us. We will always be there.'

His words are intended to reassure but his tone is almost imploring. He looks suddenly rather forlorn in his walking gear, as though he has chosen the wrong clothes for the circumstances and wants to change his mind, wants to join Cathy and me for a day of gossip and family bonding. I give him a peck on the cheek. 'I know you will, Stan. And I'm immensely grateful for your goodness and your support.'

He brightens and says: 'And I'll see you tomorrow in the pub.'

'We'll see you tomorrow in the pub.'

'Make sure you're there. You, I mean.'

'Don't worry. I'll be there.'

He turns and crosses the road. We watch him walk along the grass verge. He gives a quick wave and disappears into the trees.

I will be there. We will be there. We will welcome him, buy him his triumphal drink and make a fuss of him as we used to back then, on his birthdays or on the day he returned from Newcastle having got the job. He didn't expect the unusually elaborate meal and the special bottle of wine, and was immensely pleased and grateful. After the meal we transferred the fuss-making onto Annie, carried her up to bed, the pair of us sharing legs and arms, and tucked her in. The family reunited!

I am not inclined to nostalgia. Nor to families for that matter. But I remember those moments with great joy for I revere whatever the past has given me in the way of tenderness and love.

So we will be there, Annie and I. We will sit him between us, buy him his drink and shower him with congratulations. It will be an echo of those old times, an echo of the best of those old times. There will be other such moments for I will visit more often than I have of late.

It is the best solution, it will have to do. He will understand. He always did.

# Acknowledgements

I would like to thank my friends Lynn Barrett and Jean Davies and my wife and children, Ros, Elsie and Joe for reading and commenting on the manuscript of *Rambling Man.* I owe special thanks to Elsie for her cover design.

I would also like to thank Tom and Megan of Pen2Print for their excellent work in licking the book into its final shape.